THE IRISH
SOCCER
SPLIT

THE IRISH
SOCCER SPLIT

CORMAC MOORE

ATRIUM

First published in 2015 by Atrium
Atrium is an imprint of Cork University Press
Youngline Industrial Estate
Pouladuff Road, Togher
Cork, Ireland

ISBN-978-1-78205-152-7
Printed in Malta by Gutenberg Press
Typeset by Tower Books, Ballincollig, Co. Cork
www.corkuniversitypress.com

Contents

Contents

Contents

Acknowledgements

My interest in researching the Irish soccer split came about through a series of conversations I had with Dr Paul Rouse of University College Dublin (UCD) who offered invaluable advice and guidance to me on how to approach the project and for that I am very grateful.

Professor Mike Cronin of Boston College, Ireland, was also of huge assistance to me. From every meeting I had with Mike, I came away with new ideas and directions on the topic. Mike's vast knowledge and readiness to help at all times is particularly appreciated.

I would like to thank Dr Mark Tynan for sharing his PhD thesis with me, *Association Football and Irish Society During the Inter-War Period, 1918–1939* from NUI, Maynooth. Mark's research covers similar topics and themes as mine. I found his thesis to be an excellent study which contributes greatly to a better appreciation and understanding of soccer history in Ireland.

Tom Hunt, Pat Bracken and Dónal McAnallen were also very helpful in sharing their research on different areas within the field of Irish sports history. A huge thank you is owed to Margaret Ayres, Gráinne Daly, Ciarán Mollohan, Frank Mulcahy and Brendan Coleman for reading the original draft and offering many suggestions for improvements that have contributed greatly to the final version.

I am very appreciative to the Deputy Keeper of Records, Public Record Office of Northern Ireland (PRONI) and the Irish Football Association (IFA) for granting me access to the extensive IFA and Irish Football League records. I am grateful for the assistance I

Acknowledgements

have received from all of the staff at PRONI on my many trips to Belfast. I wish to thank Sarah O'Shea and Rea Walshe from the Football Association of Ireland (FAI) for granting me access to the FAI records located in UCD. I would like to acknowledge the assistance I received from the staff of the UCD Archives, the National Library of Ireland and the National Archives of Ireland who were very helpful on every visit. I am also grateful to David Barber of the English Football Association (FA) in Wembley and to Mark Reynolds of the GAA Archive in Croke Park.

I wish to thank Berni Metcalfe from the National Library of Ireland, Michelle Ashmore from the National Museum of Northern Ireland, Norman McCloskey from *Inpho Photography* and Philip Kinane from *Sportsfile* for their help in the sourcing of images for this book.

To Maria O'Donovan and Mike Collins of Cork University Press who have been a pleasure to deal with throughout the publishing process, a huge debt of gratitude is owed.

Finally, I would like to thank all of my family, friends and work colleagues who have supported me throughout this venture.

Abbreviations

AAA – Amateur Athletics Association

AAUE – Amateur Athletics Union, Éire

AIFA – All-Ireland Football Association

BBC – British Broadcasting Corporation

BLE – Bord Lúthchleas na hÉireann

CAP – Cercle Athletique de Paris

CBAI – Contract Bridge Association of Ireland

CCAI – Cross Country Association of Ireland

CRE – Cumann Rothaidheachta na hÉireann

FA – The Football Association (England)

FAI – Football Association of Ireland

FAIFS – Football Association of the Irish Free State

FFF – French Football Federation

FIFA – Fédération Internationale de Football Association

GAA – Gaelic Athletic Association

GUI – Golfing Union of Ireland

IAAA – Irish Amateur Athletics Association

IAAF – International Amateur Athletics Federation

ICA – Irish Cycling Association

ICU – Irish Cricket Union

Abbreviations

IFA – Irish Football Association

IFAB – International Football Association Board

IFU – Irish Football Union

IHU – Irish Hockey Union

IOC – International Olympic Committee

IRA – Irish Republican Army

IRFU – Irish Rugby Football Union

LFA – Leinster Football Association

MFA – Munster Football Association

NACA – National Athletics and Cycling Association

NCA – National Cycling Association

NCU – Northern Cricket Union

NFU – Northern Football Union

NICF – Northern Ireland Cycling Federation

RDS – Royal Dublin Society

RIC – Royal Irish Constabulary

RUC – Royal Ulster Constabulary

UCI – Union Cycliste Internationale

UEFA – Union of European Football Associations

Introduction
Windsor Park, Belfast,
17 November 1993

The Republic of Ireland soccer team was looking to secure its place at the USA World Cup of 1994. Under Englishman Jack Charlton, the team had experienced heights never before realised. Qualification for the European Championships in West Germany in 1988 followed by a quarter-final positioning at the World Cup in Italy two years later had cemented the team in the hearts of the Irish public. The Republic of Ireland had never secured qualification to any major tournament previously.

Qualification for USA '94 came down to the last match. The Republic of Ireland needed a win, or at least a draw, to secure qualification. After eleven matches of Group Three of the European qualification groups, Denmark was top with eighteen points, followed by Spain and the Republic of Ireland with seventeen points each. Goal difference was tight too. Denmark had a positive goal difference of fourteen, Ireland thirteen and Spain twenty-two. The last match was against one of the Republic's most bitter rivals, Northern Ireland.

Northern Ireland's international record had totally eclipsed the South's before the Charlton era. In the 1958 World Cup in Sweden, Northern Ireland reached the quarter-finals. Under the stewardship of Billy Bingham, Northern Ireland made it to the second round of the World Cup in 1982, securing a memorable win against the hosts, Spain, along the way. The team also reached the World Cup in Mexico in 1986. The match against the Republic of Ireland in November 1993 would be Bingham's final match as manager. Although Northern Ireland could not secure World Cup qualification, being on twelve points, the team and the fans wanted to give Bingham a send-off to remember for his achievements as manager. The opposition of the night also contributed to Northern Ireland's desire to win.

The Northern Ireland of 1993 had been engulfed in the Troubles for over twenty years, with no apparent end in sight. The former British Prime Minister, Margaret Thatcher stated in October 1993 that she believed there would be no peace in Northern Ireland in her lifetime.[1] October 1993 had been a particularly dark month for a province that had experienced many dark ones before it. The Irish Republican Army (IRA) bombing of a fish shop on the Shankill Road in Belfast on 23 October, killing eight people, was followed by Ulster loyalists killing seven customers at the Rising Sun bar in Greysteel, County Derry, seven days later. Twenty-six people were fatal victims of the Troubles in the last week of October 1993.[2]

The crucial match in November was due to be played at the home of Northern Ireland football, Linfield Football Club's ground, Windsor Park in Belfast. The escalation of violence experienced in October put the venue in jeopardy. Many saw the security risk to the Republic of Ireland team and fans from the South as too great to host the match in Belfast. Even though no tickets had been distributed to southern fans it was expected many would still make it to the match through contacts in Northern Ireland.[3] It was felt in early November that the Fédération Internationale de Football Association (FIFA), soccer's world governing body, would rule that a change of venue to a neutral location was required,[4] most likely in England, but venues such as Rome were also touted.[5] After submissions from the North's governing body, the Irish Football Association (IFA), and the South's governing body, the Football Association of Ireland (FAI), to FIFA, it was decided in early November to host the match in Windsor Park on the condition that no atrocity similar to the Shankill Road and Greysteel ones occurred in the intervening period.[6]

In the build-up to the match, Bingham called the Republic of Ireland team 'a bunch of mercenaries', as a significant portion of the Republic team were not born in Ireland. Of the eleven players who started against Northern Ireland in November 1993, only four were born in the Republic of Ireland (Packie Bonner, Denis

NORTHERN IRELAND MANAGER, BILLY BINGHAM

argues with his Republic of Ireland counterpart, Jack Charlton, during the World Cup Qualifier match in Windsor Park in November 1993. The tense and bitter atmosphere that night highlighted the divide in Irish society and in Irish soccer.

Courtesy of Inpho Photography

Irwin, Roy Keane and Niall Quinn).[7] To avoid unnecessary provocation, it was decided not to fly the Irish tricolour in the ground nor to play the Irish national anthem, 'Amhrán na bhFiann'. The *Irish Press* commented that Northern Irish fans were changing in common with their Republican counterparts and were now behaving a lot better, concluding that 'perhaps we are getting to know each other a little better.'[8] The night in Windsor Park would prove this to have been optimistic in the extreme.

It was a cold bitter night in Belfast, with the crowd contributing to that more than the weather. A 'terrible tension' engulfed the stadium.[9] Fans with southern accents were advised to keep quiet throughout the match. *The Irish Times* journalist Fintan O'Toole was in the crowd that night:

> To be a Republic supporter in that stand, is to live in a surreal, semi-conscious dream. You have to be somebody else, to divest yourself of your voice and still your reaction. To put your

conscious, waking self into a state of suspended animation like a machine with the power on but all the controls turned right down, lest it leap out and betray you. With the Billy Boys left and right, with the screams of 'Fenian scum' and the palpable waves of hatred breaking over your back, you have to act a role. You have to think and feel like them, to be outwardly a Billy Boy yourself.[10]

The *Irish Independent* poetically wrote:

The old wooden stand creaked and rumbled to a raucous, unholy anger. Forefingers jabbed fiercely into the tense night air and harsh, Shankill voices dredged up the bile that poisons this sad city . . . And there was a faintly surreal glare as the kindly grandfather shape of Billy Bingham paraded the tram-line with wrist sweeping provocation to the assembled.[11]

The *Belfast Telegraph* also mentioned that Billy Bingham was gesturing and whipping the crowd up before the match, to urge the Northern Ireland team on.[12] The Fine Gael TD Austin Deasy believed Bingham 'should be indicted for incitement to national hatred' as his gestures were 'definitely an attempt . . . to inflame passions, which were already running very high.' This claim was denied by Bingham and the IFA, his gestures in their opinion being a mere encouragement for the public to get behind the team.[13] In a debate in Seanad Éireann, the atmosphere in Windsor Park was seen as an example of 'the depth of the bigotry and hatred in what may be only a small segment of the population' and it was also described as 'the low level energy of real tribal hatred. That is precisely the atmosphere or environment which permits violence. Having seen and listened to that we can understand how and why people are murdered. The display was absolutely irrational.'[14] Eamon Dunphy, RTÉ TV pundit, believed Bingham's behaviour was the worst he had seen at an international match.[15] Another commentator ventured that Bingham 'must have thought he was Glenn Miller such was his orchestration of the crowd.'[16]

Some of the Republic of Ireland players were singled out for abuse, including Paul McGrath and Terry Phelan, on account of the colour of their skin.[17] The player who suffered the most verbal abuse was Alan Kernaghan, who was born in Northern Ireland, as he was seen as 'a turncoat, a Northerner in Fenian clothing, a

Introduction

Belfast boy made bad.'[18] The following day RTÉ Radio had a steady stream of callers complaining about the attitude of the Northern Ireland fans at Windsor Park. Listeners said they were 'shocked and repelled by the behaviour of the crowd, who had labelled some of the players "England's rejects", "Fenian scum"and "Taig bastards".'[19] John Haughey, journalist with the *Irish News*, writing a few days after the match, commented that he was still in a disturbed state from what he witnessed, claiming the fans had gone way beyond the normal tribal posturing typical of soccer matches.[20] Jack Charlton, writing years later, could still recall the incredible tension that existed that night in Windsor Park.[21]

The poisonous atmosphere clearly affected the Republic of Ireland players who performed poorly on the night. Northern Ireland took the lead after seventy-three minutes with Jimmy Quinn scoring a spectacular volley. The crowd erupted. With the game reaching its closing stages, it looked like Northern Ireland was going to deny the Republic of Ireland World Cup qualification. Substitute Alan McLoughlin came to the rescue equalising with a well-executed goal. McLoughlin described Windsor Park that evening as 'a very strange place' with 'the safest place' being on the pitch.[22] Spain defeated Denmark by a goal to nil and the Republic of Ireland secured qualification, beating Denmark on goal difference to secure second spot in the group.

Looking back at those events that night, still etched in the memories of all who witnessed them, why had soccer in Ireland come to this? Why was there so much hatred between North and South? Was soccer a reflection of the political conflict? The purpose of this book is to explore those questions by detailing the split in soccer in 1921, when the southern part of Ireland broke away from the IFA to found the FAI.

The book will look at the foundations of soccer in Ireland, starting in the north-east part of the country and eventually moving southwards. The IFA was founded in Belfast in 1880 to govern soccer for all of Ireland. The early years were dominated by teams from the North. With the founding of the Leinster Football Association (LFA) in 1892, Dublin teams, particularly Bohemians and Shelbourne, began to challenge the North's supremacy. The Leinster Football Association and the Munster

ROY KEANE CELEBRATES WITH ALAN McLOUGHLIN

after the World Cup Qualifier match in November 1993 between the Republic of Ireland and Northern Ireland. McLoughlin's equalizing goal saw the Republic of Ireland qualify for the World Cup in the United States the following year.

Courtesy of Inpho Photography

Football Association (MFA), formed in 1901, were affiliated to the IFA from the outset. The alliance was an uneasy one from the beginning, with many in the South believing the IFA to have a Belfast bias in the selection of players for representative matches, venues and Council members.

This book will look at the relationship that existed between the IFA and its southern affiliated bodies during the last years of the nineteenth century and the first years of the twentieth, and at the incidents that shaped opinions and perceptions which would colour the bond and eventually culminate in the split of 1921.

Introduction

The year 1912 was significant for Belfast and for soccer in the country. It was the year of the Titanic disaster, the world's largest ship sunk, built in the Harland and Wolff shipyards of Belfast. The introduction of the third Home Rule Bill, significantly, with no more permanent House of Lords veto, meant Home Rule would become a reality in 1914.[23] Northern Unionists became more militant and tensions rose sharply throughout the year. The First Lord of the Admiralty, Winston Churchill, came to Belfast in February 1912 to promote Home Rule. Unionist Belfast felt betrayed that the son of Randolph Churchill, who had been the darling of Ulster Unionism in the 1880s, would come to preach the opposite of what his father did. They forced him to change the venue for his speech from Ulster Hall to Celtic Park, the ground of the nationalist leaning football club, Belfast Celtic. The football club was then seen as a direct sponsor of Home Rule. In September 1912, a vicious riot took place at the same ground, when Belfast Celtic played Linfield, one club representing nationalism, the other unionism. The riot was the worst ever seen at a soccer match, a political and sectarian riot that left over fifty people injured. Days later, on 28 September, Ulster Unionists' resistance to Home Rule reached its zenith with the signing of the Solemn League and Covenant by the majority of Ulster Protestant men and women, many signing with their own blood.[24]

Nineteen-twelve also witnessed a split in soccer when many of the senior clubs left the IFA and set up a new association rivalling the supremacy of the IFA. The Leinster Football Association stood steadfastly by the parent body. The split was healed before the start of the 1912–1913 season with the rebel clubs winning many of the concessions they were looking for. The IFA, in its darkest hour up to that point, received solace from its sister associations in Britain, the football associations of England, Scotland and Wales. Their support would help to shape future actions of the IFA in the troubles that lay ahead.

Ireland reached the holy grail of soccer in 1914 by winning the British Home Championship outright, for the first time in its history. With a young team, it was felt Ireland would realise regular success in the coming years. Alas, it did not transpire as the world became engulfed in a war months later, with the start of the First World War. Soccer in Ireland, like everything else, was severely affected by the war, with many players and fans joining the front, and clubs struggling to survive. It was decided in 1915 to impose a division of sorts, to cancel the Irish Football League for the duration of the war, and to hold regional leagues in its stead. Belfast and Dublin had separate leagues. This too would have repercussions for division in future years.

By the time war did end in 1918, Ireland had changed irreversibly. Ireland's path towards independence was reaching its climax; her route towards partition was close at hand. Soccer was fundamentally affected.

The catalyst that led to the split revolved around the choosing of a venue for an Irish Challenge Cup semi-final replay between Dublin club Shelbourne and Lurgan club Glenavon in 1921. The first match, played in Belfast, resulted in a draw. It was believed the replay would be played in Dublin. The IFA's Senior Clubs' Protest and Appeals Committee ruled that, because of the violence in Dublin (with the War of Independence raging), it was too unsafe for the Glenavon team to travel to Dublin. The replay would be held in Belfast instead.[25] Shelbourne and the Leinster Football Association resisted and ultimately left the IFA, leading to the formation of a new association, the FAI.

The FAI would spend the following decade fighting for recognition internationally from the British Associations and from FIFA. It would also spend those years establishing itself as an association and spreading the game throughout the Free State, whilst the IFA consolidated itself within the new Northern state.

Given the political climate at the time, was the split inevitable? How was it that soccer divided but many other sports, like rugby and cricket, remained or became unified after partition. Were other factors at play in causing and cementing the split? The thrust of this book is an in-depth analysis of the split, the people who were the main protagonists and the incidents that caused the rift to take the course it did. Many attempts were made by the IFA and the FAI to heal the split, some coming tantalisingly close. All failed, leaving soccer in Ireland today, as it is politically, divided North and South.

CHAPTER 1

The North Began

Recorded evidence exists of football being played in Ireland from the sixteenth century onwards. The playing of football was mentioned to have taken place in areas such as Dublin, Galway and Waterford, amongst others.[1] It experienced a decline in the late eighteenth and early nineteenth centuries, primarily due to political suppression and a decline in activities devoted to amusements after the Great Famine of the 1840s. Would-be reformers also helped to curb the growth of football, taking a dim view of its perceived association with rioting, revelry and hard drinking. In 1793, the *Freeman's Journal* complained that:

> Stephen's green (Dublin) was never so badly taken care of as of late. It is become a general resort of all kinds of ruffians and vagabonds, every day. The Sabbath is there profaned by them with hurling and football matches – and in the week-days herds of low ragamuffin vagrants, basket-boys, and servants, disgrace the walks, playing pitch-and-toss, and bellowing forth blasphemy and obscenity.[2]

Neal Garnham in his book, *Association Football and Society in Pre-Partition Ireland* states, 'It seems . . . that social, economic and political factors conspired to create a situation in which, by 1850, football in Ireland was, if not completely extinct, something of a rarity.'[3] It would be a number of decades before the first recorded match of association football, or soccer, would take place in Ireland and it would be under very different rules from previous forms of football played on the island.

Organised soccer came later to Ireland than to anywhere else in the UK. The Football Association in England was founded in 1863; Scotland's first club, Queen's Park, was formed in 1867, with

1

the Scottish FA following in 1873 and the Football Association of Wales was up and running with a domestic trophy by 1877.[4]

The man most responsible for the introduction of codified soccer into Ireland was County Down man, John McCredy McAlery, manager of the Irish Tweed House gentleman's outfitters in Belfast.[5] It is believed that, whilst on honeymoon in Scotland, McAlery witnessed a game of soccer.[6] So enthralled was he with the sport that he invited the captain of the Caledonians football club, J.A. Allen, to bring a match to Belfast.[7] Allen brought Caledonians to Belfast where they played an exhibition match against Queen's Park of Glasgow on 24 October 1878 at the Ulster Cricket Ground. This is considered to be the first game of football played in Ireland under association rules. Queen's Park was believed by many to be the great innovating club of the game at the time, pioneering the passing or combination game which soon overtook the dribbling game favoured by teams in England.[8] The club also helped promote the Football Association of England and is the only Scottish club to have reached the English FA Cup Final.[9]

Despite a rough passage over from Scotland, both teams offered a good exhibition of soccer, watched by one thousand spectators, with Queen's Park coming out on top by three goals to one.[10] Reporting on the match, the *Belfast Newsletter* commentator was clearly unfamiliar with the game and was still getting to grips with the different nuances of soccer as demonstrated by the following passage:

> The ball was then taken by the Caledonian men to the other end of the ground, where, with the help of the wind, they kept it for a considerable time, and ultimately succeeded in securing a goal, thus making matters even ... In the second half, when ends were changed, the Queen's Park had the wind in their favour, and kept the ball almost continually in the neighbourhood of the Caledonian goal. Several good attempts were made by the Caledonian players to carry the ball to the other end of the ground, but the Queen's Park backs invariably returned it.[11]

McAlery, who was Treasurer of the Cliftonville Cricket Club, established a soccer team within Cliftonville, based on the rules of the Scottish Football Association, it not being uncommon for soccer

CLIFTONVILLE FOOTBALL GROUND

Cliftonville was the first soccer club established in Ireland and was at the
forefront in the founding of the Irish Football Association in 1880.
Courtesy of the National Museum of Northern Ireland

clubs to develop from cricket clubs at the time.[12] Cricket was considered Ireland's most popular team sport in the 1860s and 1870s,
its decline in popularity within the country commencing only the
following decade.[13] 'Cricket was standardised in the late eighteenth
century, and in the 1820s it was the first of the codified field sports
to gain a footing in Ireland', spawning from the British army and
young men returning from English public schools or universities.[14]
One of the representatives of the Irish team from the first recorded
cricket match that took place in Ireland in the Phoenix Park, Dublin
in 1792, is believed to have been Arthur Wellesley, the Duke of
Wellington, future Prime Minister of Britain and victor at
Waterloo.[15] He was a member for Trim, County Meath, in the Irish
Parliament, Grattan's Parliament at the time.[16]

An article appeared in the *Belfast Newsletter* on 20 September
1879 asking for 'gentlemen desirous of becoming members' of
Cliftonville Association Football Club to turn up for opening
practice that day.[17] The club was soon playing practice matches

against other clubs. Cliftonville played Quidnuncs, a team of rugby players, on 29 September 1879, the first time two Irish teams played a soccer match.[18] McAlery busied himself procuring rivals for Cliftonville to play against. He played a significant role in helping set up Knock FC, a club that was composed of existing lacrosse players.[19] By 1880, four clubs were regularly playing against each other: Cliftonville and Knock in Belfast; Moyola Park in Castledawson, County Derry; and Banbridge Academy from County Down. There was also a club founded in the midlands, at St Stanislaus College in Tullamore, with the hope that more clubs would be formed in the midland and southern counties the following season.[20]

In its first season, Cliftonville played fourteen matches, winning eight, drawing two and losing four. One of the draws came from Scottish opposition, the Ardee Club from Ardrossan.[21] Scottish clubs were regular visitors and helped soccer in the north-east of Ireland to gain a solid footing. Clubs like Caledonians, Ardee, Ayr and Portland (from Kilmarnock) were soon either visiting Belfast or receiving teams from Belfast in Scotland.[22] Local clubs saw these exhibition matches as potential revenue earners and generally charged sixpence entry to the matches, with ladies being allowed in for free.[23] At one such match between Cliftonville and Ayr, it was reported that Cliftonville would have better results if the players 'learned more co-operation, and . . . got rid of what may be called selfishness in their play', as well as training 'to keep the ball at the toe instead of kicking, and are more alive to the advantages of passing – often back.'[24] The Scottish played a huge role in helping the growth of soccer in Ireland, and have contributed far more significantly in spreading the gospel of sport around the world than they have often been credited with.[25] When the IFA was established in 1880, the Scottish FA donated £5 towards purchasing a trophy for a cup competition.[26]

The IFA was established to organise, govern and promote the game of soccer in Ireland. Cliftonville sent an invitation to other clubs in the Belfast and District area, with the first meeting taking place on 18 November 1880, in the Queen's Hotel in Belfast.[27] In attendance were representatives from seven clubs: Cliftonville FC,

Avoniel FC, Distillery FC, Knock FC, Oldpark FC (all Belfast), Moyola Park FC (Castledawson) and Alexander FC (Limavady). At that meeting, a sub-committee was 'appointed to draw up a code of rules for the Association and also cup competition rules and submit to meeting of representatives for confirmation.'[28] It was also agreed, after 'a good deal of conversation', that clubs affiliating to the Association should pay an entrance fee of ten shillings and an annual subscription fee of the same amount.[29] Finally, it was decided to invite Major Spencer Chichester to become the Association's first president. Chichester, who formed the Moyola Park football club in Castledawson, although not a particularly political man, did have close family Unionist links. His grandson, James Chichester-Clark, would become the second last Prime Minister of Northern Ireland.[30] With business concluded, it was felt that if 'the spirit which pervades those present be acted upon the result will be a strong Association for promoting the game which they have espoused.'[31]

The first IFA meeting of 1881 centred on the new cup competition, the Irish Challenge Cup.[32] This competition would grow to become the Blue Riband competition in Irish soccer, the one all clubs most dearly wanted to win at the start of each season. The IFA had learned from the English FA, whose growth had been stinted before the initiation of the FA Challenge Cup in 1871. The introduction of a cup competition helped the English Association experience a period of sustained growth from which it never looked back.[33] The IFA realised from the beginning, it needed a vibrant competition to allow soccer to grow, with a reputable cup worth fighting for to be awarded to the winner. The IFA commissioned William Gibson & Co. in Belfast who designed a trophy:

> Of solid silver, vase shape, of most artistic design, and high-class workmanship, being richly chased with Irish shield, surrounded with shamrocks, and its beauty is much enhanced by being surmounted with a finely-modelled athlete holding an association ball, the whole resting on a handsome ebony plinth, ornamented with silver.[34]

It was worth £30. The first-round draw for the competition was next on the agenda, with seven clubs entering their names in the draw.[35] At a later meeting of the IFA, it was decided to award the players of the winning team medals; gold ones being seen as too extravagant, silver ones were opted for instead.[36] This decision was later rescinded and gold medals were awarded to the winners, as the funds of the Association were in a healthier position than first thought.[37]

The first year of the competition was not without its moments of controversy. Avoniel made a complaint against Moyola Park, as a player from the latter club's team was 'found wearing boots having large nails' during a first-round tie.[38] A player suffered from a leg fracture during another of the cup ties, and the IFA awarded him one pound for his troubles.[39] The competition in its inaugural year was eventually won by Moyola Park, surprisingly beating Cliftonville in the final. Commenting on the win many years later, one of the people associated with Moyola Park, John Downey, told the newspaper *Ireland's Saturday Night*: 'It was the greatest night ever seen in Castledawson. The victorious team were met by a band and hundreds of people from the village and surrounding districts, and the procession was headed by Lord Chichester himself, who was a proud and satisfied man at his team's achievements.' Lord Chichester, first president of the IFA and patron of Moyola Park was singled out for praise:

> Being an ardent supporter of all sorts of athletics, he himself donned the jersey, and, with the assistance of a few others, taught the young men of the village the rudiments of the game ... Lord Chichester always accompanied the team and paid their expenses. When his Lordship was Sheriff of the County he honoured some of the players by placing them on his staff as escorts.[40]

Downey also commented on the roughness of the game in its early years, when it was 'a matter of "take the man" and "get the ball", no matter whether there was an arm or a leg smashed in the encounter.'[41]

The IFA could look back with satisfaction on its first year in operation. It had successfully organised a cup competition, albeit with some unsavoury moments, and at its first annual general meeting it boasted a balance in the black of thirteen pounds, one shilling and five pence.[42] At that meeting, another meeting was mentioned, one involving the 'kindred Associations throughout the United Kingdom to be held in Manchester on 25 April.'[43] It was agreed at the meeting in Manchester, a Conference of Football Secretaries, chaired by C.W. Alcock of the English FA, to arrange for internationals against England and Wales the following year.[44] The links created on that day in Manchester would foster relationships crucial to the IFA over the coming years, both domestically and internationally.

Ireland's first foray into international soccer took place on 18 February 1882.[45] Ireland played England at Bloomfield, the ground of Knock football club, in Belfast. In a preview of the match, the *Freeman's Journal* described it as a meeting of Ulster versus England, a 'semi-international match in Belfast between an association eleven picked from the various local clubs and the English international team.' The paper concluded by saying, 'the affair is likely to prove a financial success, but a football failure.'[46] The *Belfast Newsletter* also expressed doubts that the match would go well for the Irish team considering most players representing Ireland had about two years' practice, pitted against the experienced Football Association team from England.[47]

The fears were to prove well-founded as Ireland slumped to a thirteen to nil loss. Dressed in royal blue jerseys and socks, with white shorts and wearing a badge consisting of an Irish cross, with a harp in the centre and surrounded with a wreath of shamrocks, the Irish were no match for the all-white Saxons.[48] To make the score line even more humiliating, it came immediately after England's largest ever home defeat, to this date, a six-one rout by Scotland.[49] It has been commented that McAlery, who was captain that day, wept at the result.[50] In Ireland's defence, they were unlucky in having the disadvantage of a heavy wind against them in the first half, to be removed in the second half as an advantage for them because of the wind dissipating. The Irish team consisted of players from four clubs, all recently founded: Cliftonville, Knock, Distillery and Avoniel. England fielded a team made up of players from seven clubs: Cambridge University, Oxford University, Blackburn Rovers, Nottingham, Aston Villa, Swifts and Royal Engineers from London.[51]

Ireland played Wales in Wrexham a week later and lost by seven goals to one. There would be no international victory for five years, the first coming against Wales in 1887.[52] To compete internationally, the game needed to expand, numerically and geographically.

Preceding the match against England came a request from McAlery 'asking if the English team would agree to play their International match with them under the Scotch rule of "throwing in".' It was met with the haughty rebuke of the English FA 'that the Association recognises no other rule than their own and as they have always strictly adhered to them they cannot deviate from their principle for the match in question.'[53] This request from the IFA may have prompted the English FA to seek uniformity on one code being played throughout the United Kingdom. It called for a conference with the Scottish FA a few months later in Sheffield to come to such an agreement, a conference the Scottish FA declined to attend.[54] This rejection stung the English FA deeply and it responded with the following rebuke:

> That the answer of the Scottish Association to the letter of this Association respecting the announcement of withdrawing from the Conference is not at all satisfactory and as it is the almost unanimous desire of the Football Association to have one uniform code of rules throughout the United Kingdom and the present diversity of the rules is not conducive to the interests of the game; the Committee of this Association cannot take any further steps towards arranging the International match until the Scottish Association appoints representatives to meet representatives of the Football Association, the Irish and the Welsh Associations.[55]

Fearing the loss of international fixtures, the Scottish FA soon agreed to change their minds and a conference of the four home nations was held in December 1882 in Manchester where a new uniform code was agreed upon.[56] Despite misgivings from some English FA council members on the wisdom of the potential of 'Associations having no authority as compared with this one (the parent Association, the English FA)' to dictate the rules of the game, most council members welcomed the move and soccer journeyed on the path towards uniformity.[57]

This led to the formation of the International Football Association Board (IFAB) to approve changes to rules on football, a body which met for the first time in 1886. This body still exists today and includes in its membership the football associations of England, Scotland, Wales and now Northern Ireland, since the split within soccer in Ireland, as well as FIFA.[58] It was also decided that an annual championship should be played between the four home countries which became the British Home Championship. Ireland played Scotland in the first ever match of the tournament, held in Ormeau Road, Belfast on 26 January 1884. In the build-up to the match, the *Belfast Newsletter* was optimistic that Ireland would perform well 'on account of the great popularity of the dribbling code' with 'new clubs ... springing up in all parts of Ireland, several clubs playing in and around Dublin, the head centre of Rugby football.' The paper went further by predicting that Ireland would soon 'be "second to none" in the exposition of association football, and those "knowing ones" who prophesised its downfall and utter annihilation must feel small as they see its bright prospects and increasing popularity.'[59]

Despite this optimism, Ireland lost to Scotland by five goals to nil. This was followed up with a six to nil defeat to Wales and an eight to one drubbing against England. The score lines did not get better anytime soon. Ireland's first win in the competition was in 1887 against Wales; their second win another four years later in 1891, also against Wales.

A major reason for Ireland's poor showing in international competitions was the slow progress of soccer in Ireland. It was initially geographically confined to Belfast and its surrounding areas. By 1886, there were still fewer than forty clubs affiliated to the IFA.[60] By contrast, the English FA by the mid-1880s was an association of county and regional associations with a membership of over one thousand clubs.[61] In central Scotland alone, club membership increased from 66 in 1880 to over 500 by 1890.[62]

The IFA did look to attract others to soccer by organising exhibition matches in different areas, mainly limited to Ulster in its early years. At an IFA Council meeting in 1881, it was decided to organise such matches in Limavady in Derry and Strabane in Tyrone. A representative IFA team did travel to Limavady; but not to Strabane, however, as the latter couldn't muster a team together.[63] The IFA was also willing to help the local community by organising charity matches[64] and subsequently a Charities Cup was started to help local hospitals.[65]

The sport in Belfast started to gain momentum and by 1890 was significantly more popular than it had ever been. It did have many disputes in the intervening period and the occasional threat from clubs to disaffiliate, such as Alexander FC threatening to leave the IFA in 1884, unless its protest against Moyola Park winning their Irish Cup tie was taken seriously.[66] It was, though, on an upward trajectory. The IFA now had 124 clubs affiliated to it. A demand for more fixtures led to the formation of the Irish Football League in 1890, with seven clubs from Belfast and Milford from Armagh competing in its first year. William McCrum, a member of Milford, instigated the introduction of the penalty kick to the game of soccer in 1891.[67] Greater urbanisation allowed for more sports meetings to be attended by more spectators and the vast improvements in rail transport allowed for more events to be held in areas inaccessible previously.[68] Increased literacy levels and an expanding press, including media outlets dedicated solely to sport, helped to grow all sports including soccer. It is estimated that over 88 per cent of the Irish population were literate by 1911.[69] As the IFA expanded, the need for substations grew and regional divisions were born in Antrim, Down, Derry and north Armagh.[70]

Given Belfast's status in the late nineteenth century, it is understandable that soccer did blossom there over everywhere else. Many changes happened that facilitated the growth of sport and soccer in the late 1800s for all of Ireland, amplified more in Belfast. The introduction of the Factory and Workshop Acts gave workers more free time to enjoy leisure activities.[71] With its shipbuilding and linen industries, Belfast had many workers, from around 1874, who could enjoy their Saturday afternoons off by going to see a soccer match. The shipbuilding industry also provided Belfast with a disproportionate amount of skilled labourers who had more money to spend on leisure activities.[72] Many of their colleagues were Scottish and English immigrants who introduced them to their favourite pastime, soccer.[73]

On 13 October 1888 Belfast became a city in recognition of it being 'the fastest growing urban centre in the United Kingdom in the nineteenth century.'[74] Belfast's population had mushroomed

BELFAST CITY HALL

By the late nineteenth century, Belfast had become a city, the most populous at one stage in Ireland and one of the most thriving in the United Kingdom. A potent symbol of the huge strides Belfast had made was the construction of its impressive City Hall, completed in 1906.

Courtesy of the National Library of Ireland

from 20,000 in 1800 to just under 350,000 in 1901. It had overtaken Dublin as the most populous city by the time of the 1891 census.[75] The ever increasing population of a thriving city was able to devote more and more time to soccer.

Belfast and its surrounding areas also had less competition from other sports compared to the regions in the South. The other main football code imported from Britain, rugby, also experienced a North-South split before eventual union. Rugby was introduced earlier to Ireland than soccer. Recent research suggests that Ireland could boast the oldest existing rugby club in the world in the guise of Trinity College Dublin, founded in 1854.[76] Rugby in Ulster started some years later with the formation of the North of Ireland Football Club (spawned from the North of Ireland Cricket Club) in 1868.[77]

Ireland, seeking to play a rugby international against England, was advised by the latter body this request would be granted on the condition that a national union was set up. This led to the formation of the Irish Football Union (IFU) in 1874. At the first meeting of the IFU on 10 December 1874, membership comprised of the clubs Trinity, Wanderers, Bray, Engineers and Lansdowne from the Dublin area and Monaghan, Dungannon and Portora from Ulster.[78] The Northern Football Union of Ireland (NFU) came into being the following month. Although not part of the IFU, the northern body did support the international match against England, held in March 1875. This support was aided by the IFU who proposed, for the selection of the Irish team against England: 'In order to guarantee that the Northern clubs' interests would be duly regarded in the selection of the international twenty [twenty players formed a rugby team at the time], that the Irish Union shall nominate seven men to play on the twenty, and the Northern Union a like number and that each Union would then submit the names of ten further players each from which the remaining six players would be chosen.'[79] The remaining six players were chosen by a committee of six, three from the IFU and three from the NFU. For Ireland's first ever international rugby match, twelve players came from Dublin (nine from Trinity College alone) and the remaining eight from Ulster. The match, played in London, was won convincingly by England.

Rathkeale from Limerick was the first Munster club to join the IFU, doing so in March 1875.[80]

The IFU, looking to form a single union for all of Ireland, sent proposals to the northern body in 1875. One of the proposals was to rotate the annual meetings of the union in the North, Dublin and the South (Limerick). The NFU rejected the proposed amalgamation for that season, and instead recommended a sub-committee of ten, five from each union, to choose the Irish team for the return trip of England to Dublin in December 1875. The IFU agreed to the proposal with the one proviso that Munster and Connacht players must also be considered for selection.[81] None was selected for Ireland's second international, which had eleven from Leinster and nine from Ulster.

Thwarted initially, the IFU sought again, in 1877, an all-Ireland union. It proposed that the union would consist of branches in Ulster, Leinster and Munster, the committee of the union to comprise of nine members, three from each branch and when possible, the committee would meet in Dublin.[82] Again the proposals were rejected by the NFU, who according to Edmund Van Esbeck in his officially sanctioned book from the Irish Rugby Football Union, (IRFU), *The Story of Irish Rugby*, rejected equal representation being offered to Munster.[83]

Rules agreeable to Ulster did emerge in November 1878 which did form the basis of the IRFU. They were: that the union be called the Irish Football Union with the objective of promoting and fostering the game of rugby football in Ireland and to arrange international and interprovincial matches; branches to be formed in Leinster, Ulster and Munster; the union committee to consist of eighteen members, six from each province, to be elected annually and that the annual subscription for each club to be £1, with an entrance fee of one guinea.[84]

One caveat was added. Munster would have only four members on the committee until they drew or defeated Leinster or Ulster in an inter-provincial match, the other two seats remaining vacant before that occurred. The union finally came into being in February 1879, its first general meeting was held in 1880.

It has been ascertained that union did not come about until 1879, due to political factors. This claim is refuted by Liam

O'Callaghan in his book, *Rugby in Munster: A Social and Cultural History* who maintains, 'Given that the contemporary powerbase of Dublin rugby was Trinity College and a number of surrogate clubs, it seems likely that those in positions of power in southern rugby may have had a great deal in common with their Belfast counterparts politically and socially.'[85] He believes there was a bias towards Ulster and Leinster instead, to the detriment of rugby in Munster. In 1892, a slimmed-down international selection committee was formed consisting of six members, two each from Ulster, Leinster and Munster. This was reduced to five in 1895 when Munster was deprived of one of its seats for not paying subscription fees and for not having comparable club strength to Leinster and Ulster.[86] The players chosen to play for Ireland reflected Munster's lack of representation within the IRFU. Of the 250 men who played for Ireland before 1900, 220 were from Ulster or Leinster, with just twenty-nine from Munster. There is clear evidence, though, that before 1900, club rugby in Ulster and Leinster was far more vibrant than in Munster.[87]

Soccer enthusiasts from the southern provinces faced far greater threats, not just from rugby, but also from the newly established Gaelic Athletic Association (GAA). The GAA quickly spread in the southern part of Ireland, but not so much in Ulster, particularly in the northern half of the province. 'The general disapproval of Sunday games in Protestant areas of Ulster, together with the strength of association football in the province, meant that the GAA had more external opposition to deal with in Ulster than in the other Irish provinces.'[88]

There is no doubting the pivotal role played by the north-east of Ireland in introducing and spreading the game of soccer in Ireland. The other large urban centre, Dublin, was a latecomer to the game and had a lot of catching up to do before it could challenge the hegemony of Belfast as the central hub of the game on the island.

CHAPTER 2

'The South has been Invaded'

A letter appeared in the *Freeman's Journal* in September 1880 calling for the adoption of soccer in Dublin:

> Will you allow me through your columns to suggest to one or more of the Dublin football clubs to play the Association as well as the Rugby game in the coming season. I think that thereby they would get many new members who have been accustomed to play the dribbling game, which is so popular in England and Scotland, said would be the means of introducing Association football into Ireland.[1]

Despite these calls in the same year the IFA was founded, it would be another three years before a soccer club was formed in Dublin, the Dublin Association Football Club, established in October 1883. The club asked 'gentlemen knowing association and desiring to join' to meet at Tyrone Restaurant, Tyrone Place on Sackville (now O'Connell) Street at 8pm on 19 October.[2] Despite one Dublin paper describing the players as 'butting at the ball like a pack of young goats' and stating it unlikely that 'the natives will take kindly to the innovation',[3] the first practice match in the Phoenix Park did attract 'over a score of players, all of whom were old "association" men'. It 'was attended with a large share of success', according to another newspaper, with a finishing score line of five goals to three between the two teams selected on the day.[4] Players that day came from clubs in England and Scotland such as Carthusians, Pilgrims', Notts County, St Mark's College, Old Westminster and Glasgow City, as well as from Cliftonville in Belfast.[5]

At an early committee meeting of the club, it was proposed to secure a ground at the Hospital for Incurables in Donnybrook. The governors of the hospital allowed the club to play matches on their grounds with profits from the gate receipts going to the hospital. Other benefactors to the hospital included Lord Powerscourt, who gifted it with a hamper of apples on one occasion.[6] At one meeting a swipe was made at the press for 'the suppression of fixtures, letters, and reports concerning the club by some of the metropolitan papers, and [it] considered that the Dublin Association Football Club were as much entitled to recognition and space in the columns of those journals as Rugby clubs of equal standing.' This may have been in reference to an *Irish Times* article condemning the establishment of a soccer club, believing it would detract from rugby:

> Without wishing in any way to condemn the game, we must say that we would regret extremely to see the Association game in Dublin, for the simple reason that there hardly is any room for it . . . Any split in the ranks would only injure the Rugby game, without materially benefiting the Association. We question strongly are there many men who desire the dribbling pastime.[7]

The meeting ended with a rallying call for all gentlemen with experience in soccer to play the game and for even those without, to come and watch 'and thus endeavour to push the real game of football' in Dublin.[8]

Opposition was initially hard to find for the Dublin Association Football Club. It was also more difficult to attract players and spectators in Dublin than Belfast. Belfast was significantly more industrialised with more skilled labourers available to devote their free time to soccer. In Dublin, less than a quarter of the male population were employed in any kind of manufacturing by 1881, and they were less likely to avail of the factory acts that allowed for more time off work. More unskilled people in Dublin meant less time and resources for leisure activities.[9] The growth of the game in the capital was reliant on immigrants from England, Scotland and Belfast as well as the British army and educational institutions.

At one committee meeting of the Dublin Association Football Club, the secretary was tasked with a scouting mission to contact a soccer club believed to be based in the army camp at the Curragh in Kildare.[10] The second match the club played was against Belfast opposition, Belfast Athletics, on the grounds of rugby club Wesley College in Donnybrook. Much to the surprise of the experienced Belfast opposition, the Dublin club went two nil up by half time. Belfast Athletics eventually won by three goals to two. The 'plucky play' by the Dublin club 'augurs well for the future of the Association game in the metropolis', according to the match report of the *Freeman's Journal* , which also mentioned the presence of another soccer club from Dublin, based in Trinity College, Dublin University Football Club.[11]

With two clubs in Dublin, John McAlery, in his secretary's report at the IFA Annual General Meeting of 1884, claimed 'the South has been invaded, the stronghold of opposition besieged, and clubs started in the proud metropolis, the attempt to boycott the dribbling code having been defeated, thanks to the intelligent action of this association and the energy of some few gentlemen in the city.'[12] Later that year at an IFA Council Meeting, due to 'the increasing popularity of the dribbling game in Dublin, it was felt that the time had come to institute an inter-provincial match between Ulster and Leinster, the first encounter to take place in Belfast early in the new year.'[13]

The IFA could rightly take credit for helping to spread the game in Dublin by actively encouraging clubs in the north-east to play against clubs in Dublin. The initiation of inter-provincial contests also allowed Leinster players to compare themselves to the best in Ulster and to put themselves in the shop window for international selection. 'Between 1884 and 1891, nine players from Dublin University were capped for Ireland. F.D. Moorhead and A.L. Eames were the first players from Dublin to be selected for a game against Wales in 1885.'[14] Belfast people living in Dublin also contributed significantly to spreading the game in the capital. The IFA helped grow the game in other regions also, such as Derry. From its inception, the IFA used St Stephen's Day as a day for inter-county matches. Up until 1884, Antrim played against Down. Due to the great strides soccer was making in Derry, it was decided to pit Derry against Antrim on 26 December 1884 to see how the Derry clubs would fare against a team composed of Belfast-based players and to also see if any Derrymen were 'deserving of international honours.'[15]

BRITISH ARMY FOOTBALL TEAM CIRCA 1908

Although not as influential as some critics have claimed, the British army was instrumental in spreading and fostering the game throughout Ireland in its early years, particularly outside of the Northern region.

Courtesy of the National Library of Ireland

Soccer in Ireland has been described by many as 'The Garrison Game' due to its perceived close links with the British army. Some commentators believe this term is an exaggeration of the impact the army had on spreading soccer in the country, the military being notable by its absence at the genesis of the game in Ireland (no military team was affiliated to the IFA by 1888), and the lack of significant success experienced by military teams in most competitions, Gordon Highlanders winning the Irish Cup in 1890 being the one stand-out success.[16] It is undeniable, though, that the military played a significant part in helping to foster the spread and growth of soccer in Ireland in its early years, particularly outside of the northern region. Civilian clubs were reliant on teams from the army to form opposition during the genesis phase of soccer in

Dublin and elsewhere in Ireland. Michael Cusack, the founder of the GAA, commented in 1896 that soccer players came to 'learn their game by fagging the ball for soldiers in the [Phoenix] Park.'[17] On the same day that the GAA was founded in Thurles, 1 November 1884, the Dublin Association Football Club played against a team from the 71st Regiment of the British army in Sandymount.[18] A list of fixtures for one Dublin club, Montpelier, in 1890, shows half of the opposition being from the army. The club played against the 3rd Hussars, the Sussex Regiment and Gordon Highlanders as well as some civilian clubs.[19] The reliance on military opposition was more pronounced in rural Ireland. Most of the opposition for Athlone Town, formed in 1887,[20] in its early years, was from the army, including Royal Artillery, Royal Irish Rifles and Royal Irish Fusiliers.[21] Soccer led to 'considerable interaction' between the rank-and-file soldiers and the middle and lower classes of Athlone.[22] One of the first ever soccer matches played in Munster was in November 1879 between teams from the 7th Hussars and the 15th Regiment held in Tipperary Barracks.[23] Soon afterwards civilian clubs in Tipperary were playing against army regiments.[24] One of the most prominent players was the goalkeeper of the Carrick-on-Suir Athletic, Cricket and Football Club, Tom Davin, brother of Maurice, who would become the first president of the GAA in 1884. The first recorded game of soccer in Kerry was between the Durnham Light Infantry Regiment stationed in Tralee and the employees of the Commercial Cable Company in Waterville in 1894.[25] The initiation of the Army Cup competition also helped to spread the game in previously uncharted territory.[26]

Educational institutions also played a pivotal role in spreading soccer in Dublin and elsewhere. As well as Trinity College Dublin, the second club to be formed in Dublin, clubs emanated from schools such as St Vincent's College in Castleknock and Clongowes Wood. St Vincent's College provided many of the players of a new club formed in the capital in 1890, Bohemians.[27] St Helen's, Montpelier, Chapelizod and Terenure Schools also formed teams, considering soccer as a new form of physical exercise beneficial for their pupils.[28] In Athlone, Ranelagh school was one of the early proponents of soccer.[29] It was believed, by the 1890s, that 1,500 Irish boys travelled each year to English public

TRINITY COLLEGE DUBLIN

The second soccer club in Dublin was founded in Trinity College Dublin. Educational institutions played a pivotal role in the growing of soccer in Dublin and elsewhere.

Courtesy of the National Library of Ireland

schools and upon their return spread the gospel of soccer. One such sponsor was Thomas Kirkwood Hackett, who learned the game at a school in Dorset. He became a founding member of the Leinster Football Association in 1892.[30] Some of the schools that had contributed handsomely to the growth of the game in Dublin, such as Clongowes and Castleknock, would abandon the association code in the early years of the twentieth century, seeing soccer as 'beneath contempt'.[31]

The stinted growth of soccer outside the north-east of Ireland can in many ways be attributed to the formation and spreading of the GAA, particularly in the GAA's heartland, Munster. The GAA waged an aggressive war against sports it deemed as foreign, with the introduction of bans in the early years of the GAA, rescinded in the 1890s and reintroduced in 1901. It was claimed 'there was not so much as a soccer ball . . . in Cork County' courtesy of the GAA-imposed bans.[32] By 1907 there were 270 GAA clubs in Munster, in contrast to just ten affiliated to the IFA. Soccer and the GAA had a more peaceful co-existence in Dublin and Ulster.

The South has been Invaded

Soccer and other sports were granted a welcome reprieve in the 1890s when the fortunes of the GAA plunged, almost disbanding. Its politicisation, manifested most vividly through its support for Charles Stewart Parnell during the divorce proceedings against his lover Katharine O'Shea and her husband William O'Shea in 1890, brought the GAA on a collision course with the Catholic Church, a battle it badly lost. The GAA became, to all intents and purposes, extinct in all parts of Ireland with the exception of Dublin, Cork and Galway. In 1890 there were between sixty and seventy clubs affiliated to the Dublin County Board of the GAA, this was reduced to a low of just eight clubs in the early 1890s.[33] Soccer benefited from the GAA's collapse and gained a foothold in more areas in the country as a result. Many of the GAA clubs that disbanded took up soccer instead.[34]

One of the clubs that did not benefit from the GAA's dip in support was the first club formed in Dublin, the Dublin Association Football Club. The club which had entered the Irish Cup competition for the first time in the 1884–85 season, reached the semi-final stage in 1890. Losing to Cliftonville, the club protested that one of the match umpires was a member of the Cliftonville club. The IFA ordered a replay which Cliftonville also won. Not happy with many of the referee's decisions during the game, the Dublin Association Football Club decided to disband.[35] Many of the club's members would go on to form the Leinster Nomads. This new club became the foremost team in Dublin by 1892 when it reached the Irish Cup semi-final. The club was also not slow to criticise the IFA, claiming the parent body could do more to promote the game in Leinster. One of the club's members, Thomas Kirkwood Hackett, after another humiliating international defeat, stated, 'All this has come upon us because of the prejudice of five men [International Selection Committee members] who select the teams preventing anyone outside the Belfast area being chosen to represent their country.'[36] The club was the main driving force in forming the Leinster Football Association in 1892. The first meeting of the new body was held in the Wicklow Hotel in Dublin on 27 October. Along with Leinster Nomads, Bohemians, Montpelier, St Helen's School and Dublin University, were also in attendance. Ironically, considering the future history

21

of both bodies, the move was welcomed by the IFA, 'which was only too willing to encourage the growth of soccer clubs in Ireland in general and Leinster in particular, and it donated £50 to help with the financial side of setting up the association.'[37] Reverend T.V. Morley from St Helen's School was elected the first chairman and Dudley Hussey from Bohemians, the first honorary secretary. Rules and a cup competition were quickly agreed upon. The formation of the Leinster Football Association led to a more formalised structure for the game in Leinster and helped spread its reach to places other than Dublin such as Athlone, Kilkenny and Dundalk.[38] It also led to a significant development for the game in the South. Teams from outside of Ulster were now competing, reflected in Irish Cup Final appearances for Bohemians in 1895 and 1900. The club lost by ten goals to one to Linfield in 1895, a losing margin for a final which still stands as the highest to date, reduced to a loss of 2–1 to Cliftonville in 1900. Cliftonville beat another Dublin team in the final the following year by the same margin, defeating Freebooters 1–0. Freebooters were the first Leinster team to tour the European continent when they visited Belgium in 1902. They won all six games played, including an impressive 13–0 victory over Brussels which consisted of most of the Belgian international team.[39] The arrival of Shelbourne Football Club in 1895 as a serious rival to Bohemians' dominance in Dublin, also helped improve the standards of the game in Leinster and levelled the playing field between the Ulster and Leinster teams.[40]

By 1900 there was 'a Leinster Senior League, Leinster Junior League, Junior Alliance, Junior Combination League and Leinster Senior, Junior and Minor Cup competitions'; competitions allowing the standards of the game to continue on an upward curve in the province.[41] The year 1900 was seminal for football in Dublin. For the first time an Irish international match was played in the capital. It came about after a request was made by the Leinster Football Association to have the match between England and Ireland played in Dublin, on 17 March, St Patrick's Day, instead of in Belfast, as Belfast already had a rugby international scheduled for that day.[42] The IFA consented and the Leinster Football Association began its preparations for its biggest day in the spotlight to date. As no soccer pitch could accommodate the projected crowds, the match was played at Ireland's rugby head-quarters, Lansdowne Road, with patronage being offered by Earl Cadogan, the Lord Lieutenant of Ireland. Ireland lost 2–0 to England on the day. Just one player from a Leinster club, Dr George Sheehan of Bohemians, played for Ireland. He was selected as captain. Eight players came from Ulster and the other two were Irish players plying their trade with English clubs.[43] One of the two, Matthew Reilly, goalkeeper for Portsmouth, was the first profes-sional from Leinster to join an English club. He was also a distinguished Gaelic footballer.[44] The match was considered a financial success with gross gate receipts amounting to over £312.[45]

The strides made by Leinster were acknowledged at the IFA Annual General Meeting of 1900, held on 14 May, where it was stated:

> Owing to the rapid and remarkable interest evinced in the game in the Dublin district your committee decided to alter the venue of the semi-final of the Irish Challenge Cup and International match versus England, hitherto played in Belfast, to Dublin. Your committee are happy to say that the experiment proved a highly satisfactory one.[46]

Despite the 'experiment' proving to be a success, Dublin would still experience little change in the amount of international fixtures it hosted.

Undoubtedly, great strides had been made in Leinster in the 1890s. However, the province still lagged considerably behind Ulster in every area. Other than Gordon Highlanders, Ulster teams made up all the winners of the Irish Cup up to 1900. The Irish Football League, established in 1890, would only ever see winners from Ulster right up to the split of 1921 and beyond. The game in Ulster was considerably more advanced than in the South, manifested most vividly by its acceptance of profession-alism into the game a full decade before professionalism was introduced into Leinster. The IFA legalised professionalism in 1894, the Leinster Football Association didn't do so until 1905. In many ways, Leinster's progress compared with Ulster's, mirrored Ireland's progress compared with the other home nations, with the IFA almost a decade behind the English FA's introduction of

professionalism in 1885.[47] Football in Munster lagged behind
Leinster by a greater margin again, with a Munster Football
Association not established until 1901.[48] An illustration of these
similarities was the results of the Irish national team against its
rival home nations compared with the results of the annual
Leinster-Ulster inter-provincial matches. Most years saw Leinster
aping the Irish international team, suffering heavy defeats against
their northern rivals.

Many in Leinster saw the administrative structure of the IFA
as a major factor in contributing to Leinster's lack of competitiveness against Ulster, the IFA Council a stumbling block to
accelerating the progress of the game in Leinster and beyond. The
IFA was seen as a body favouring the County Antrim Association
to the detriment of every other region. Many in the Dublin press
accused the IFA of giving 'as little encouragement . . . as they possibly can to football in Leinster' prompting one Leinster delegate
at the IFA AGM of 1899 to claim that there was 'sectional warfare
and internecine strife between the provinces.'[49] Leinster joined
forces with the North-West Association to increase regional representation on the IFA Council, the primary decision-making
body for soccer in Ireland. A victory of sorts was achieved in 1901
when it was decided, at a specially convened conference, to
divide the IFA Council's twelve seats with six from Belfast and
three each from Derry and Dublin. Supporting the new structure,
James Sheehan, the chief advocate of change from Leinster, at the
Leinster Football Association AGM of 1901, commented on 'the
long standing dispute which existed between Derry and Dublin
on one side and Belfast on the other,' which he stated had now
been settled.[50] The new format was unanimously supported by
the delegates. The increased representation on the IFA Council
for Dublin and Derry helped to smooth relations between the
parent body and its regions. It was not long before this relationship would be tested, almost leading to the Leinster Football
Association leaving the IFA.

Familiar with losing to Ulster, Leinster suffered a particularly
galling defeat in 1902, losing by eight goals to nil against the
northern team. Four players who had been selected to play withdrew from the match. Reasons cited were illness through blood

poisoning and work commitments.[51] Humiliated by the nature of the defeat, the Leinster Football Association decided to make scapegoats of the withdrawn players and suspended them for a month. This rash decision was soon questioned by the IFA who claimed the Leinster Football Association had broken protocol by suspending the players without inviting the perceived offenders to a meeting to defend themselves. Also, the IFA's approval had not been sought, which it needed to be in order for the suspensions to stand.[52] The Leinster Football Association was forced to back down and the suspensions were removed, all excuses offered by the players now deemed satisfactory. This also led to a Leinster Cup tie between Bohemians and Freebooters being replayed, Bohemians having lost the original tie due to two of the club's players being wrongfully suspended.[53]

Following immediately after that run-in with the IFA, came another decision by the parent body that irked many in Leinster. The IFA ceded to Richmond Rovers' (a club from Rathmines in Dublin) request to play a professional footballer, M. Bruton, as an amateur. The Leinster Football Association ruled that as it was an amateur body, unlike the IFA, Bruton was not allowed to play for Richmond Rover's.

These incidents led directly to the following motion proposed by J.M. Duggan at the Leinster Football Association Committee meeting of 12 March:

> That as the Irish F. Association has allowed a sub committee of its own to interfere with the internal arrangements of the Leinster F. Association contrary to the Rules governing the IFA and also the Rules of the LFA, we, as a protest withdraw from the membership of the Irish F. Association, that we also request the English, Welsh and Scottish Associations, to bring our case before the International Board at its meeting in June; and that all competitions under the jurisdiction of the Leinster F. Association shall be continued as heretofore and further that we call upon all clubs connected with the Leinster F. Association who are also connected with the Irish F. Association to resign membership of the latter body at once.[54]

Demonstrating a lack of conviction in supporting his own motion, Duggan decided to absent himself from all committee meetings for a month, leading to one committee member questioning when Duggan planned to put forward his motion.[55] When the motion did come before the committee, a tied vote ensued. It took the casting vote of the chairman (J. McConnell) to ensure that Leinster Football Association would remain within the IFA fold.[56] The rift highlighted the volatile nature of the alliance with the IFA, a rift caused largely by Leinster itself in its clumsy and rash reaction to an embarrassing defeat to Ulster. The next decade would see many more disputes between Leinster and the parent body, the uneasy alliance tested severely on numerous occasions.

CHAPTER 3

An Uneasy Alliance

The first decade of the twentieth century saw a huge upsurge in the popularity of football across the country, especially in Ulster and Leinster. There were 110 clubs affiliated to the IFA in 1900. By 1910, there were 420.[1] More and more people attended matches. Sixteen-thousand spectators attended a soccer match between England and Ireland on the same day as five thousand witnessed Ireland play Wales in a rugby match in Belfast in 1904.[2] Irish Cup and League matches were also drawing bigger and bigger crowds. Of all regions, Leinster witnessed the most spectacular growth, with 119 clubs affiliated to the IFA by 1910, just fifteen shy of the largest region, the north-east.[3] The Leinster Football Association went on to overtake the north-east as the largest region of the IFA in 1913.[4]

Munster did not see a comparable uptake in soccer. In 1910 there were forty-three clubs from Munster affiliated to the IFA,[5] a year later just thirty.[6] Munster was dominated by British army teams. Cork's representation in the new Munster Football Association comprised of a large contingent of army and navy teams based in Cork, including Royal Engineers, 6th Provisional Battalion from Fermoy, HMS Black Prince, RE Camden, and the Army Service Corps.[7] At an inter-provincial match between Leinster and Munster in 1910, 'the Munster team was composed principally of military players, their [sic] being eight soldiers in the side.'[8] The province's reliance on the British army was disheartening for many locals, drawing them to rugby and Gaelic games instead.[9] Although the army did help local economies and became part of communities, relations were often strained. Many saw

27

troops having little to do 'but get noisy in a pub or try to lure a girl under a hedge.'[10] The changing political environment and the GAA's aggressive campaign banning 'foreign sports' also contributed to the stinted growth of soccer in Munster. J.J. Walsh, chairman of the Cork County Board during the 1900s, in his autobiography, explained the effects the GAA's campaign had on 'foreign games':

> With this intensely organised instrument, war was declared on foreign games which were made to feel the shock so heavily that, one by one, Soccer and Rugby Clubs began to disappear. In a few years there was not as much as a Soccer ball, outside the British garrison, in Cork County . . . and only one or two Rugby Clubs, already in a groggy condition.[11]

It was also felt the parent body, the IFA, did little to nurture the growth of soccer in the province, bemoaned by a *Sunday Independent* correspondent in 1906:

> Last week I drew attention to the grant of £50 by the IFA to the Fermanagh and Tyrone Association, and criticised the neglect at the same time of the parent body of an equally deserving branch, the Munster Football Assoc., who since their formation has had to struggle hard for existence. Matters are even worse than I thought, and with the exception of a paltry £10 in 1903–4 the IFA has left the Southerners to their own mercy. True; they sent a team from Ulster to Cork last season, but, although the gate was a poor one, the IFA walked away with their small half; which with great advantage to the Munster FA and at little loss to the IFA, might have been handed over in toto to the former.[12]

In 1913, a motion at an IFA Council meeting was defeated, 'that the Munster Association be given a grant of £20 to keep the game alive in Munster.'[13] Yet, the same council had no problem in granting £25 to a council member, G.M. Small, for a testimonial in his honour at the very next council meeting.[14] The council eventually reluctantly did offer Munster a grant, 'the sum of £35 on condition that the Munster Football Association raise the balance to clear their debt, and further recommend that this grant be considered final as far as this Association is concerned. Grant to be forwarded as soon as the Association receive assurance that the

Balance is raised.'[15] Connacht did not even get any recognition from the IFA. According to Garnham, 'In 1910 the IFA decided "not to interfere in the project" of setting up a Connacht FA to encourage the game in the west of the country.'[16] The Munster Football Association did receive support from their colleagues in Leinster, though, who provided them with grants on occasions[17] and provided the province with much-needed competition and funding through annual inter-provincial contests.[18]

Leinster, with some similar slights at the hands of the IFA, enjoyed better fortunes than Munster and Connacht, experiencing a decade of progress from the turn of the century, both on and off the field. One of the main contributing factors to this turnaround in fortune was its eventual acceptance of professionalism in 1905.

Professionalism officially came into Irish soccer at the IFA AGM of 1894 by a vote of sixty-four to thirty. Ironically, it was the votes of the staunchly amateur club, Cliftonville, and the Leinster delegates who would not introduce professionalism for another decade themselves, that saw the motion pass. One of the clubs opposing professionalism that night was Linfield, a club to all intents and purposes that had introduced it previously. In 1890, Linfield advertised in the *Belfast Evening Telegraph*, offering work to '5 whitewashers, 2 tar spreaders and 4 handymen' at a football ground in the city. While no experience was deemed necessary, potential applicants were required to 'be expert players' and to give details of their 'age, weight, last club and wages expected.'[19]

Professionalism would be slow to take off in Ireland. By 1903 there were just 104 professionals in Ireland, all confined to Ulster, many of them part time, and most of them professional for just one season.[20] It did lead to larger crowds at matches and improved standards, most aptly demonstrated by Ireland's sharing of the British Home Championship with England and Scotland in 1903, its best season in that competition to date by a considerable distance. The IFA granted each regional division a lot of autonomy on introducing professionalism, the north-west introducing it in 1902 followed three years later by Leinster.[21] It did lead to some tensions between the parent body and the Leinster Football Association. Leinster disagreed with the IFA's ruling on Richmond Rovers

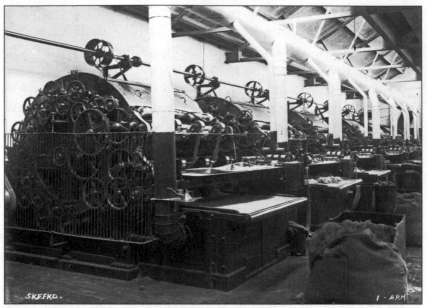

LINFIELD SPINNING MILLS

The Linfield Football Club was formed by the staff of the Linfield Spinning Mills in 1886. It would go on to be the most successful club in Ireland.
Courtesy of the National Museum of Northern Ireland

fielding a professional player, M. Bruton, in 1902 (see Chapter Two). The same club's attempt to introduce professionalism in Leinster at the AGM of 1902 was defeated.[22] Months later the Leinster Committee took great exception to the decision of the IFA Council to delete the word 'amateur' from the rulebook of the Leinster Football Association.[23] The IFA replied, accepting the Leinster Football Association's right to remain an amateur organisation, insisting, though, that Leinster would have to accept dealings with professional players and clubs considering the IFA had legalised professionalism.[24]

Leinster's eventual acceptance of professionalism in 1905 led to almost immediate rewards on the field, when its first professional club, Shelbourne, became the first Dublin team to win the coveted Irish Cup in 1906, defeating Belfast Celtic 2–0 in the final. Frightening scenes were experienced that day in Dalymount Park when hundreds were hurt after a makeshift wooden stand collapsed.[25] But it didn't stop the celebrations for the Shelbourne supporters. 'Tar barrels blazed in Sandymount and Ringsend that night.'[26] That success was followed two years later by the first all-Dublin final when Bohemians defeated Shelbourne 3–1 in a replayed final, also held in Dublin. Shelbourne would gain revenge on Bohemians in 1911, defeating them 2–1 in another replayed final.

Bohemians, who would retain their amateur status until 1969, joined the Irish Football League in 1901, followed by Shelbourne in 1903.[27] Although neither team would ever go on to win an Irish League title, the experience of playing teams from Ulster on a weekly basis did stand to both teams, and helped immeasurably in bridging the gap in standards between the two provinces. The annual inter-provincial matches started to reflect this with Leinster, on the back of some drawn fixtures, finally defeating Ulster by the late 1900s, recording their first victory against Ulster in 1909 by 3–0. At the subsequent Leinster Council meeting, the clubs of Bohemians, Shelbourne and Lancashire Fusiliers were thanked for providing the players for Leinster. The IFA was also thanked 'for granting the net receipts of the match' of £72–2s–0d.[28] The IFA had somewhat redeemed themselves with this gesture following a bitter dispute between Leinster and the parent body that almost caused a split in Irish soccer, a dispute centred on the outgoing secretary of the Leinster body, William Sheffield, and an abortive attempt by Leinster to obtain a loan of £200 from the IFA.

Sheffield had been secretary of the Leinster Football Association from its early years and initially enjoyed cordial relations with the body. A Special General Meeting was convened to organise a testimonial for his marriage, where he was awarded a gift of £5 which was warmly received by Sheffield.[29] He also was the recipient of cash advances[30] as well as regular salary increases as secretary.[31] The first hint of trouble to come occurred in 1903 when Sheffield threatened to resign as secretary. The main reason he wished to resign was that his attendance was deemed necessary at all Leinster Cup semi-finals and finals. He did not want to go to every match. He withdrew his resignation once it was established he could appoint a substitute at those matches in his stead.[32] Relations between Sheffield and the rest of the committee did continue to deteriorate. It finally came to a head in 1907 when it was revealed that Sheffield had not forwarded twelve Leinster clubs for affiliation to the IFA, even though some of their applications had been received by him six months earlier.[33] The IFA rejected the clubs for membership unless details of matches the clubs had played in were forwarded to the parent body, in effect questioning the validity of the twelve clubs.[34] This was a particularly sensitive issue for the Leinster Committee, as claims had been made throughout the 1900s of clubs and regional associations creating bogus clubs to boost their numbers, with the aim of wielding more power within the IFA.[35] The Leinster Committee replied that 'through an oversight on the part of the Secretary, the Council regrets the clubs were not sent on sooner and in future the Council will see that a repetition does not occur.'[36] At that same meeting it was decided, on a vote of nine to one, to advertise the position of secretary at a salary of £40 in the papers inviting applicants for the post.[37] Forty applicants were received for the post. A special committee shortlisted six names, including Sheffield. On a final ballot, Jack Ryder, who would oversee many changes in soccer in Ireland as Leinster Football Association and first FAI secretary, was announced as the new secretary.[38]

In early 1908, the Leinster Football Association was in dire financial straits and it decided to canvass the IFA for a subsidy of £200.[39] The IFA agreed to send the £200 loan to Leinster on terms to be agreed by a sub-committee set up by the IFA. It was agreed that the sub-committee would consist of five trustees, three elected by the IFA Council and two elected by the Leinster Football Association. The Finance Committee of the Leinster Football Association unanimously chose P.H. Stewart and William Fitzsimons as their representatives.[40] After lengthy protracted conferences and discussions, one of the trustees proposed by Leinster, Stewart, was deemed unacceptable to the IFA. The IFA suggested T. Kearney, who was deemed unacceptable to Leinster.[41] Unable to come to an arrangement between both parties, the Leinster Football Association decided to withdraw their interest in receiving a loan from the IFA, securing a bank overdraft instead.[42] They had proposed a number of money-making and cost-saving measures earlier in the year including reduced fees from the IFA (the request was rejected):[43] an annual match between Bohemians and Shelbourne with the clubs to get 10 per cent of the gate receipts; and the Leinster Football Association to receive one third of the gate receipts for preliminary rounds of the Senior Leinster Cup, one half for the semi-finals and 80 per cent for the final.[44]

At the same time as the loan discussions were ongoing, William Sheffield complained to the IFA that, as a former secretary of the Leinster Football Association, he was entitled to be co-opted onto the Leinster Council, something that had not happened after he lost his job as secretary.[45] After the IFA enquired on the matter, the Leinster Football Association informed the IFA 'that it came to the knowledge of the [Leinster] Council in going through the books that certain monies had not been properly accounted for and also, having regard to his conduct as secretary to the Council, he was not considered a proper person to sit on the Council.'[46] The IFA ruled that Sheffield still should have been co-opted as Council member and threatened to suspend the entire Leinster Council. At a heated Leinster Council meeting, evidence was produced of Sheffield retaining money owed to the Leinster Football Association on a number of occasions. After a lengthy discussion, the following resolution was passed: 'In accordance with the direction of the IFA contained in their resolution of the 6th inst, we hereby co-opt Mr Sheffield a member of this Council but . . . we consider that it is against the interests and purity of football that Mr Sheffield should become a member of this Council.'[47] The resolution was immediately followed by seven Council members handing in their resignation which were rejected by the Chairman.[48] Sheffield's co-option was one of the main discussion points at the following Leinster Football Association Annual General Meeting. With Sheffield in attendance, the treasurer, Stewart produced evidence that Sheffield had not handed over affiliation fees as secretary. He also failed to get elected onto the Leinster Council for the following year. The following proposal was passed unanimously: 'That having regard to the irregularities declared in Mr Sheffield's letters read at the Annual Meeting, this Council suspend him from taking part in the management of football in Leinster.'[49] The IFA, on subsequently asking the Leinster Council what rule Sheffield had broken to be suspended, received this reply from Leinster: 'that as Governing Body they have to make decisions for the good of football management. If the IFA weren't [sic] happy, they could hold an investigation into the matter.'[50] The IFA never followed up on this suggestion.

The IFA had also taken exception to Leinster describing their loan terms of 1908 as insulting.[51] Looking back on the sagas involving the loan and Sheffield's status as Leinster Council member in 1908–09, it would be hard to draw any conclusion other than that the Leinster Football Association was shown huge disrespect in both instances by the parent body. On asking Leinster to choose two of the five names as trustees for the proposed loan, and subsequently attempting to impose a trustee not agreeable to Leinster, the IFA went back on the terms it had drawn up and presented a scenario Leinster was never likely to consent to. The Sheffield case, following immediately after the loan fiasco, added further fuel to the contention of bullying from the IFA, that the IFA was interfering unfairly in internal Leinster affairs. In many ways it is surprising that Leinster did not secede from the IFA at this juncture. Instead of seceding, Leinster came to the IFA's rescue when soccer in Ireland was engulfed in its largest crisis in 1912, with most of the senior clubs breaking away from the parent body to form a new association.

CHAPTER 4

The First Rupture

The first major split in Irish soccer was neither religious nor political in nature. It revolved around power and money. All of the senior clubs, with the exception of Linfield and Bohemians, seceded from the IFA in early 1912 after their demands for a greater say in the running of the IFA as well as increased gate receipts for international and other marquee fixtures were rejected by the parent body. There was also dissent amongst clubs by the Irish Football League's decision to create a new tier in football, a second division. The IFA Council permitted clubs from this second division entry into the Irish Cup, resulting in the senior clubs being unhappy with the prospect of reduced gate receipts from playing newer less established clubs, and the second tier clubs were unhappy that they would now be considered as senior clubs without entry into junior competitions.[1] The split caused a shockwave for the game in Ireland. The bitter dispute lasted for months, with the seceding clubs forming a new association to rival the IFA. If we look back at IFA Annual Meetings over the previous ten years, the seeds were clearly sown for the 1912 conflict.

The IFA Annual Meetings were often acrimonious affairs during the first decade of the twentieth century. Explosive arguments and melees were commonplace. The 1904 Annual Meeting was dominated by disagreements over the cancelled annual inter-provincial matches between Leinster and Ulster, as well as a motion by Belfast Celtic to allow grounds to be opened on Sundays for other sports.[2] The Annual Meeting a year later in Derry was a far more torrid affair. The meeting started with arguments over the perception of Derry Celtic and Belfast Celtic being shunted from the IFA Council through pacts with other regions; the integrity of the International Selection Committee was called into question for selecting players for international matches who had not 'toed a ball for the season'; and the finance report was challenged, particularly for the extravagant bill for cigars, leading one attendee to jibe, 'Has the Association been smoking cigars all year round?'[3] Proceedings disintegrated when a free fight ensued after one member of the four-hundred-strong audience struck another, with many breaking chairs and using them as their weapon of choice. The melee lasted for minutes, order eventually restored when two young men were removed from the hall. One member claimed the meeting was 'not to the credit of the citizens of Derry', the 'meeting had been part and parcel of rowdyism', a remark he was forced to withdraw.[4]

The Annual Meeting in 1906 witnessed more acrimonious scenes with the press table being rushed by over-eager and angry delegates demanding their voting cards so that they could vote and then get the last train home.[5] The 1910 Annual Meeting was a long night that opened with offerings of condolences to the new king George V on the death of his father Edward VII as well as offering loyalty to the new king.[6] The finances of the IFA then came in for close scrutiny with many criticising the lavish expenses on hotels and other travelling costs. One council member, Thomas Moles claimed that 'the Football Association had been too liberal, and he suggested that the Association should be run as a business organisation, and not as a philanthropic society.'[7] Out of total receipts of £3,092 14s 9d, there was just a balance of £4 10s 1d, seen as extraordinary by many delegates, with some claiming the IFA would soon end up in the bankruptcy court if the finances were not brought under control.[8] One of the delegates suggested, as there was such an extravagant outlay incurred in the Irish Cup semi-finals, the organisation of those matches should be left entirely in the hands of the competing teams.[9] At the same Annual Meeting, a proposal to hold the Annual Meeting in Belfast every year was lost as was an attempt 'to ensure that James McAnerny, a Catholic journalist with the *Irish News* and a representative of the Belfast Celtic club, was excluded from the IFA Council.'[10]

At the Annual Meeting the following year, a proposal by Shelbourne to awards clubs more gate receipts for Irish Cup finals and replays was defeated. Shelbourne had proposed:

> That in the final tie for the Senior Cup the Association shall take half the net receipts, and the remainder shall be equally divided between the two competing clubs. In the case of a replayed final tie the net receipts shall be divided, the Association to take 10 per cent, and the remainder to be equally divided between the two competing clubs.[11]

By 1912, many of the senior clubs, most of them professional, saw the parent body as an amateur-run organisation which wantonly squandered the finances of the game on frivolous items. It was felt by many in the senior clubs that a time for change in the governance of soccer was needed.

In February 1912, Linfield demanded 20 per cent of the gate receipts from the IFA for the international match against Scotland, due to be played at its ground, Windsor Park, the following month, instead of the usual 10 per cent it was entitled to receive under the IFA Articles of Association.[12] This decision led to four members of the Linfield Club Committee being suspended for two years by the IFA and the decision reversed, with the rest of the Linfield Committee and Trustees agreeing to accept the 10 per cent offered by the IFA.[13] Subsequently, at a meeting held on 12 February, between members of the Cliftonville, Belfast Celtic, Distillery and Glentoran clubs they passed the resolution 'that, if the remaining members of the Committee and the trustees of the Linfield Club grant the use of their ground at 10 per cent, and desert their suspended colleagues, the Belfast senior clubs do not take part in any match against the Linfield Club.'[14] The four clubs were either hoping to compel Linfield to leave the IFA and set up a new association or hoping the IFA would back down and agree to 20 per cent gate receipts for the clubs.[15] They were to be disappointed on both fronts. Linfield remained within the IFA and at an IFA Emergency Committee two days later, it was ruled that all members from the four Belfast clubs who attended the meeting at which the Linfield boycott was agreed upon were suspended for a period of three years.[16] Describing the magnitude of the crisis unfolding, Dublin newspaper, *Sport* claimed, 'Not since "soccer" was first introduced into Ireland, away [sic] as far back as 1879, has the governing body of the game received such a shock as has been the case during the present week.'[17] The paper also contended that the powers of the IFA Emergency Committee were as absolute as the full council and because of the serious nature of the crisis, it was felt the whole council should have convened to reach a decision and not just the Emergency Committee.[18]

One prominent Leinster representative believed the action of the IFA Emergency Committee would end the matter: 'the League clubs have played their last card and must accept defeat, as the Linfield Club, one of the most influential in the North, has practically acknowledged the justice of the IFA's case',[19] – an assertion that would prove to be erroneous. Events were set in motion where calm and reasoned voices would not be heard: soccer in Ireland was split. Cliftonville, followed soon after by most of the senior Belfast clubs, resigned from the IFA. It was agreed to hold a meeting in the Grand Central Hotel in Belfast on 21 February with a view to setting up a new association.[20] In attendance were representatives from Glentoran, Distillery, Belfast Celtic, Derry Celtic, Glenavon, Cliftonville and Shelbourne, the sole Dublin club. It was decided to establish a new association for the governance of soccer in Ireland. 'It was further decided to insert advertisements in the local Press inviting applications from clubs desirous of joining the new association, also from referees willing to act under its auspices.'[21] The IFA Emergency Committee responded by 'suspending those clubs from this date from taking part in football or football management under the jurisdiction of the Irish Football Association', in some ways a mute action as the clubs had already left the association.[22]

The IFA now had in its fold, just two senior clubs, Linfield and Bohemians, ironically the two clubs most affected by the IFA using club grounds, being the proprietors of Windsor and Dalymount Parks respectively. It did, though, have the support of many regional associations including Leinster and Munster. At a meeting of the Leinster Football Association, a resolution was passed 'to assure the IFA Ltd of their support in the present crisis and further that the Council considers it their duty to urge upon the clubs and players under their jurisdiction the necessity for remaining loyal to the IFA Ltd.'[23] As well as being suspended from the IFA, Shelbourne was also suspended from the Leinster Football Association. The IFA welcomed Leinster's 'kind resolution in reference to the present football trouble.'[24] The IFA also received a letter of loyalty from the Munster Football Association.[25]

Other key support bases for the parent body were the other home nation football associations, whose loyalty and assistance during this difficult period would not be forgotten when soccer in Ireland was subsequently plunged into fresh crises. The IFA approached the English, Scottish and Welsh Associations and a decision was made to recognise each association's suspensions, based on an international agreement reached in 1894. This agreement was authored by the IFA according to a previous IFA secretary, Jack Reid. It was reported in *Sport* that when Reid on behalf of the IFA:

> ... introduced it, the other bodies could not understand why an English or other player not of the IFA should be dealt with by the latter, presuming he committed an offence in Ireland. But the argument was that we were likely to have internal quarrels often in the Emerald Isle, and it was to prevent suspended players taking part in matches across the Channel that the rule was desired, and therefore the agreement was come to. Unquestionably it is useful to-day, and had it not been in operation there is no doubt but that the authority of the IFA would, as the governing body in Ireland, have been seriously menaced, if not altogether undermined.[26]

This agreement left players who played for any of the suspended clubs in a precarious position. It left them bound to their present club or the other suspended clubs with no prospect of transferring to a club associated to any governing body of the home associations.[27] The prospect of international football was also removed. One player was reported as using the present crisis to his advantage. James McKnight of Glentoran, applied to the IFA for reinstatement as soon as Glentoran was suspended, his wish was granted. Without uttering a word to Glentoran, McKnight left for England and joined Preston North End on what was effectively a free transfer. With his transferrable fee estimated at £300, Glentoran, as a suspended club, instead received nothing.[28]

A prominent journalist in England, James Catton, editor of *Athletic News*, suggested that the associations of England, Scotland and Wales convene a conference with the IFA and the seceding clubs to resolve the dispute, a suggestion initially rejected by the IFA who claimed there was nothing to arbitrate about.[29]

Instead of a resolution being sought, the dispute escalated. Most matches were suspended. The Leinster Cup semi-final match between Bohemians and Shelbourne, scheduled for 9 March was cancelled, replaced by Bohemians playing the Rest of Leinster instead,[30] a game Bohemians won easily by seven goals to two.[31] Linfield was particularly ostracised, devoid of practically all local opposition. As the only non-suspended club left in the Irish Cup, the other semi-finalists, Cliftonville, Glentoran and Shelbourne all being suspended, Linfield won the Irish Cup of 1912 by default.[32] Linfield, along with Bohemians, were reliant on opposition from overseas to sustain them financially during the crisis. Prominent cross-channel clubs including Everton, Glasgow Rangers, Preston North End, Derby County, Greenock Morton, Blackpool, Leeds City, Renton and Clyde all sent teams over to Ireland to play against Linfield and Bohemians.[33] The presence of such luminary visitors was seen as a boost by some to soccer in Leinster:

> Notwithstanding the extraordinary state of affairs which pre-vailed, it may be said that the season in Leinster was a very successful one, and the public may be said to have benefitted somewhat by the crisis insomuch as several prominent cross-Channel clubs visited the metropolis to play Bohemians, and in each case the matches were very well patronised.[34]

As well as agreeing to clubs under their governance visiting Linfield and Bohemians in Ireland, the home associations refused to recognise the new breakaway Irish association and the clubs affiliated to it.[35] At the subsequent International Football Association Board Annual Meeting, held in Aberystwyth, Wales on 8 June, an extraordinary gesture of support was offered to the IFA by the other home nations:

> A vote of sympathy was accorded the Council of the Irish Association in its troubled times, and a hearty vote was passed to stand loyally by the Irish FA, and give it the support of the other Associations. It was further unanimously decided by the

delegates present to urge their respective Associations to play
the International Matches with Ireland for the ensuing season
in Ireland, and thus give the Irish FA valuable support.[36]

This decision was fully endorsed by the Football Associations
of England, Scotland and Wales, and all of the Irish international
matches for 1913 were held in Ireland, offering a huge boost to the
beleaguered IFA coffers.[37] The level of support received by the IFA
from the other home associations during the crisis of 1912 would
also imbue the IFA with a sense of security should another crisis
befall it, powerful friends would be at hand to help.

The new Irish football association, despite being bereft of international competition, had distinct advantages over the IFA. Most
of the senior clubs in Ireland were now under its governance. A
new cup competition was quickly established and put in motion,
with the provision of a 'magnificent trophy' for the winner.[38]
Belfast Celtic went on to be the first and only winner of the cup
competition for the new association, defeating Glentoran in the
final. 'The Celtic people were so delighted that they nearly
"mobbed" the team.'[39] Although this would be the only year the
new cup competition was held, the trophy would not be lost to
Irish football, it subsequently became the prize for the Gold Cup
competition.[40] Two other trophies acquired by the new association, the McElroy and Junior Cups, were subsequently offered to
the second division of the Irish Football League.[41]

The IFA tried to combat the lack of local competition available
to Linfield and Bohemians by introducing new clubs to the Irish
Senior League to replace the suspended clubs. A special committee of the IFA convened to agree on the new clubs and
guarantee the necessary capital to allow the new clubs to survive
and strive in a league competition to commence the following
season. It was decided that the league would consist of two clubs
from Dublin and Belfast, and one each from Derry, Lurgan and
Portadown, as well as Linfield and Bohemians.[42] The clubs that
finally agreed to form the new IFA league were Linfield,
Bohemians, St James' Gate, the Guilds from Derry, Portadown,
Lurgan Celtic, Ulster and Old Park.[43]

Throughout the spring and early summer of 1912, the two competing governing bodies for soccer in Ireland pitted themselves

41

against each other, on many occasions organising matches to coincide with those being organised by their rival. On the same day as Ireland played Scotland at Windsor Park, a benefit match was held for Shelbourne in Grosvenor Park in Belfast between Glentoran and the Rest of the new League with an attendance of 10,000, just 2,000 shy of the full international. The Lord Mayor of Belfast, MP R.J. McMordie, was at the Shelbourne benefit match instead of the international between Ireland and Scotland. The rival match led to reduced gate receipts for the IFA, significantly down on what it would expect from a home international. The Scottish FA was aggrieved by the actions of the new association, believing the perpetrators as unpatriotic and discourteous. As the Scottish FA sided with the IFA, it is doubtful if the new association was overly concerned by the Scottish viewpoint.[44]

The IFA attempted to return the favour in May, when Distillery was scheduled to play Belfast Celtic in the Charity Cup Final, by inviting Blackburn Rovers over to play a selected Irish team on the same day, in aid of the Titanic Disaster Fund, the ship having sunk in the North Atlantic the previous month. This move, intended to spoil the Charity Cup Final, was considered particularly dis-tasteful by some, as echoed by *Sport*, ''Tis a strange football world we live in after all. Charity is kind in an old and trite saying, but underneath the surface of all that is charitable to-day lie deep feel-ings of animosity in the game. The pity of it all.'[45]

By the time the IFA held its Annual Meeting in Portadown in May, the dispute had been raging for three months, with no end in sight. Deep regret was expressed for 'the serious crisis', seen as 'detrimental to the future working of the game as a sport in this country.'[46] It was also felt that 'the time has arrived when the seri-ousness of the position should be gone into and a settlement of the unfortunate dispute be made in the interests of the game.'[47] A motion was passed accepting:

> As Arbitrators in the present dispute, the Chairman or Deputy of the English Association, Scotch Association and Welsh Association, also Chairman or Deputy of the English League and Scottish League . . . to hear all the evidence required and grievances (if any) from both sides, their decision to be final and binding on all concerned.[48]

One delegate from Leinster commented that if they were going to have a settlement it should be one with honour on both sides.[49] This volte-face by the IFA was picked up by *Sport*:

> Now the period which led up to the dispute was one of great suspense. During that time the clubs said they had a lot of grievances, but the Association were of opinion there was really nothing then to settle. The clubs were insistent that there was, and said they were quite prepared to leave all matters in dispute to an Arbitration Board like that suggested at the meeting in Portadown last Friday night, but, alas! that offer was rejected, and then came the split. If the Association felt there was nothing to arbitrate about, then it seems strange they find out at the eleventh hour this is highly desirable.[50]

Both sides agreed to enter into negotiations during the summer of 1912 to resolve the dispute, despite a claim at one IFA Council meeting that such negotiations were not of interest to the chairman of the new association, J.D. Reid.[51] After a number of meetings, both sides came to an agreement in August and the dispute was settled.[52] The major points agreed upon were representation on the IFA Council for all senior league clubs; the senior clubs to organise the Irish Cup except for Protests and Appeals and the finances for the final tie, which would be under the remit of the whole council; reduced representation on the IFA Council for the regional associations: clubs from the second division to be eligible for the Intermediate Cup Competition; 10 per cent could only be agreed to for 1912 for gate receipts to clubs; no punishment to be meted out to Linfield and Bohemians for siding with the IFA; and all suspensions to be automatically rescinded. The IFA also agreed to discharge the liabilities of the new association to the value of seventy pounds.[53] The new association wrote to the IFA accepting the terms and in the process it dissolved itself.[54]

The first major dispute in Irish soccer was now at an end with many of the concerns of the senior clubs dealt with in a satisfactory manner. The IFA had been stunned by the resolve of the clubs to secede and survive as a new association and finally consented to many of their demands. The IFA also saw the unwavering support received from the other home associations in its hour of need, support the IFA would not hesitate to call for again in the future. Another of the bodies that had supported the IFA throughout the crisis, the Leinster Football Association, was somewhat perturbed by the IFA as it received no official notification detailing the settlement.[55] It also was at loggerheads with the parent body which refused to grant Dublin club, St James' Gate, entry into the Irish Cup even though the club had just won the Intermediate Cup.[56]

One of the clubs that did secede from the IFA, Derry Celtic, was soon no longer involved in the sport in any guise. It switched its allegiance to the GAA. In a massive coup, the GAA celebrated 'a big Soccer landslide . . . in Derry City, where no less than fifteen clubs, including Derry Celtic and the Catholic Guilds, have adopted the Gaelic code.'[57] 'So as to deprive the soccer association clubs of having any ground to play on', Luke O'Toole, GAA general secretary, proposed and received 'a grant of £30 in the form of a loan so as to have sole control of the ground in question.'[58] Despite efforts by the IFA to lure Derry Celtic back to soccer by offering £10 to compete in the Irish Cup in 1914, the club remained committed to the GAA.[59]

The soccer dispute of 1912, neither political nor religious in nature, was just one dispute bubbling in that fraught year of 1912. Most of the other ones were political, as the prospect of Home Rule became more real than it ever had before during that year – a year that changed the fate of politics in Ireland irrevocably, and with it, the fate of Irish soccer too.

CHAPTER 5

1912

The year 1912 was a significant one for Ireland, particularly for the part of the Ireland that would become divided from the rest of the country less than ten years later. Central to many of the seismic events that occurred that year was Belfast Celtic, the leading nationalist-leaning club in Belfast, whose sometimes accidental involvement in key events of 1912 helped to illustrate the bitterly divided society in the North of Ireland that would intensify in the years ahead.

The catalyst for the change in mood in the northern region of the country was the introduction of the Third Home Rule Bill. This Home Rule Bill was very different to the previous two of 1886 and 1893, both being defeated through the normal parliamentary procedures, the first defeated in the House of Commons and the second making it to the House of Lords where its progress was halted. Ulster Unionists were able to confine their resistance to the Houses of Parliament in Westminster, knowing victory was assured.[1] Everything changed with the passing of the Parliament Act of 1911, allowing the Conservative-controlled House of Lords to veto bills for just two years from thereon, no longer permanently.[2] The John Redmond-led Irish Parliamentary Party supported the Liberal government after securing a promise of a new Home Rule Bill, one that would become law by 1914. Ulster Unionists were now forced into action with the objective of avoiding Home Rule at any cost. The resistance would involve a huge propaganda campaign spearheaded by James Craig, future Prime Minister of Northern Ireland who led a:

> Propaganda blitz against Home Rule between 1912 and 1914
> . . . conducted on the lines of a two-year advertising campaign
> utilising every available media resource including newspa-
> pers, cartoons, books, postcards, placards, posters, pamphlets,
> leaflets, songs, banners, photographs, film, badges, brooches
> and even towels. There were also lectures, parades, demon-
> strations, guided tours and sermons in church.[3]

The Unionists were ably assisted by the leader writer of the *Belfast Telegraph*, Thomas Moles, who would become managing editor of the same newspaper and an MP for Ormeau and Belfast South in the Westminster parliament.[4] Moles wrote many of the anti-Home Rule pamphlets published by the Ulster Unionist Council as well as ghosting pro-unionist articles for the British press.[5] He was one of the leading assistants of Edward Carson, leader of the Ulster Unionist Party, and amongst his notable pamphlets were 'The Ulster Situation' and 'The Real Ulster'.[6] He was also a keen soccer enthusiast and served on the IFA Council and International Selection Committee both for Fermanagh and Munster.[7]

To combat the anti-Home Rule propaganda, the Ulster Liberal Association, organised by William Pirrie, chairman of Harland and Wolff and a Home Rule supporter, arranged for a pro-Home Rule rally to be held in Ulster Hall in January 1912, with Winston Churchill, First Lord of the Admiralty and John Redmond as guest speakers.[8] 'The meeting incensed Unionists, who booked the hall the night before and refused to vacate it for the Liberals' meeting.'[9] The Ulster Hall, placed in the centre of the Protestant quarter, was seen as a symbol of Ulster Unionism. Holding a pro-Home Rule rally there was seen as a crass and insensitive move by some, akin 'to denouncing the monarchy from the steps of Buckingham Palace.'[10] The choice of venue was the subject of a subsequent debate in the House of Lords.[11] The main guest speaker in favour of Home Rule, Winston Churchill, also came in for severe criti-cism: 'Unionists were outraged that the son of such an anti-Home Rule advocate as Sir Randolph Churchill, who in 1886 coined the phrase "Ulster will fight and Ulster will be right", would have the audacity to come to "their" city to preach for Home Rule.'[12] It was commented that the Ulster Unionist Council was 'threatening to

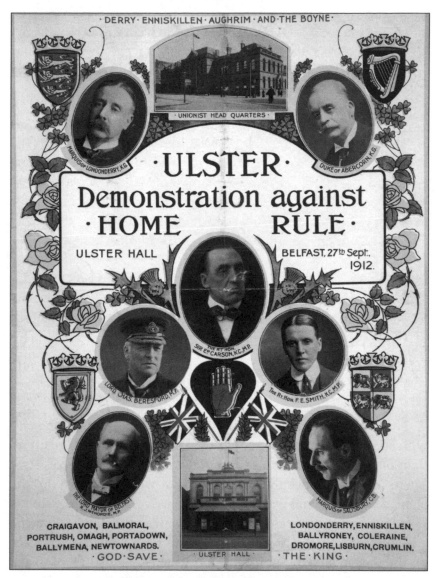

POSTER FOR AN ANTI-HOME RULE RALLY
held circa 1912 including the Marquess of Londonderry as one of the speakers. A staunch Unionist, he was the second president of the IFA.
Courtesy of the National Museum of Northern Ireland

raise a riot and commit murder if Winston dares to speak in the Ulster Hall.'[13] The pro-Home Rule rally now had to be rescheduled and in a different location. It was decided to hold the meeting on 8 February in 'Paradise', Celtic Park, the home ground of Belfast Celtic.

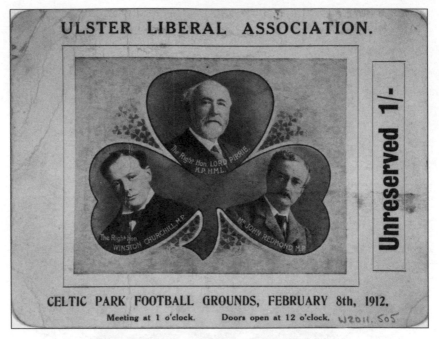

UNRESERVED TICKET FOR A PRO-HOME RULE RALLY
held in the grounds of Belfast Celtic Football Ground on 8 February 1912
with Winston Churchill as the main guest speaker.
Courtesy of the National Museum of Northern Ireland

The build-up to the rally saw heightened tensions in the city
with some claiming there would be sixty thousand men ready to
fight on the day, thirty thousand of them armed with revolvers.[14]
There were wild speculations as to what would happen on 'the
eight' when Churchill was scheduled to arrive, many of the stories
were fed and exaggerated by the press. It was believed that the
'"Islandmen" . . . the horny-handed and hard-souled employees
on the Queen's Island shipbuilding yards . . . mostly Unionists'
were intending to cause disturbances in Celtic Park.[15] It was
reported in the *Freeman's Journal* that 'one enterprising firm of
armourers . . . actually distributed to the Unionist clubs a large
number of envelopes filled with circulars regarding the cost price
of quantities of all kinds of firearms, from pinfire revolvers to the
very latest rifles.' It was contended in the same article that the
blame for whatever violence may occur rested with Unionist
politicians, including the Marquess of Londonderry, president of
the IFA up to 1909, who had 'recreated a feeling amongst their

dupes which had almost faded out of existence during the past ten years.'[16] The Marquess of Londonderry had replaced Major Chichester as president of the IFA in 1897. He was a leading opponent of Home Rule who once claimed in the House of Lords that 'the one and only pledge that I gave to my constituents was that to my dying day I would stand by and maintain the Union between England and Ireland.'[17] It was also allegedly claimed that he was regarded even by some of his own family as being a trifle dim, and he was described by one contemporary as one of 'the two stupidest men in Britain'.[18]

The Ulster Liberal Association commandeered Celtic Park a few days before the rally, immediately after an Irish Cup first-round tie between Belfast Celtic and Cliftonville had taken place on the ground,[19] to prepare for the rally. This included erecting a giant marquee on the ground with a capacity of four thousand, shipped over from Scotland. Posters proclaiming 'Churchill for Paradise' were also distributed around Belfast.[20] The threat of violence, potentially towards a cabinet minister, forced the authorities to increase security for the event. Special police units guarded Celtic Park on the days leading up to the rally.[21] Extra army troops were drafted in for the event, a measure which came to a cost of £2,700.[22] In total eighty-five additional officers and 2,486 additional troops were assigned to Belfast for Churchill's speech – a normal measure when a breach of the peace was threatened according to one government minister when questioned on the wisdom of such a move.[23] This was met with the retort, 'Would it not . . . lead to public economy if, in cases where there is likely to be grave disorder, Ministers are warned beforehand and asked to postpone their visit?' to which the minister countered with, 'No, sir . . . I think the rights of free speech have got to be safeguarded.'[24]

Churchill arrived, with his wife Clementine, in Belfast at 8:40am on the morning of 8 February to a chorus of hissing and booing from opponents of Home Rule. Churchill was considered to be 'exceedingly nervous and ill at ease . . . As he emerged from the railway premises the crowd groaned heartily.'[25] From the train station he was scuttled to the Grand Central Hotel to meet the chief organiser of the event, Lord Pirrie, and from there to Celtic Park. 'All sorts of tricks had to be resorted to, so that he might elude publicity, except when within the friendly shelter of the "Scottish tent".'[26] At one point his car was nearly overturned by a jostling crowd.[27] On the way to Celtic Park, Churchill and his cortege were received by protests from Unionist supporters in Unionist quarters.

Upon entry into the Falls Road and the nationalist quarter, Churchill was finally welcomed to Belfast. 'A great many of the houses were decorated with wet [rainfall, a constant throughout the day], bedraggled looking bunting, and small flags of various descriptions, the Union Jack being conspicuous by its absence.'[28] Fearing the prospect of disturbances, many businesses were closed, the city a sea of drawn blinds, 'and in place of the usual class of persons seen about on a week-day, central streets were thronged by shipyard workers and mill girls.'[29] Large contingents of army troops were visible at all points of Celtic Park.

Churchill's speech was considered a dull speech by *The Irish Times*, which commented that it lasted for an hour and ten minutes and he appeared to read the speech without indulging in any 'rhetorical gesture'.[30] The paper also stated that the content of the speech was not well received by the pro-Home Rule audience either who listened to Churchill speaking of the impossibility of separation from the United Kingdom, 'not only for sentimental and national reasons, but also because Ireland's economic dependence on Great Britain was complete.'[31]

This was followed by a speech from John Redmond, leader of the Irish Parliamentary Party, who effusively praised Churchill and accepted everything he had promised, even though many in the audience felt the promises to be hollow ones.[32] On the content of Churchill's speech, Redmond was quoted as saying, 'I accept every word of it.'[33] Churchill also had to contend with some suffragettes who interrupted his speech occasionally asking, 'will you give self-government to the women of Ireland?'[34] The *Freeman's Journal* felt differently, considering the reception accorded to Churchill as very enthusiastic: 'Eight thousand Ulster Home Rulers, chiefly Protestant Liberals, defied the lawlessness of Londonderry and Carson yesterday in Belfast, and gave Mr Churchill a welcome such as he never before experienced.'[35] The *Southern Star* agreed:

> Mr. Churchill's meeting in Belfast was a magnificent success. The threatened Orange interference was a complete fiasco. A few rather disreputable hostile groups paraded the street in the Unionist portions of the city, but in the Nationalist quarters a welcome of the warmest kind was extended to Mr. and Mrs. Churchill.[36]

After the rally, still fearful for his safety, Churchill left secretly by train to Larne and from there back to London. His clandestine movements in leaving Belfast were mocked in the House of Commons by Ronald McNeill:

> Armed with this safe conduct from the Ulster Unionist Council and protected with 4,000 troops, the right hon. Gentleman effected his escape from Belfast by leaving the football field by devious back paths and taking a special train from Belfast to avoid the dangerous necessity of waiting an hour for the ordinary train.[37]

The rally may have concluded with few incidents of trouble reported. It was clear, though, that there was a rancorous mood in the air of the city of Belfast, a mood that would only deteriorate with each passing month as the prospect of Home Rule loomed larger and larger. Belfast Celtic, by offering the venue for such a prominent display of support for Home Rule, had in many ways become more politicised, more associated with nationalism and more of a target for those opposed to Home Rule. Celtic Park would be the venue again for an ugly riot just months later, offering another example of increased disturbances along sectarian and political lines.

As the divisions became more pronounced over Home Rule in the city of Belfast and the introduction of the Third Home Rule Bill to the House of Commons was fast approaching, the city was dealt with a huge psychological hammer-blow in April 1912. The pride and joy of the Harland and Wolff shipyard, the *Titanic* was sunk on its maiden voyage, struck by an iceberg in the North Atlantic. Harland and Wolff was established in 1861 when Edward Harland partnered with Gustav Wolff to create a company that would cause a sensation worldwide with their revolutionary shipbuilding designs.[38] The company and the ships it built were the most potent symbols of Belfast's supremacy, gaining it a worldwide reputation for its industrial might. Even though the chairman of Harland and Wolff in 1912, William Pirrie, supported Home Rule, he was in a minority. Most of the workers of the company were Protestants and Unionists; Catholic shipyard workers were becoming more and more marginalised and were victims of sectarian prejudice.[39] Certain myths started to appear about the *Titanic*, including an assertion that the ship's hull displayed the number 3909 04, which, when reflected in the water, read 'no pope'.[40]

The loss of the *Titanic* and with it over fifteen hundred lives was a huge blow to all in the United Kingdom, particularly felt by those closely aligned to Harland and Wolff. Amongst the many expressing their grief at the tragedy was the IFA, which, at the first meeting after the disaster, recorded 'its sorrow at the terrible disaster which has plunged the civilized world into mourning, and renders to the bereaved relatives of the victims its deep sympathy in the tragic and awful bereavement they have sustained.'[41] A minute's silence was accorded the victims of the sinking at the subsequent Annual Meeting.[42] The new football association also paid homage to the victims with the finalists of its one and only cup final wearing crepe black armbands.[43] The IFA organised a match between Blackburn Rovers and a selected Irish team for the Titanic Disaster Fund on 11 May. The choice of this date came in for some criticism as it coincided with the Belfast Charity Cup final organised by the new football association (see Chapter Four).

The English FA decided to offer the proceeds from the Charity Shield match between the champions of the Football League and the champions of the Southern League, to the Titanic Disaster Fund as well as contributing two hundred guineas. It also recommended that clubs affiliated to the FA make collections at their matches for the fund.[44] A total of £2,235 was raised by the FA's endeavours.[45]

Just days before the *Titanic* sank, the British Prime Minister, Herbert Asquith, had introduced the Third Home Rule Bill to the House of Commons, on 11 April.[46] The debate in the House of Commons would rage on for months. The public campaign to resist Home Rule by the unionist community would escalate over the intervening months too, culminating in the signing of the Solemn League and Covenant on 'Ulster Day', 28 September 1912, when 471,414 men and women signed the covenant in opposition to the Third Home Rule Bill. They pledged 'to stand by one another in defending for ourselves and our children our cherished position of equal citizenship in the United Kingdom and in using all means which may be found necessary to defeat the present conspiracy to set up a Home Rule parliament in Dublin.'[47] At a ceremony in Belfast's City Hall, Sir Edward Carson was the first to sign the covenant, followed by the Marquess of Londonderry, former president of the IFA.

The build-up to 'Ulster Day' witnessed an event that saw soccer become directly involved in the political and sectarian tensions that engulfed Belfast at the time. It involved two of the city's most prominent clubs, Belfast Celtic and Linfield, whose fans were involved in an ugly riot on 12 September in Celtic Park, the most vicious football riot ever witnessed up to that point in the whole of the United Kingdom. Both clubs were no strangers to incidents of violence in the past, although never on the scale of September 1912.

Belfast Celtic, the leading Catholic club of Belfast, was an amalgamation of junior clubs on the Falls Road, a predominantly Catholic area, such as Milltown, Millvale and Clondara. It was formed in August 1891, based on the Glasgow Celtic model, a club that gave the new club a sizeable donation.[48] From its early days, there was always a threat of sectarian violence any time Belfast Celtic played Linfield or Glentoran in particular.

Linfield was founded in 1886, formed by the staff of the Ulster Spinning Company's Linfield Mill,[49] located in Sandy Row, a predominantly Protestant area of Belfast – 'Up Sandy Row where the Fenians never go.'[50] Both clubs were seen as representing opposite sides in politics. A person's religion was often ascertained by knowing which team they supported.[51] On becoming professional, both clubs chose to hire staff of the religious persuasion to which the clubs were most closely aligned. From 1899 to 1903, Belfast Celtic hired one Protestant; Linfield no Catholics. As Neal Garnham contends, Linfield:

> . . . with its roots in the overwhelmingly Protestant area of Belfast's Sandy Row, [and which] continued to hold its general meetings in that area's Orange Hall, perhaps saw its Protestant identity as reinforced by the nature of its professional playing

staff. By 1912 Celtic and Linfield were simply identified in the English press as Belfast's Catholic and Protestant teams.[52]

Many of the early incidents of violence Belfast Celtic was involved in, pitted the club against Glentoran, another club with a predominantly Protestant make-up which had James Craig, future Prime Minister of Northern Ireland, as one of its shareholders.[53] Celtic supporters were involved in brawls and stone-throwing with followers from the Glentoran Seconds team at a Robinson and Cleaver Junior Final in 1895. 'After the final whistle, the crowd invaded the pitch and a number of Glentoran officials and players were attacked, with some being hospitalised.'[54] A year later, when Celtic was admitted to the Irish Football League for the first time, Celtic supporters clashed with Linfield and Glentoran fans on separate occasions, incidents including attempted assaults on referees and pitch invasions.[55] At an Irish Cup semi-final tie between Celtic and Glentoran in 1899, more violence ensued when the 'the match ball was stolen and cut to pieces by knife-wielding men.' A bricklayer passing by was also attacked, forced to fend off his assailants with his trowel.[56] One local newspaper saw this incident as the introduction of 'the "curse of party bigotry" to football, and thus "threatening to destroy not only the reputation of footballers, but the peace of the community".'[57] 'In 1902, fans from the Linfield and Belfast Celtic clubs were chased down Belfast's Donegall Road by the police after throwing stones and exchanging "party tunes" rather than blows.'[58] In December 1903, two matches involving Celtic were marred with violence. After a match against Distillery, the crowd at Celtic Park invaded the pitch, throwing mud and gravel at the players.[59] A week later it was reported by *The Times* of London in a match between Celtic and Linfield:

> Shortly after the beginning of the second half some of the spectators encroached on the field and made a rush for some players. Stone-throwing followed, and the small force of police on duty were unable to separate the crowds. Reinforcements of constabulary had to be sent for, but considerable time elapsed before the disturbance was quelled. Several baton charges were made and some arrests effected.[60]

To curb crowd trouble, clubs put notices out condemning violent conduct, prices were increased to keep out the lower classes, who were seen as responsible for a lot of the crowd trouble, and police and stewards also started to appear at games. The IFA and clubs started to impose fines too. The measures seemed to have the desired effect as fewer incidents of violence at matches were reported up to 1911.[61] Celtic and Linfield were even enjoying more of a cordial relationship. In April 1908 and March 1910, Linfield and Celtic played benefit matches for some of the Celtic players, with Joseph Devlin, nationalist MP for West Belfast even kicking off one of the games. No crowd trouble was recorded at either of the matches.[62]

By September 1912, the mood of the city was significantly more volatile, though, with very few people in the city politically neutral. The more convivial atmosphere witnessed at soccer matches the previous decade had evaporated. A league fixture involving Celtic and Linfield, two teams representing polar opposite views on the Home Rule debate, should have alerted the authorities to the dangers this match represented. It didn't, the police and authorities were caught cold. There was even rumour that the spectators would be treated to a fly-past that day during the match.[63]

Over twenty thousand were in attendance at the match. The match kicked off at 3:30pm sharp. It was an exciting match hotly contested by both teams.[64] Linfield led by a goal to nil at half time. It was during the interval that the trouble started. An *Irish Times* correspondent wrote:

> A scene unprecedented in the annals of Irish football occurred. A party of Celtic supporters in the unreserved area; carrying the club colours – a green and white striped flag – marched through the crowd in the direction of the Linfield supporters, who carried aloft a Union Jack. Their approach was resented, and a fight ensued. The disturbance rapidly developed into a riot, and the crowds overran the playing pitch. Stones were thrown, and [the] air soon became filled with flying missiles. In the melee a number of revolver shots were fired, and this so terrified the other spectators that they scattered in all directions, and many were knocked down and trampled under foot. The riot raged for about half an hour, and the ground resembled a battlefield owing to the number of men lying about in all directions. The ambulances were summoned, and about sixty men were conveyed to the two city hospitals, five

of whom, it is stated, were suffering from revolver shot wounds . . . The police force on the ground and the officials were unable to cope with a riot of such magnitude, and reinforcements of constabulary were sent.[65]

Many of the wounded received injuries from 'Belfast Confetti', the Belfast shipyards being a great source of nuts, bolts, rivets and other debris.[66] Celtic Park was also under construction which provided more weapons according to the *Sunday Independent*: 'All kind of missiles were, of course, lying handy. There were stones, half bricks, and huge clinkers, for the unreserved side of the ground has lately been in the hands of ground makers, who have been laying it out, and the materials were loose and ready at hand.'[67] Describing the scenes on the pitch, a correspondent from *Donegal News* commented:

> The scene was beyond description, hundreds of the rioters had scaled the iron fences and the field was covered with a seething mass of humanity, rolling on the ground kicking and disfiguring each other in a most brutal manner. Whenever the mobs could find opponents they set upon them, and dragged them to the ground, and left them senseless.[68]

Certainly the most worrying element to the riot was the use of revolvers with the most serious wounds treated at the hospitals being gunshot wounds. *The Irish Times* stated:

> The most regrettable affair was the free use made of revolvers and the indiscriminate shooting into a surging mass of humanity. The large number of revolvers now in the possession of more or less irresponsible youths of both parties in Belfast is one of the most appalling facts, and in view of the high feeling which occasionally breaks out in the city, it is a factor laden with the most dangerous possibilities.[69]

The Celtic executive approached the referee and it was decided to abandon the match. A rock flew in through the window as the referee was having his half-time tea break.[70] Reinforcements of police finally arrived 'and two companies were formed up in the enclosure, one at the Donegall road end and one at the Falls road end. Both forces charged out onto the road, and after using their batons freely they chased them back to their own quarter.'[71]

One witness to the events that day was Ina Heron, daughter of James Connolly, a man who would play a pivotal role in the Easter Rising of 1916. Years later she recounted the events that day in Belfast:

> There was a football match in Celtic football grounds a couple of months later. During a final match the supporters of the winning side waved a green flag with a harp inserted in the corner. This was the signal – I don't mean intentional. It gave the opposition the excuse for losing their sense of reason and a very serious riot ensued. The police mounted on horseback took command of the moving throng and rushed the Catholics up the bog meadows towards the Falls Road and the Unionist element down the Donegal Road towards Sandy Row. This was our first experience of mob rioting; shots were fired, people beaten and trod upon as they lay on the roadside. This we could see from our back windows. The cries and screams of people as they reached the trams! People were pulled off and left cut and some with bones broken lying in the street. Military were called out. This led to more excitement and con-fusion; everything was broken up that was moveable in the district; shops looted, and only after hours of unlawful destruction was peace restored. Things had taken on a dif-ferent complexion for us. Here we found ourselves up against a situation unheard of in our short lives and, believe me, a somewhat frightening atmosphere.[72]

There were about one hundred people injured, with sixty treated in the hospitals. Serious wounds included gunshot wounds, fractured skulls (including to a sixteen-year-old), severe injuries to eyes, faces and arms and many scalp wounds.[73]

The riot dominated the news stories in the following days, with many condemning one or other of the parties involved. *Sport* blamed the police and the system of policing in particular. In an article entitled 'Useless Police', the paper claimed:

> Belfast is cursed with officialism [sic] and red tape, as far as the police are concerned. The men themselves are not to blame – it is simply the system. A football ground is a private house in the eyes of the RIC. A man may do everything short of murder under the very eyes of the police on a football ground, and they look calmly on. They have not the power to arrest anyone there, the onus lying on the club to give the man, or those offending in charge, or the alternative of issuing a

summons and taking the risk themselves and bearing the expense ... Several times members have called attention to this gross dereliction of duty, for I hold it is nothing else, but those responsible for the Irish Government wring their hands and do little else. It is an unsavoury subject at the best, and I hope we won't have any more trouble like it this season. It is time some strong action was taken.[74]

Many newspapers believed the main blame lay with a section of Celtic fans who caused the riot by marching over to the Linfield fans hoisting emblems and flags of a provocative nature. *The Times* blamed the Roman Catholic Celtic mob.[75] Others believed the Celtic fans were incited by the Linfield fans 'carrying purple and Orange coloured flags, and singing party songs, and cursing the Pope.'[76] *The Irish Times* believed there were no winners coming from the incident:

> The whole affair, no matter how it is regarded, is not likely to go to the credit of sport in the city or add to the honour of Belfast ... Linfield and Belfast Celtic, as everyone in Belfast is aware, are supported by a following opposed on almost every conceivable question. When two crowds of such a character come together the situation, to say the least, is one requiring careful handling ... It was wrong, therefore, for both parties to display flags – whether a green and white striped flag, or a Union Jack – as these could easily be construed into a means of providing provocation. That was the first error of judgement, and the officials might have made some effort to induce these men not to hoist flags.[77]

It concluded by stating: 'All the elements which go to make up a party riot were present, and this mixture of football and politics, no matter how one may look at it, is certainly not good for sport, and is undoubtedly bad for politics.'[78] Other newspapers including the *Daily Express*, the *Irish News*, the *Irish Weekly* and the *Ulster Examiner*, blamed Edward Carson, who they believed had inflamed tensions so much in the build-up to 'Ulster Day 'that it was almost inevitable such incidents would happen.[79] The *Irish News* commented: 'The tuition of Sir Edward Carson and the gospel of hatred so zealously expounded in the Belfast Unionist Clubs have so far affected the minds of their dupes that even the area of sport is not considered sacred from mob violence.'[80] The

Gaelic Athlete, the GAA mouthpiece, always quick to denigrate soccer, in describing a green flag being hoisted as the catalyst for the riot to begin, quipped: 'The phrase "A red rag to a bull" can now be altered to "A green flag to a Soccerite".'[81]

Reacting to the riot, the Irish Football League issued a manifesto to the football public condemning 'in the strongest possible manner the action of those followers of football who, by their rowdyism, created the deplorable and disgraceful scenes which took place at Celtic Park.'[82] An order was issued 'that under no circumstances will any banners, flags, or other emblems of any kind be permitted inside our respective grounds at football matches, and any attempt to display such will be treated as an offence, and will be severely punished.'[83] It was signed by representatives of all the senior clubs of the Irish League, including the directors of Belfast Celtic and Linfield. A Round Table Conference was called by the City Commissioner of Belfast, inviting all clubs to meet to formulate plans to stamp-out 'football hooliganism.'[84]

There were some follow-up incidents at football matches after the riot in Celtic Park. Only one match was held on 'Ulster Day', 28 September between Celtic and Distillery in Grosvenor Park, seen as an attempt to keep the nationalists quiet.[85] Heavily policed, there still were some disturbances. Revolver shots were fired into the air, there were 'one or two fights between spectators in the unreserved area', an attempt was made to hoist a Union Jack and Celtic fans shouted, 'Home Rule', whilst holding a green flag.[86]

In a peculiar incident just weeks after the Celtic Park riot, Linfield was invited to Dublin by local club Tritonville to play a match, a fixture that normally would attract a large crowd. The gate receipts were a paltry £3, hardly anyone attended. In the opinion of Linfield, this was the result of a carefully orchestrated boycott due to the club's involvement in the riot of two weeks previously.[87] The corresponding fixture between Celtic and Linfield in Windsor Park in November 1912 resulted in Celtic lodging a protest against the 'gross intimidation by the spectators', mainly in the firing of revolvers.[88]

In the build-up to the First World War, 'the inevitable demonstration of revolver music' was heard at many matches, despite the threat of matches being abandoned.[89] The events precipitated by the introduction of the Third Home Rule Bill in 1912 were a mere portent of what was to come. Divisions between those seeking and opposing Home Rule widened over the following years. Irish soccer, dealing with its own division on top of external events, was powerless to avoid the politicisation of the sport as the country looked to be spiralling towards civil war. Of all sports, soccer appealed to people from all religions and political persuasions, a factor that allowed it to become a sport of mass appeal; but it was a factor that also made the sport more susceptible to getting caught up in events outside of its sphere. Soccer in Ireland did receive a respite from the trying political climate not long after the challenging year of 1912: the sport experienced a moment of unity as Ireland, for the first time, won outright the British Home Championship in 1914.

CHAPTER 6

Ireland – Soccer Champions of the World

In March 1914, Ireland won for the first time outright, the premier soccer tournament in the world at the time, the British Home Championship. This annual tournament was the first ever international soccer competition, established in 1883 and first played in 1884. Ireland's record up until 1914 was abysmal, only once sharing the title, with England and Scotland in 1903. Most years consisted of heavy defeats to England and Scotland, punctuated with the odd moral victory and a yearly scrap with Wales for the wooden spoon that Ireland invariably lost.

It was believed by many that this was the tipping point, heralding a bright future for the Irish team. Events unforeseen intervened, however. Months later the world was plunged into war, dashing all hopes of this young Irish team ever repeating the success of 1914.

Ireland's overall record in the British Home Championship up until 1914 makes for very grim reading. Out of a total of ninety matches played over thirty years, Ireland lost sixty-seven, drew nine and won just fourteen, scoring ninety-nine goals and conceding 331, a goal difference of –232.

TABLE 1.1

Ireland's British Home Championship Record: 1884–1913[1]

Played	Won	Drew	Lost	For	Against	+/-
90	14	9	67	99	331	–232

A major contributory factor, believed by many, for such poor results lay in the IFA's selection policy for the international team, leaning heavily towards selecting people from Belfast and its surrounding environs. One of the reasons the Leinster Football Association was formed was to combat this discrimination (see Chapter Two). The national side was often just referred to as 'Belfast' in the media. The Dublin-based newspaper, *Sport*, blamed the IFA for 'behaving most unfairly' in 'overlooking the Dubliners.'[2] It was countered that it was better to select Belfast people for matches held in Belfast and Dublin people for matches played in Dublin. However when Dublin was finally offered a chance to host an international, against England on St Patrick's Day 1900, there was just one player from a Dublin based team selected, Dr George Sheehan from Bohemians. Eight of the players played for Ulster based clubs, and the other two were based in England. The capital would host just six internationals before the outbreak of the First World War.

The one country that mirrored Ireland was Wales and this was reflected in the two countries' results in the Home Championship compared to England and Scotland. Wales did not win a Home Championship outright until 1907,[3] a team that included the legendary Manchester City and Manchester United player, Billy Meredith, the original 'Welsh Wizard' before Ryan Giggs. Like Ireland, the popularity of the game was concentrated in the north of Wales, the south choosing the ball-carrying game of rugby as their football of first choice. The Welsh clubs were also considered weak, and they, like the Irish clubs, haemorrhaged players to the more lucrative English and Scottish ones.[4]

The IFA became more reliant on players based overseas from the start of the twentieth century onwards. It started to include players based abroad once professionalism was accepted. Eleven of the 605 international caps awarded between 1882 and 1900 went to players based at clubs outside of Ireland. However, of the 462 caps granted between 1901 and 1914, 207 went to overseas professionals who played against English and Scottish internationals on a weekly basis; 204 caps went to players based at Ulster clubs, with the remaining fifty-one going to players based at clubs in Dublin (see Appendix C).

The releasing of players from the English and Scottish clubs for international duty to Ireland and Wales was often not granted, leading to both countries fielding weaker teams than England and Scotland, whose FAs did not encounter the same problems. This led to the IFA proposing, at the International Football Association Board Annual Meeting of 1909, held in the Great Northern Hotel, Bundoran, County Donegal, the motion: 'That each Association . . . must arrange that any player or players (playing under their jurisdiction, and of a different nationality) selected to play in International matches be released for such matches.' The motion was withdrawn 'on the understanding that each Association, when requested, would use its influence to have players allowed off when selected in International matches.'[5] It would transpire that each sssociation, particularly the English and Scottish FAs, was ineffective in convincing clubs to release their players for international duty, a factor that almost derailed Ireland's efforts to win the championship in 1914.

The Irish soccer team was becoming competitive by the early 1900s. Instead of losing matches by margins of five goals or more, Ireland was now losing by just the odd goal or two. This closing of the gap was echoed at an IFA Council Meeting in 1910:

> It is rarely that we are permitted to raise a jubilant note in con-
> nection with our International matches, but we can, without
> anything of undue egotism do so upon the present occasion.
> No one who has followed football in this country has ever
> seen an Irish team put up such displays as did the team which
> met the chosen representatives of England and Scotland this
> year. Never before has an Irish team succeeded in defeating
> the very cream of Scottish football upon Irish soil.[6]

Despite playing all of their games at home, following a decision by the other home associations to help the IFA following the split of 1912, Ireland finished bottom of the table in the 1913 Home Championship. Ireland did achieve something that year it had never done before, defeating England for the first time. Ireland beat England by two goals to one on 15 February 1913 in Windsor Park, with debutant Billy Gillespie, who played for Sheffield United in England, being the hero of the day, bagging both Irish goals.[7] It was decided at the following meeting of the IFA's

International Selection Committee to award the players with a memento of the victory, commemorative medals being granted to each player.[8] The win was lauded at the IFA's Annual Meeting the following May:

> The year has been an epoch-marking one in Football. For the first time in the history of the game four Internationals were played in this country, and for the first time similarly in the history of the game Ireland achieved the ambition of 32 years by securing a victory over England, and this is more creditable when it is taken into consideration that Ireland played the major portion of the game with only ten men.[9]

The victory over England did give the team a much-needed confidence boost going into the 1914 Championship, an optimism that would transpire to be well founded as the team reached the holy grail of becoming Home Champions outright for the first time.

Ireland's first match of the 1914 Home Championship was against Wales, held at the Wrexham Racecourse on Monday, 19 January, with a crowd of 5,000 in attendance. It was reported in *Sport* that, 'the game was changed from a Saturday to a Monday in order to let both sides, the Welsh body especially, call on any Anglo players in the service of English or Scotch clubs.'[10] Ireland won by two goals to one, Billy Gillespie being the hero, again scoring both goals.[11]

Born in Kerrykeel, Donegal in 1891, Gillespie has gone down in history as a legend of Sheffield United, making almost five hundred appearances with nearly 130 goals over a twenty-year period for the club. On top of winning the Home Championship with Ireland in 1914, his other standout honour was captaining Sheffield United to FA Cup Final victory in 1925. Such was the esteem in which he was held, that when he moved from Sheffield United to Derry City in 1932, his new club adopted the red and white stripes of his old club, the Candystripes, the colours they wear to this date.[12]

In the build-up to the second match against England played on Valentine's Day, at Ayresome Park in Middlesbrough, the *Freeman's Journal* reported that 'the only occasion on which the [same] match was played at Middlesbrough a drawn game was the outcome, and it is hoped that Ireland will improve on that record. The Irish team is not considered to be a strong side, owing to the changes that will have to be made.'[13] As many of the players were based with English and Scottish clubs, the IFA were unable to field a full strength team. Val Harris was injured after the game against Wales; Jim McAuley, from County Laois, was not released by Preston North End; Bradford Park Avenue refused to release Jack McCandless; Glasgow Celtic refused to release William Crone and Brighton and Hove Albion refused to release Charlie Webb.[14] Regardless of being deprived of these players and perhaps emboldened by Ireland's victories over England the previous year and Wales a month earlier, the newspaper *Ireland's Saturday Night* 'raised hopes of a victory to an even chance.'[15] *The Irish Times* was not so optimistic: 'There is much speculation about a second win over England but it is hardly likely that the team will be caught napping, as did the side who did duty for England last year.'[16]

If the first victory over England a year earlier was considered in some quarters to be a fluke, there was nothing lucky about the victory in Ayresome Park in 1914. Watched by 27,500 spectators with gate receipts of £1,200, Ireland won by three goals to nil. It was reported that England's best players were the goalkeeper, Sam Hardy, and the two full-backs, Rob Crompton and Jessie Pennington, such was the dominance of the Irish team. Ireland's goal-scorers were Billy Lacey with two and Billy Gillespie, continuing where he left off against Wales, scoring one.[17] Wexford-born Billy Lacey had a distinguished career with Shelbourne, Everton and Liverpool. He moved from Everton to Liverpool in 1912 and won two First Division Championships with Liverpool in 1922 and 1923.[18]

The result was lauded by the Irish press and also by many in the British press who also condemned the English team, it being reported that the English fans were 'disgusted' with their team. *The Times* stated that Ireland was the better side and deserved to win. *Athletics News* highlighted individuals from Ireland including Lacey, Galway-born 'Sandy' Craig, Mickey Hamill and Paddy O'Connell, whilst also claiming that Ireland played together as a unit and worked harder than England.[19] O'Connell, or Don

Patricio O'Connell as he was known to Catalans, had an impressive career as a player with Manchester United and Hull City and an even more impressive career as a manager, particularly in La Liga in Spain. He guided Real Betis to its one and only La Liga title in 1935 and also managed Barcelona during the dark days of the Spanish Civil War.[20]

Sport was fulsome in its praise of the Irish team:

> Ireland's first victory over England on English soil was a remarkable achievement. After many years of struggle, of shattered hopes and profound mortification, she has at length burst through in a veritable blaze of triumph. England had not the tiniest loophole of excuse for her failure on this occasion. It was a memorable victory insomuch as the sporting Press is unanimous in its verdict that the best possible talent was opposed to our lads, and the result was the complete supremacy in all departments of the Irish team. The game at Middlesbrough was a revelation, particularly as one of the Irish players selected could not turn out at the last moment, and Rollo, the Linfield full-back, had to be requisitioned, and had to play in an entirely new position for him – namely, outside right.[21]

The *Irish Independent* claimed that the victory over England was 'sensational' and showed 'the game has made great progress in recent years.'[22] The *Freeman's Journal* declared that 'the great achievement of Ireland at Middlesbrough on Saturday has been the solo topic for discussion ever since the result was declared.' It continued by claiming that the result 'makes it obvious to even the "man in the street" that the time has come when the representatives of the Shamrock can claim an equality with the representatives of the Rose . . . The time has come when Ireland has to be reckoned with in International Association warfare.'[23] Although declaring Ireland's win 'a remarkable victory' that beforehand 'no one, except a candidate for a lunatic asylum' would have 'prophesised', *The Irish Times* focused more on the Goliath slayed rather than the victorious David. The paper remarked that 'something is wrong with English football' and predicted 'a remarkable change of tactics on the part of the English team-builders' by bringing back a few of the first-class amateurs from the famous amateur-only Corinthians team, a prediction that proved spectacularly wrong.[24] At the first IFA Council meeting after the match against England, 'nearly all the [Council] members spoke in congratulatory terms of the players in this match.'[25]

The Irish team now had amassed four points out of four and should they beat Scotland on 14 March, at Windsor Park in Belfast, not only would they win the Home Championship outright for the first time, they would win the Triple Crown too. The build-up to the match garnered significantly more interest than normal, with the *Freeman's Journal* declaring that 'the sons of Erin have a chance of showing what they can do in the world of sport, and if they happen to succeed they will have conquered the football nations' of the world.[26] Acknowledging the difficulty of the task ahead against a strong Scottish side, the *Irish Independent* believed that, 'with ordinary luck, Ireland will win the Triple Crown for the first time.'[27] *Sport* too was optimistic of a favourable result, stating that the match:

> Is the talk everywhere, and it will attract all classes and condi-
> tions of people . . . A team that can beat England and Wales
> across the water ought, in the ordinary course, to beat Scotland
> – at Belfast. In 1903 we tied with England and Scotland for the
> Championship, and in 1910 we had a splendid chance pro-
> vided we beat Wales at Wrexham, but we failed. There were
> extenuating circumstances, however, because we lost two
> famous players through injuries after we had drawn with
> England and beaten Scotland. I refer to William Scott and Sam
> Burnison; and therefore we were a victim of circumstances in
> Wales . . . The cross-Channel clubs employing Anglo-Irish
> players have been generous, and let their men away . . . The
> Scottish team is, on paper at all events, the heaviest team, and
> possibly the finest they have ever put up against us.[28]

Ireland was dealt a blow on the Thursday before the match when, because his team, Sheffield United, drew against Manchester City in an FA Cup Quarter Final tie, Ireland's perilous forward, Billy Gillespie was not allowed to travel to Ireland to play against Scotland.[29]

On the same day that Ireland played Scotland in the Home Championship soccer match on 14 March, Ireland played Wales in rugby, both games being held in Belfast, the former at Windsor Park, the latter at Balmoral Showgrounds. The IRFU was not happy with this clash of fixtures, having scheduled the rugby match long before the soccer international against Scotland was set for 14 March. 'In the ordinary course the IFA game with Scotland should have been played in Scotland. By the desire of the Irish body, the Scottish people agreed to come to Ireland again, making it the third successive year they have done so.'[30] Attempts by the IRFU to have the date of the soccer match changed or even for the match to start at a later time than the rugby fixture were not realised: the match remained fixed to start at 3:30pm on 14 March.[31]

Commenting on the Home Rule crisis and on the rugby and soccer matches and their potential as a unifying power, the *Manchester Guardian* remarked:

> At a time when the 'two races' argument is being passed to breaking point the sporting passion of the common people should supply a not insignificant instance of the strength of the national sentiment. Next Saturday both teams will be drawn from the whole of Ireland, and the native Ulsterman, who in all matters except political discussions will have you know that he is just as good an Irishman as they raise in Leinster or Munster or Connaught, is exulting in the hope of cheering a united Ireland to victory.[32]

Due to the large interest both matches garnered, Great Northern Railway scheduled special trains from Amiens Street in Dublin to Belfast to facilitate the large crowds expected.[33] One of the 'special' trains broke a new record too that day by reaching Belfast from Dublin in two hours and one minute.[34]

In front of an estimated crowd of 30,000, the highest ever at an Irish soccer international up to that point, which provided a record gate of £1,650 according to some reports, the match itself was played under miserable weather conditions. According to the *Irish Independent*, 'the ground in Windsor Park was covered with water in several places, and the rain, which had been coming down throughout Thursday and Friday, was still unabated most of the time the game was in progress.'[35] *Sport* reported:

> There never was a game played under more remarkable circumstances. In the first instance, the ground was in parts covered with water. It rained in Belfast for practically forty-eight hours previous to the match, and during it as well. The Scottish side, a heavily-built one, were more at home on it. They, let me say, did not scruple to use their weight.[36]

Reflecting the weather was the fortune of the Irish team during the match. The physique of the Scottish team also caused difficulties. Three of the Irish team's players got injured, the goalkeeper Fred McKee, Paddy O'Connell and full-back Bill McConnell. Whilst O'Connell and McConnell limped on, McKee was forced to retire and was replaced in goals by McConnell. With Ireland reduced to ten men, Scotland took the lead half way through the second half. The Irish responded strongly and with seven minutes to go, Sam Young of Linfield scored the equaliser that ensured Ireland won the Championship outright for the first time.[37]

The press, in general, was gushing in its praise on the achievement of the Irish team. *Sport* wrote: 'Ireland, International champions. Yes, that was the verdict of last Saturday. After thirty years' struggle in the face of extreme difficulty and in the face of adverse circumstances, few would begrudge old Ireland the success in this the greatest prize of the professional football nations.'[38] In a follow-up article in the same paper, headlined 'The World's Champions', it stated:

> The Irish Association team, which won the International Championship this season, has rightly been acclaimed the World's Association Football Champions, and the question has arisen how are the IFA to suitably recognise the fact. That recognition of a substantial character is due all the players who so nobly battled and won fame for Ireland is a matter that cannot be gainsaid.[39]

There were a few exceptions to the glowing plaudits received by the Irish team, including one correspondent who wrote a rather tongue-in-cheek letter to the *Irish Independent*:

> Being a son of the Bulldog breed of Britons . . . I can take an impartial view of Saturday's games. I don't want to rub it in, but I do feel sorry for Ould Oireland . . . Of course, I went to the water polo at Balmoral . . . it was more aquatics than rugger – and no two ways about it Wales walloped Ireland all ends up . . . From all I hear your soccer chaps at Windsor Park wiped the floor with Scotland at every part of the game, except goal getting. 'Twas hard luck to miss the Triple Crown by making a drawn game in it. But, cheer up, Paddy! Ireland will have a double crown soon – King Carson in Belfast and King Redmond in Dublin.[40]

At the following meeting of the IFA Council it was passed unanimously, 'that some recognition on the winning of the International Championship be made to the players, International Selection Committee, Chairman and Secretary.'[41] The Annual Meeting of the IFA was a celebratory affair with the council, stating that they were:

> Able to sound a note never heretofore uttered in connection with Irish Football. It has never fallen to the lot of any previous Council to be able to record that the honour of champions had deservedly been won by Ireland. For 32 years succeeding Councils have striven for this honour and now it has at length been attained, and it was only ill-luck that prevented us from winning the still greater honour in International Football – the 'Triple Crown', but this does not exceed the features that make the year unique. Never have the other three countries been placed in a position of having only the combined total of two goals to their credit.

The Council singled out the players:

> Who so splendidly upheld the honour of Ireland in these International contests. The Council and the entire football public owe a debt of gratitude; they entered into the game with a manliness and determination that were invincible, and as a result Irish football to-day occupies a position that at one time seemed perfectly unattainable.[42]

Commenting on the proceedings at the IFA Annual Meeting, *Sport* compared the status of soccer in Ireland in 1914 to just a few short years previously when the game was in utter turmoil:

> To-night the annual meeting of the IFA, Ltd, takes place in Belfast. When one thinks of the last Association meeting held in the Northern City and compare it with this one, there will be a marked difference. In the 1910 meeting we were in the throes of a revolution amongst the senior clubs as against what was termed the interference of the junior element in football, and it afterwards took place, and almost ruined the game. But for the staunch attitude of Linfield and Bohemians, who alone remained loyal to the governing body, dear knows what might have happened. The firm support of the other three countries, of course, counted. Then England played their annual match two successive years in Ireland and [in] Scotland three. In the match this year, thanks to our victories over England and

Wales, we met Scotland in a battle for either the triple crown or
the championship. It is history now that we won the latter . . .
The meeting therefore, should in every way be a pleasant one,
as I am sure it will. When one considers the united sphere in
which the IFA from a senior point, has been, this return is a
splendid one.[43]

As Table 2 illustrates, there was a truly all-Ireland nature to the
Irish team when birthplace is taken into account. Of the fifteen
players who played at least once that season, five were born in
Belfast and Dublin, two in Galway, one in Wexford and one, Louis
Bookman, moved from his native Russia (present-day Lithuania)
at a young age to Dublin. The IFA had been accused on many occasions, with good justification, of having a clear bias towards Belfast
players, selecting a token player or two from Dublin. This assertion
could not be laid at the association's door in 1914. The teams
selected, represented a balance of players either based in or from
Belfast and Dublin – a team unified with one common goal, to win
for Ireland the British Home Championship. Perhaps it was this
unity and all-Ireland flavour to the team that was a significant
factor in bringing Ireland victory for the first time

TABLE 2

Irish players used during the British Home Championship of 1914[44]

Player	Club in 1914	Birthplace	Matches played in 1914 Championship
Fred McKee	Belfast Celtic	Belfast	3
Bill McConnell	Bohemians	Dublin	3
Sandy Craig	Greenock Morton	Galway	3
Pat O'Connell	Hull City	Dublin	3
Sam Young	Linfield	Belfast	3
Billy Lacey	Liverpool	Wexford	3
Mickey Hamill	Manchester United	Belfast	2
Val Harris	Everton	Dublin	2
Dave Rollo	Linfield	Belfast	2
Frank Thompson	Clyde	Galway	2
Billy Gillespie	Sheffield United	Donegal	2
Ted Seymour	Bohemians	Dublin	1
Harry Hampton	Bradford City	Dublin	1
Rab Nixon	Linfield	Belfast	1
Louis Bookman	Bradford City	Present-day Lithuania (Grew up in Dublin)	1

Ireland overcame years of hurt and humiliation in securing the British Home Championship outright for the first time in 1914. That Ireland won the championship in 1914, so soon after a bitter dispute in 1912 that led to the secession of most senior clubs from the IFA, was a remarkable achievement. The standout fixture on their way to victory was the three-nil victory away to England in Middlesbrough, a repeat of the result the previous year. Ireland's journey on its way to the title captured the imagination of the Irish people, the final match against Scotland in Belfast attracting the biggest crowd ever at an Irish international up to that point. Winning the championship for the first time that year, the premier international soccer tournament in the world at the time, gave the Irish public and press great grounds for optimism for the future. It was felt that this young team could dominate international fixtures for some years to come. Events outside of soccer's control, however, intervened. The world became immersed in war by late summer 1914, a war that would last for four long years and irrevocably change Ireland and indeed the world.

CHAPTER 7

The World goes to War

On 25 May 1914 the Third Home Rule Bill was finally passed in the House of Commons.[1] It was introduced into the House of Lords a month later on 23 June: 'Proposing that the six temporarily excluded counties in Ulster would be controlled by a makeshift administration under the Lord-Lieutenant in Dublin, for unionists, it was tantamount to Home Rule by stealth.'[2]

Five days later, in Sarajevo, Franz Ferdinand, the heir to the Austro-Hungarian throne, was assassinated. That event triggered the start of the First World War. As international tensions escalated and many European countries mobilised over the following weeks, Ireland was more concerned with internal affairs: its path towards war, a civil war. Opening the Buckingham Palace Conference, a conference established to bring about agreement on the Irish Question,[3] King George V warned that 'the cry of civil war [was] on the lips of the most responsible and sober-minded of my people.'[4] It was hoped in Britain and Ireland that war on the Continent could be avoided.

Tuesday 4 August was therefore a momentous day across the United Kingdom. A variety of emotions were felt: shock, despair, panic, a thirst for news and a sense of stoic necessity, among many others. There was, however, one distinctive feature of the Irish response: war abroad meant peace at home. It is one of the paradoxes of modern Irish history that the outbreak of war in Europe may have prevented conflict in Ireland in 1914.[5]

Both unionists and nationalists answered the call to arms to the British flag, both for different reasons. Unionists did so to emphasise their loyalty to the United Kingdom, to enhance their status as an integral part of the Empire. Nationalists went to war to pave the way for a smooth transition to Home Rule, as well as endeavouring to protect the rights of small nations such as Belgium and Serbia. 'In both communities, unionist and nationalist, the war was a palpable presence – from silk embroidered postcards of the Allied flags to disparaging portraits of the enemy.'[6] The majority of people from Ireland who participated in the war were Catholic. Enlistment was sluggish from farmers and people from the poorer western counties, most brisk from both Catholics and Protestants in the industrialised north-east.[7]

The First World War is believed by many to be the most pivotal event in modern Irish history. The war fundamentally transformed Ireland and was the catalyst that led to the current political make-up of the island.[8] Over 200,000 men from Ireland served on the different fronts and anywhere from 35,000 to 40,000 are known to have died on duty.[9] Tens of thousands more returned home with severe physical and mental disabilities. There were close to 30,000 Irishmen who were in the regular forces of the British army and another 30,000 who were reservists at the outbreak of the war.

Regular and reserve soldiers would never be enough to help the French take on the mighty German infantry. New volunteers were needed – thousands of them. All across these islands recruiting posters adorned with the picture of the War Secretary, Lord Kitchener, announced the formation of battalions in a 'new army' to be filled with ordinary citizens, each being promised training, a uniform and a gun.[10]

Posters appeared in all newspapers including ones specialising in sport. One such poster appeared on the front page of *Sport* in October 1915, calling on 50,000 Irishmen not to:

> permit your Regiments to be kept up to strength by other than Ireland's sons! It would be a deep disgrace to Ireland, if all her regiments were not Irish, to a man . . . Lord Kitchener has told you – his fellow-countrymen – that Ireland has done magnificently; and all the world knows of the splendid valour of the Irish Regiments, horse and foot. So glorious is the record that it must be maintained by the men of our race – by Irishmen alone.[11]

The message concluded by mentioning that volunteers only had to serve for the duration of the war, their families would be looked after, they would be fed, clothed, boarded and paid, they would get to see other parts of the world and pensions would be given to disabled soldiers.[12] Approximately 150,000, on top of the forces already in existence before the war, would answer the call and volunteer to serve.[13] According to David Fitzpatrick, 'no war or conflict had ever involved so many Irish participants, making the revolutionary events of 1916–23 appear as minor skirmishes by comparison. Think of the 1916 Rising, involving 1,600 rebels, or the Anglo-Irish War of Independence, fought with about 3,000 rifles and 80 sub-machine guns.'[14] Michael Laffan described the Anglo-Irish War as 'a small affair. The crown forces lost 550 men and the total number killed was under 2,000. Ten or twenty times as many soldiers had often been killed in one day's fighting on the western front during the first world war.'[15]

The regular forces were shipped off from Ireland swiftly once war broke out. Perhaps the most visible evidence of war was the departure within three weeks for England and the Continent of some 40,000 British soldiers who had been stationed in Ireland . . . Eye-witness accounts of the send off that British troops received as they left Ireland during the first weeks of war contradict later myths about indifferent or hostile Irish reactions to the outbreak of the conflict. Cheering crowds were common.[16]

The Second Battalion of the Royal Irish Rifles was sent to the front in France, and was amongst the first to experience engagements in the war. The Royal Dublin Fusiliers were sent to Madras, and the Royal Munster Fusilier battalion sent to Rangoon.[17] All of those divisions had active soccer teams, many of which would have members who perished in the war.

> Many excellent footballers joined such Irish regiments as the Royal Irish Rifles, Inniskillen Fusiliers, Irish Guards, Dublin Fusiliers, and many others. Many young Dublin men never got the chance to pull on the jersey of their local club again while many never returned, others were so badly gassed or injured that they would never be the same again.[18]

The war did not just affect those who fought. Everyone was affected by the war, and all parts of society were consumed with the war effort.[19] It had an immediate economic impact. Banks were closed, food prices rose and unemployment steadily increased, peaking in September 1914.[20] Those who remained at home established fund-raising events and sent comforts to the troops at the front. The sum of £2,610 18s 10d was raised in Cork alone by 28 September 1914.[21] News of the horrific nature of the war was not long in filtering home to Ireland, as Catriona Pennell notes:

> The industrialised killing and horrendous casualties were revealed from the outset. Indeed, the mortality levels of 1914 were never to be surpassed on the Western Front, even in 1916, the year of Verdun and the Somme. Although the BEF [British Expeditionary Force] (with 100,000 men) was at this stage only a small component of the allied forces, it was decimated.[22]

Although Ireland did experience rationing during the war of commodities such as bread, butter and beer, it was not as affected by the war as most other countries, due to its strong agriculture sector.[23] The shortage of available men presented women with work opportunities. It was not uncommon to see women in roles unheard of before, including bus conductors, ambulance drivers, farm hands, clerks and 'munitions girls.'[24]

Most forms of entertainment were severely affected by the war. With the exception of cinema which 'flourished as civilians flocked to watch battle films and newsreels', recreational travel and public entertainments were significantly curtailed.[25] There was also a shortage of train services, limiting people in going to events. Sport did not escape the effects of war, in many cases suffering more than most civilian elements of society.

Once war was declared in August 1914, some sports immediately answered the clarion call to duty. Chief amongst those sports was rugby. Nine Irish rugby internationals would lose their lives in the war.[26] After a committee meeting, the IRFU, echoing a previous statement from the English Rugby Union, declared, that 'all football fixtures for this season be abandoned, save school boy fixtures'. It concluded by stating that the resolution would not 'interfere with the organisation of charity matches or matches for the war relief funds.'[27] A detachment, 120 strong, of the Irish Rugby Union Volunteer Corps was then sent to the army headquarters in the Curragh, enthusiastically sent off by families and friends.[28] The decision to abandon all rugby matches, with the exception of school fixtures, did meet with some resistance from the Leinster branch of the IRFU. At a meeting of the branch, many clubs expressed a desire to play matches against each other. *Sport* agreed with this stance:

> Most of the clubs were in favour of playing matches, and after all why should they not do so. A large number of members of the various clubs have enlisted, Clontarf, for instance, having given no less than thirty-four to the army but if a club has a sufficient number left to get together a fifteen, why should they not play matches?[29]

The IRFU refused to allow matches to take place; it wanted to be seen, like the English Rugby Union, as totally committed to the war effort. This did not stop an unofficial league in Dublin and local cup competitions in Munster being run during the war years.[30]

The GAA was also affected by the war, with many of its members joining the British army, even though the GAA had a ban on members of the British armed forces being members of the GAA.[31] Many were from working-class backgrounds who enlisted for economic reasons. In Ulster, two former inter-county players, Patrick Corey from Tyrone and William Manning from Antrim, died on the front.[32] The Laois County Board proposed at the 1915 Annual Congress 'that volunteering in the army for the present European War shall not entail any disqualification from playing under the Gaelic Athletic Association',[33] a motion it later withdrew, as debate on that motion would certainly test the Defence of the Realm Act's prohibition of holding two opinions on the war.[34] The British military also occasionally used GAA grounds for manoeuvres. A ground in Limerick, used as a cavalry encampment, was 'so cut up as to be more adaptable for the "plough" of a cross-country championship than for a hurling encounter.'[35]

The English Rugby Union's reaction to the outbreak of war was quite different to that of the English FA: 'The Rugby Football Union took its cue from the *Evening Standard*, who ran the headline "Duty before Sport", and abandoned its playing programme for the duration of the war.'[36] The FA believed the war would be over by Christmas and there was no need to halt all football, a perfect distraction and recreation on the home front. At a meeting of the FA shortly after the declaration of war, the FA made a statement:

> The Football Association earnestly appeals to the patriotism of all who are interested in the game to help in all possible ways in support of the Nation in the present serious crisis, and particularly to those who are able to render personal service in the Army and Navy, which are so gallantly upholding our national honour. To those who are unable to render personal service the Association would appeal for their generous support of the funds for the relief and assistance of the dependents of those who are engaged in serving their country. Clubs having professional players are urged to give every facility for their temporary release.[37]

The English FA contributed £1,000 towards the Prince of Wales' War Fund and £250 towards the Belgian Relief Fund.[38] The IFA responded in kind by contributing 150 guineas to the Prince of Wales' Relief Fund and fifty guineas to the Belgian Relief Fund.[39] The English FA also advised clubs to offer their grounds to the military for use, except on match days, for 'well-known public men' to address the crowds to encourage recruits and for the gate receipts for any special match to be offered to the War Relief Fund. Justifying the FA's decision not to cancel all of football, the English FA chairman, Charles Clegg, commented, 'It has been suggested that all games should be stopped. Having regard to the great anxieties which all must feel during the continuance of the war I think total suspension would be mischievous rather than good.'[40] The War Office, on receipt of the FA's proposals for the war effort, appeared to agree with the FA's decisions, saying the 'suggested schemes meet with their full approval' as well as:

> The question whether the playing of matches should be entirely stopped is more a matter for the discretion of the Association, but the Council quite realise the difficulties involved in taking such an extreme step, and they would deprecate anything being done which does not appear to be called for by the present situation.[41]

According to David Goldblatt:

> *The Times* claimed that over 100,000 men, led by professionals who took the King's shilling on the pitch before a game, had

signed up by November 1914. This meant that around half of the country's whole recruiting drive had been achieved through football clubs. Two thousand players out of around 5,000 professionals had joined the armed forces and only 600 unmarried professionals had not enlisted.[42]

League football in Germany also continued on a limited scale. As the war progressed and the British sea blockade saw food become more and more scarce, football pitches like all public open spaces were commandeered to grow potatoes, essentially bringing football to a standstill.[43]

The efforts of the English FA were to no avail to many who compared:

> Rugby's manly athleticism and gallant patriotism with degen-erative soccer, a game now only fit for the basest elements of the lumpenproletariat: 'the sooner the army as a whole takes up "rugger" . . . the better for Tommy. Let "soccer" remain the exercise of the munitions workers who suffer so much from varicose veins, weak knees, cod-eyed toes, fowl's liver and a general dislike for a man's duty'.[44]

Many contributors to House of Commons debates deplored the FA's decision to continue with football and called on the government to take action. Some called on the government to 'put a tax on all those attending professional football who are not in uniform.'[45] Another commented that the public were 'absolutely outraged by the fact of these matches': professional football should be discontinued immediately. He concluded by saying, 'Amateur Rugby footballers . . . have set the others a good example in not only having discontinued their play, but in having volunteered a full complement of fighters.'[46] Sir John Lonsdale, commenting on the poor return derived from recruitment drives at football matches, including one match attended by thousands that saw just 'one recruit to the Colours' obtained, asked the Prime Minister, Herbert Asquith, to introduce legislation 'to suppress all professional football matches during the continuance of the War'. Asquith replied by stating that no case for such legislation existed, however communications were ongoing with the FA. He finished by appealing 'to the general good sense of all football players' to stop the playing of football.[47] The English FA retorted by maintaining that, 'football, which is essentially the pastime of the masses, is the only sport which is being attacked. It is producing more men for the Army, and money for relief, than all the others. Other sports, and the places of entertainment, are being carried on as usual without objection.'[48] This point was raised a few months later in the House of Commons, comparing the lack of agitation that horse racing received compared to football, even though race meetings were held during the war.[49] The Jockey Club had decided to continue with racing during the war 'in the interests of the very large number of persons dependent upon racing for their livelihood.'[50] In a spirited defence, the English FA reiterated its claim that it had done more than anyone else in recruiting members for the armed forces:

> There is ground for believing that approximately 500,000 players and spectators have joined His Majesty's Service since the commencement of the War, and that no other section of the community has produced better results . . . The attendance at football matches has decreased by one-half . . . The attendance at the matches gives the opportunity of appealing to men who would otherwise be lost, and the stopping of the game would defeat the objects of the War Office in recruiting.[51]

The Scottish Association called for a conference to discuss what the home nations should do to combat the negative views of their game. The conference took place in early December 1914, where it was decided to abandon international matches, but not all matches, as it was believed:

> There is no evidence that the playing of football has hindered, or is hindering, recruiting: on the contrary, there is good reason to conclude that football has encouraged and assisted recruiting. In these circumstances . . . it is not right that football should be stopped or suspended. Further . . . to deprive the working people of our country of their Saturday afternoon's recreation would be unfair and very mischievous.[52]

The Scottish FA a day later went to the War Office to say that this statement had not gone far enough and that, at the request of the Under-Secretary of State for War, Harold Tennant, it would be willing to halt all cup competitions, on top of internationals.[53] Such a move was vehemently opposed by the other home nations, including the IFA, which believed that the Scottish FA had gone behind their backs, after agreeing to the less rigorous resolution the day before.[54]

Unlike Scotland, the IFA took its guidance from the English FA in making decisions on what should be done during the war. At one IFA meeting it was decided 'to write to the Football Association of England asking to be informed of what steps they had taken in connection with the war and football, and to say that the Irish Football Association would co-operate with the Football Association in any further steps that might be taken.'[55]

At the same meeting it was mentioned that the IFA chairman, James McElmunn Wilton had accepted a commission in the army. The council congratulated him and to show their appreciation granted him a cheque of £50.[56] Wilton would go on to distinguish himself in the war and was wounded twice, including on the first day of the Battle of the Somme, 1 July 1916, where many Ulstermen of the 36th Division lost their lives. He would also play a pivotal role as chairman once Irish soccer split in 1921.

Other council members and divisional representatives volunteered to serve too, they were commended at the following year's Annual Meeting:

> The Chairman of your Association, Mr. (now Lieut.) J.M. Wilton, set an example by volunteering at the very commencement of the war; other members of your Council who joined are: Mr. J.M.B. Wilson, Dublin, and Mr. Victor Morgan, Belfast, while from the membership of affiliated bodies, quite a list of names could be compiled if space permitted.[57]

Players and supporters also volunteered in big numbers. *Sport* in an article entitled 'Ominous Outlook for "Soccer" Football' worried for the game's future:

> Irish gate receipts for the opening month show a big decrease on the corresponding month last year, and the 'pro' clubs find themselves in a position of anxiety. Fully 20,000 young men, 60 per cent of whom were football followers, have responded to the war call, and Linfield appear to be the worst hit of the Belfast clubs.[58]

It is believed that Bohemians had forty players who 'joined Lord Kitchener's army',[59] more than half of the team enlisted in divisions such as the Royal Dublin Fusiliers, the Irish Guards and the Royal

Irish Rifles.[60] The Leinster Football Association saw the number of clubs affiliated to it cut in half due to players and supporters enlisting.[61] Glenavon, the senior club most affected financially by the war, had over a thousand supporters leave for the front just months after the war began; this rose to 1,400 by April the following year.[62] The club was on the brink of folding.[63] Over a hundred Belfast Celtic supporters joined the Irish Brigade in February 1915 alone, giving a total of 1,800 Celtic supporters who joined the Irish Brigade.[64] It was also estimated that Linfield supporters numbered 'at least 4,000 men in khaki' by April 1915.[65]

Irish internationals who enlisted included Johnny Houston and Jack McCandless.[66] Former international and Bohemians player Harold Sloan was killed in action in 1917.[67] Some people complained that not enough footballers had enlisted by the summer of 1915, and that the remuneration the players were being paid to play football was too much to lure them to join the army.[68] Numbers of players enlisting did start rising significantly from then on, though. Two months later *Sport* commented: 'Celtic and Glenavon have suffered severely through enlistments. The Celts have lost Mehaffey, Cowell and Burns to the army, and Williams is working in Liverpool, and their half-back Leatham, is not sufficiently recovered from injuries of last season to start.' Only six players of Celtic from the previous season were available at the start of the 1915–16 season. 'Glenavon have lost Manderson to Glasgow Rangers, and Clarke has enlisted. Gibson, the full-back, won't play football for twelve months. These three were the backbone of the team. It is scarcely possible for Glenavon to raise an eleven.'[69] It was also commented that Cliftonville had lost six of its players to the army from the previous season.[70]

Junior clubs played their part too. At the 1916 IFA Annual Meeting it was noted that 'it is generally understood that the Junior Clubs of Ireland have rallied wonderfully to the Colours – indeed in some districts junior football has been entirely wiped out.'[71] A year later it was reported that many junior players 'had made the supreme sacrifice in this awful War.'[72]

The IFA and soccer clubs did play their part in recruiting personnel for the war effort. Soccer in Ireland also was quick to give funding to the war effort and to organise charity matches. Shortly after the war started, the Leinster Football Association organised a match between Shelbourne and Bohemians as well as one involving the Leinster League for the National Relief Fund Committee.[73] On one such occasion, players from Bohemians, Cliftonville and Linfield who had joined the army played in a charity match for the war between Distillery and Cliftonville.[74] In a match between Belfast Celtic and Linfield in May 1915, £200 was raised in aid of wounded soldiers.[75] The minute book of the IFA provides many examples of the IFA organising or consenting to one of its divisional associations organising events for war charities throughout the war years.[76]

It was not uncommon to see many in attendance at soccer matches in uniform either preparing to go to or on leave from the front. One such soldier got overexcited at one match and struck a player with his cane when the player was looking to retrieve the ball. 'A scene resulted, the police being called on to eject the offender.'[77]

The loss of players and supporters to the war effort, the support of different war funds and the general economic turmoil caused by the war, affected the finances of the IFA and its affiliated divisions and clubs deeply, particularly in 1914, when it was felt most acutely. All matches saw a significant reduction in gate receipts compared with the corresponding fixture the previous season. A Linfield clash against Belfast Celtic in September 1914 saw a reduction in takings of £112 from the previous season; a Celtic game against Glentoran met with a reduced gate of £40.[78]

Some clubs decided to brave 'the dangers of crossing the channel' to play Scottish clubs in order to obtain funding. Glentoran embarked on one such trip to Glasgow Celtic for a guarantee of £50 and half the gate receipts of £140.[79] The first weekend of October saw similar returns with a decrease of 35 per cent on all fixtures from the same fixtures the previous season.[80] Linfield estimated its receipts were down £250 from the previous year.[81] In December, Glenavon was unable to fulfil a fixture against Cliftonville due to many supporters serving in the army. They had the team ready to play but no supporters there to watch them, and they could not afford the £15 guarantee required.[82] The club applied for financial assistance to the IFA in

January 1915, for a grant of £50. It was decided a grant could not be given to the club considering 'the present circumstances',[83] a decision condemned by *Sport*, 'No decision of recent years emanating from the IFA has left behind such a stigma as the refusal to grant Glenavon a paltry £50 in order to keep a club alive which has been hardly hit through 1,000 of its supporters answering the call of the King and country.'[84] The immediate impact for the club was the need to sell some of their best players, two of those being sold, 'their crack back, Manderson, and their centre forward, Clarke, to Glasgow [Rangers].'[85] The club was also sued for two years' rent, and an ejectment decree was granted with a stay of execution.[86] After considerable public pressure, the IFA finally relented in April 1915 to offer Glenavon a grant of £50.[87]

Shelbourne had proposed, at a meeting of the senior clubs in Belfast, that the receipts for the Irish Cup should be pooled amongst the clubs and the IFA should forego its receipts from the Irish Cup Final and hand them over to the common pool. Tunney, the Shelbourne chairman, in proposing, stated, 'The IFA must bear their share of the war situation, and at a time like the present it is their duty to help the clubs. They can afford to do without the 50 per cent accruing from the final this season.'[88]

The IFA did lose its largest potential source of income in December 1914 when, at a conference of the four home nations, it was decided to abandon all international fixtures for the duration of the war.[89] At the IFA Annual Meeting the following May, the IFA accepted this was a financial blow to the organisation but not a terminal one, due to the forward thinking of the parent body:

> The temporary abandonment of International fixtures has naturally dealt a serious blow to the Finances, for these matches were the prime source of income to your Association; it will, however, be gratifying intelligence to the sporting public to know that notwithstanding the shrinkage in receipts indicated that the Association has still in hands a balance available for the prosecution of its work for some considerable period. This happy state of affairs is due to the fact that the Council early on fully appraised the situation, and took vigorous measures to retrench and effect economies.[90]

At the same meeting it was mentioned that, due to the wave of recruiting for the army, there was a big reduction in the number of clubs affiliated to the IFA from the previous year, from 393 to 221; 104 clubs competed in the Junior Cup Competition compared to 170 in 1914.[91] The IFA also defended its decision to continue with its programme during the war:

> Acting in concert with the kindred Associations across the channel . . . as clubs had already entered into very serious financial liabilities, to lay an interdict on the game would have meant ruin; that was a course of action which could not be contemplated, notwithstanding the strong patriotic feelings which animated the Council. It is gratifying to know that, however footballers may have responded to the appeal of King and Country elsewhere, the sport of Association football in this country has made a really magnificent contribution to Kitchener's new Armies, the large number of men seen in uniform at matches is ample proof of this statement.[92]

It was also believed the pre-war salaries professional players were receiving were unsustainable during the war. Clubs tried to impose a reduction of 25 per cent, many players were willing to drop by 12.5 per cent. Dave Williams, a professional with Belfast Celtic, successfully appealed a decision by his club to reduce his salary by 25 per cent, his salary was instead reduced by his proposed 12.5 per cent.[93] His successful appeal helped to limit the loss imposed on other players too. There was great uncertainty for professional players once the season was due to end in April 1915. Summer wages could not be paid as there were no funds available to pay the players. It was felt that the days of £3 and £4 a week to players were over, 30 shillings a match as the maximum amount being seen as the most sensible option.[94]

The English FA relented to public pressure in the spring of 1915 and decided to cancel soccer for the duration of the war.[95] *Sport* believed the IFA would not follow suit:

> It is not thought in Belfast that the reported action of the Football Association – no football until the finish of the war – will have any effect in Ireland. Local football officials are optimistic that football will go on as usual next August, but it is expected conditions will be much altered . . . Unless there is a prohibition order by the Government, football in Ireland need

not be discontinued if proper precautions are taken in engaging players at a wage based on this year's receipts.[96]

The government announced in May that they had no intention of interfering with horse racing taking place, an announcement that came as a big relief to IFA officials who hoped 'to start the game as usual in September next. They hold that Belfast people, at least 15,000 of whom are engaged in the manufacture of war munitions, will need some little recreation, and that football at the week-end will probably supply the want.'[97] For football to continue the following season it was agreed that matches could not interfere with footballers engaged in war munitions manufacture work, no mid-week matches would be played and wages would be of an amount that would not hinder recruitment for the army.[98] It would also be required that all footballers must work in other jobs during the week, 'there should be no shirkers in these days of stress.'[99]

A conference was called between the leagues of the home nations for 3 July 1915 in Blackpool, to discuss the continuance or not of soccer for the duration of the war. The Irish delegation were tasked with advocating the continuance of soccer, not commiting the IFA to any course of action and reporting back on the conference outcome where a decision would be made. At the conference in Blackpool it was decided that there would be divisional competitions in England and Scotland, no national competitions would take place whilst the war was ongoing. Bohemians agreed with this stance, believing 'it would be a disgrace to play competitive football, which might attract players from employment'. Bohemians withdrew from the Irish League. Shelbourne was also forced to do so, as it was too impractical for players from Dublin to expect to travel to Belfast and back again every second week and retain another full-time job during the weekdays.[100] With the two senior clubs from Dublin no longer available, it was agreed to localise soccer in Ireland. It was divided into two distinct bodies. The Leinster League would continue and the senior clubs in Ulster would form a local league in Belfast; it was decided that Lurgan-based team Glenavon would also play all of its games in Belfast. Restricted to local competition (with the exception of the national cup competitions), the Leinster Football Association was forced to revive its financial rules for the Leinster Cup. From 1916 it insisted on 50 per cent of gate receipts from semi-final ties and 80 per cent from the final.[101]

The Irish Cup Competition would continue as normal with one exception. The IFA Emergency Committee ruled that all Irish Cup ties would take place in Belfast as it would not be possible for Belfast players who were engaged in munitions work to travel to Dublin.[102] This decision clearly only took into account the needs of clubs from Belfast, with little regard for those based in Dublin.

At an IFA Council meeting it was proposed to restrict the players' wages to £1 per match. An amendment was added that no professional soccer be played under the jurisdiction of the IFA for the coming season. The amendment was defeated by eight votes to two, it was agreed to continue with a maximum £1 per player per match.[103] At the same meeting it was also agreed that any profits made by the clubs during the season would be handed over to the war funds.[104] Belfast Celtic was also in favour of introducing amateurism for the duration of the war. The club 'did not believe in paying players while the war was in progress. It is one shared practically unanimously by the club directors, and so we are to have no football at Celtic Park while the war is in progress.'[105] It was also stated that Celtic 'suffered from enlistment more than any other club; in fact all the clubs in Belfast combined.'[106] To take Celtic's place in the league, a new club was formed, Belfast United.[107] It was set up by former Celtic manager Jimmy McGowan, and many of Celtic's players joined the club.[108]

The first season under the new structure saw the IFA experience the lowest number of clubs affiliated to it for some time. By the end of the 1915–16 season there were just 140 clubs in the IFA, eighty-one less than the previous season.[109] The Leinster Football Association suffered likewise with many teams disbanding and the clubs in existence primarily reliant on localised competition.

The Easter Rising, which took place at the end of April 1916, had little impact on soccer in Leinster, with the exception that the season had to be extended to the middle of June due to the cancellation of fixtures caused by the disturbances in Dublin.[110] The war years also saw the hegemony of Shelbourne and Bohemians challenged in Leinster with new clubs coming to the fore in the province such as Shamrock Rovers and Olympia. In 1918 Olympia became the first team other than Shelbourne or Bohemians to win the Leinster Cup since Nomads won the competition in 1892.[111]

As the war progressed, soccer's fortune started to improve. By the close of the 1916–17 season thirty-nine more clubs were affiliated to the IFA from the previous year to 179,[112] the following year saw an increase again, this time by fifty clubs to 229.[113]

Soccer in Ireland did survive the horrors of the First World War. The game had lost many players and supporters; some clubs were unable to survive the financial strain of the war and folded. The IFA was forced to alter the game significantly, effectively introducing localised leagues in Leinster and Belfast. By the end of the war, the IFA was optimistic for its future, feeling it had come through the ultimate test relatively unscathed. Many divisions between Dublin and Belfast cropped up during the war years, though, and the country, after the 1916 Easter Rising, was moving in a different direction. The IFA was about to find out that it had its most challenging days ahead of it yet.

CHAPTER 8

'The Useless Tail of an Inept and Moribund Organisation'

By 1918 Irish soldiers, recuperating at home or on leave, were shocked to discover the antipathy to them – at least in many strongly nationalist areas. One officer, returning to Limerick, found it to be 'a nest of Sinn Feinery', saw soldiers being stoned and heard pro-German slogans. Another officer, returning to Cork, found it to be a city where any girl who befriended a serviceman got labelled and abused as a 'British soldier's moll'. When the armistice came in November, there was little euphoria – more an exhausted sense of anti-climax common among soldiers of all nationalities along the Western Front.[1]

Ireland had changed fundamentally during the four years of the First World War. The spectre of partition for a portion of the north-east of Ireland was imminent and constitutional politics had been abandoned in most areas, a violent struggle for independence from Britain was about to begin. Sinn Féin had scored a spectacular success in the general election to the Westminster Parliament in December 1918, extinguishing the Irish Parliamentary Party as a political force in the process and with it the campaign for Home Rule. Deserting Westminster, Sinn Féin established its own parliament, Dáil Éireann, which met for the first time on 21 January 1919, the same day the first shots of the War of Independence were fired in Soloheadbeg, County Tipperary.[2] Soccer in Ireland would be deeply affected by the political changes taking place in the country as well as by internal factors that came to the fore once the First World War ended.

During the war, the IFA had seen old divisions between Leinster and Ulster resurface, divisions that would only deepen further in the post-war years. The Leinster Football Association sent a letter to the IFA in January 1915 complaining about St James' Gate's exclusion from the Irish Cup, even though the club had won the Irish Intermediate Cup in 1910. The IFA wrote back stating 'that the opinion of the Council was that St James' Gate would be better drawn in the Intermediate Cup Competition.'[3] This response was strongly criticised by the Leinster delegates at the following Council meeting, who claimed that the issue would be up for discussion in May when the Annual Meeting was due to be held in Dublin. A suggestion to relocate the Annual Meeting from Dublin to 'curtail expenditure' was met with deep disapproval from Leinster delegates.[4]

The IFA Annual Meeting did take place in Molesworth Street in Dublin in May 1915. It turned out to be a momentous meeting with the Dublin club Olympia FC proposing sweeping changes, most of them rejected by the IFA. Some of the changes proposed included affiliated associations to retain three-fourths of their club's affiliation fees, instead of a half; an increase in Leinster's representation to the IFA Council from three to five delegates; an increase to the IFA Council (directly elected) from fourteen to sixteen members; a reduction of the fee for obtaining the opinion of the IFA Council from five shillings to one shilling; a handing over of power to Divisional Associations from the IFA Council for the Rules of League, alliances etc; protests and referees' reports in matches played under the Divisional Associations to be taken from the jurisdiction of the IFA Protest and Appeals Committee, and dealt with by Divisional Associations; Leinster to have four delegates on the IFA Junior Committee instead of three; an increase in Leinster's representation on the International Selection Committee; a new article to allow clubs from the First Division of the Leinster League to enter the Irish Cup; copies of the IFA balance sheet to be forwarded to clubs seven days before the annual meeting; and a Junior Trial International match to be played annually between teams representative of the North and South.[5] *Sport* believed it was necessary to bring about changes to the IFA in line with Olympia's proposals: 'Belfast . . . has ruled the roost too long, and no time in the history of the IFA has been so opportune as the present to rouse them up.'[6] There was a perception that Olympia's proposals were creating panic in Belfast, particularly the article to allow Leinster clubs such as St James' Gate entry into the Irish Cup, and the Belfast clubs travelled to Dublin in numbers to vote down all of the proposals.[7] Most of Olympia's proposals were defeated at an Extraordinary General Meeting held immediately after the Annual Meeting of 1915. Proposals that were passed included increased representation for Leinster on the Junior Committee and the Junior International subcommittee, as well as a trial match between a team from the Northern Divisions playing against a team from the Southern Divisions, to select the junior international team.[8] Commenting on the results, *Sport* bemoaned 'Belfast's' treatment of 'Dublin', in failing even to recognise the increased Leinster representation within junior football:

> It is not a matter for surprise now that Dublin fought their corner at the IFA annual meeting in the metropolis. We had a sample of the treatment which, in the olden days, was the experience of Dublin to receive, at the IFA Council meeting on Tuesday week last. One solitary representative was given the metropolis on the half-dozen sub-committees which run the IFA throughout the season. Mr. Sheridan was given a seat on [sic] International Committee, and that finished Leinster's share of government. A representative on the Finance Committee was not even included, and the Dublin delegates asked for a delegate to be elected on this most important committee.[9]

Months later the IFA Emergency Committee ruled that Belfast teams should not have to travel to Dublin for Irish Cup ties, showing a total disregard for the plight of Dublin teams forced to travel, another example seen by many as a bias towards the Belfast clubs (see Chapter Seven).

When the war did end in late 1918, the IFA immediately withdrew all wage restrictions on professional players' wages[10] and approached Scotland and Wales to organise internationals; England had previously decided not to play any international fixtures that season.[11]

Many clubs and divisional associations were in dire straits, localised league competitions were still in operation, with the Dublin clubs opting not to rejoin the Irish League; Leinster-based clubs just participated in the All-Ireland cup competitions.[12] The main topic of discussion at the Annual Meeting of 1919 centred on helping those most in need of financial assistance. Leinster representative, Harry Wigoder, proposed that the sum of £200 'be granted to the Munster Football Association for the furtherance of football in Munster.'[13] His motion was defeated. Opposing the motion, another Leinster representative, Larry Sheridan stated, 'That association [Munster] had got about £400 or £500 in the last ten years. He thought it would be better that the money should be given to a live association like the LFA, who had been struggling along under difficulties.'[14]

Wigoder also proposed a motion recommending a grant of £50 to Jack Ryder from the Leinster Football Association for services rendered to the IFA, this motion was passed.[15] Ryder would, in two short years, be one of the key figures in the breakaway association, the Football Association of Ireland.

Another recommendation from a Leinster delegate (Richey), citing the plight of Dublin clubs Strandville and Franfort, to reduce the affiliation fees owed to the IFA by the divisional associations by half, was also defeated.[16] A motion was passed offering a grant of £100 to Glenavon 'for the purpose of enabling that club to enter the Irish League again next season, it being pointed out that Glenavon had furnished more recruits to the Army than any other club in Ireland, with the result that it had had to be practically disbanded.'[17] It was also decided at the Annual Meeting to set up a commission 'to consider ways and means of fostering the spread of Association Football throughout Ireland' with a fund not exceeding £1,000 to be distributed to clubs and associations who had suffered financially during the war.[18] It was mentioned in the annual report that 'the Semi-Finals (of the Irish Cup) were the most successful in the history of the cup, and for the first time since the outbreak of the War one of these matches was played in Dublin, the Belfast Clubs sportingly agreeing to this being done.'[19]

The commission was tasked with producing a report to the IFA Council within four weeks of the Annual Meeting.[20] The new secretary of the IFA, Charles Watson, who had replaced John Ferguson a year earlier,[21] wrote to the divisional associations of the North-East, Leinster, Mid-Ulster, North-West, and Fermanagh and Western, enquiring on what funding each division required. There was no mention of the Munster Football Association being sent similar correspondence.[22] Ryder, on behalf of the Leinster Football Association, which had lost half its clubs to the First World War,[23] replied with the following:

> Since the War some very prominent Clubs went out of exis-
> tence through no fault of their own, and the number of Clubs
> affiliated has fallen by one half . . . if a sum of £300 was allo-
> cated to the LFA it would help to revive and foster the game in
> this district and much good work could be done. I might
> mention that we at present suffer opposition from other quar-
> ters, which has to be worn down.[24]

The 'other quarters' Ryder was referring to was the GAA. Many members of the GAA looked to 'exploit the upsurge of national feelings to try and slow down the growth of soccer.'[25] A circular was sent by the GAA Central Council in 1917 to each county board, requesting each county 'to take advantage of the present feeling of the country . . . with the object of completely wiping out "Soccer"'.[26] A year later, the GAA even relaxed its ban on members playing or watching 'foreign games' by offering an amnesty for soccer and rugby players looking to switch from their codes to the GAA.[27] Many players did move over to the GAA from soccer and rugby because of the perceived attempt by the British administration to 'ban' the national pastimes of the GAA.[28]

The IFA received no replies from the North-East, Mid-Ulster or Fermanagh and Western Associations. The commission decided to offer Leinster £200 instead of the sought-after £300, Mid-Ulster £150 and the North-West £75. 'The Commission had no informa-
tion before them regarding the condition of Football in the Fermanagh and Munster Districts, and, therefore, were not in a position to make any recommendations in regard to these Divisions.'[29] It was reported at an IFA Council meeting in November that many efforts were subsequently made to get in touch with officials from the Munster Football Association, without success, and it was left to the commission tasked with the furtherance of the game to deal with the matter.[30] Both Neal Garnham and Peter Byrne claim that Leinster was offered just £50 instead of £300, a figure that was startling and insulting, and Byrne claims that Munster sought £200 and received nothing.[31] The evidence would suggest otherwise. Leinster received £200

from the IFA – not quite the asked-for £300 but still the largest sum given to any divisional association. Wigoder from Leinster had proposed £200 to be granted to Munster at the 1919 IFA Annual Meeting, a proposal defeated and opposed by delegates from Leinster. Watson, the IFA secretary, claimed he had tried on many occasions over a five-month period to reach out to the Munster Football Association, to get input on what Munster needed, without any joy.

At the same council meeting in November 1919, a discussion arose over disturbing scenes at an inter-provincial match between Leinster and Ulster at Dalymount Park in October 1919, with a recommendation that a commission be sent to Dublin to investigate the incident.[32] At the match in question, the Ulster team, which had reluctantly agreed to go to Dublin, eased into a five-nil lead.[33] This was the cue for members of the crowd to invade the pitch, attacking one of the Ulster players in the process.[34] Crowd troubles, although not entirely removed during the war years, now started to increase significantly.[35] At a match between Dublin clubs Jacobs FA and Olympia, players from Jacobs invaded the Olympia dressing room and attacked the club's players.[36]

In March 1919, Glentoran was pitted against Belfast Celtic, and Bohemians against Linfield in the semi-finals of the Irish Cup. Both matches took place on the same day, 8 March. Linfield travelled to Dublin to play Bohemians. Although there was a bad atmosphere, the match passed off without incident.[37] The same could not be said of the other match between Glentoran and Celtic in the Solitude ground in Belfast. Mid-way through the second half, Glentoran being in a commanding two-nil lead, disgruntled Celtic fans broke through the railings and invaded the pitch, singing the nationalist 'Soldier's Song'. Persuaded to return to the touch line, it appeared that the disturbance was over. With five minutes to go and Celtic unable to make a breakthrough, the crowd again invaded, assaulting the referee and Glentoran players with stones. The referee was escorted to the pavilion, which then became a target, practically all the windows were broken. Chairs which had been placed on the touchline for wounded war veterans were then smashed by the crowd.[38] The Celtic supporters were considered the culprits by the media and the football authorities and Glentoran was awarded the match.[39] The *Belfast Telegraph* believed there was a more sinister political element to the incident: 'The Sinn Fein element, which has made itself conspicuous at Belfast football matches in the past year, managed once again yesterday to disgrace the fair name of sport.'[40] The two teams would meet again at the same stage of the Irish Cup the following year. The match would result in the same fate, abandonment.

By 1920, the country was in open revolt, the War of Independence ongoing for over a year. Both Dublin and Belfast were host to many violent incidents, both cities becoming more and more unsafe for civilians. Violence at soccer matches was also on the increase, with Belfast Celtic, the leading nationalist club in Belfast, invariably involved in many incidents. At a Belfast City Cup contest between Celtic and Distillery in January 1920, the ground was invaded at the end of the match, the police and officials being forced to protect the referee. A baton charge disbursed the crowd, who, unable to attack the referee roughly handled one of the linesmen instead.[41] At an IFA Council meeting in January 1920, a discussion took place on violent scenes happening at different league matches with a request sent to the referees and linesmen to furnish reports on such incidents.[42]

The ugliest incident that occurred was at an Irish Cup semifinal replay match, again between Glentoran and Belfast Celtic in March 1920, the most serious incident since the mass riot in Celtic Park of September 1912. The match, strenuously fought, passed off without incident deep into the second half. With twelve minutes to go, Fred Barrett, the Celtic left-back was sent off by the referee for fouling and injuring the Glentoran centre-forward, Joe Gowdy. Immediately afterwards a spectator rushed across the field in the direction of the referee, who took notice and ran to the safety of the pavilion, soon joined by the players of both teams. The match was abandoned.[43] A section of the Celtic crowd, who had been singing party songs and waving Sinn Féin flags throughout the match, then proceeded to throw stones, soon followed by 'revolver music'. The police witnessed one of the crowd wearing a white rainproof coat and brandishing a revolver, who discharged between four or five shots. A police sergeant was shot under the chin. Using their batons, they rushed the crowd and seized the suspect, only to be met with a volley of stones from the crowd. The suspect, George Goodman, was subsequently convicted of attempted murder and sentenced to eight years in prison.[44] A melee broke out that continued for several minutes, the field finally being cleared by the police after repeated baton charges. Many people were injured and three were detained in hospital, one suffering from a fractured skull.[45] Commenting on the incident, *The Irish Times* stated: 'Owing to the attitude of the Celtic supporters at previous matches this season, the question of the suspension of the club from participation in Belfast matches has been under the consideration of the football authorities, and yesterday's disturbance will, no doubt, re-open the question.'[46]

The IFA Senior Clubs Protests and Appeals Committee met on 19 March to discuss the incidents at the match between Celtic and Glentoran. The meeting was held in private, with a number of policemen stationed outside the room to ensure order was maintained.[47] Celtic protested, 'saying that John McIlveen, who played in the match for Glentoran, was not included in the list of players supplied to Celtic in accordance with Rule 3 of the Irish Challenge Cup Rules.'[48] Once no objection was received from Glentoran and the list of players supplied to Celtic was shown, the protest was upheld and Glentoran was disqualified from the Irish Cup. Fred Barrett, the Celtic player sent off during the match, sparking the riot, was then suspended for the remainder of the season.

The riot itself then came up for discussion. The referee believed the Celtic supporters were to blame: 'I have no doubt it was the Celtic spectators who caused the match to be abandoned. At half time I had to get some spectators put over the railings; these were Celtic spectators and one of them said if I did not give Celtic fair play I would not get off the field alive.'[49] Two directors of Celtic, Robert Barr and Joseph Donnelley, were next called to give evidence. Both were quick to claim that the disturbance had nothing to do with the Glentoran fans. Donnelly claimed there was little the directors of Celtic could do outside of their home ground, Celtic Park. He also acknowledged that the club's supporters had been involved in many other incidents that season: 'In fact I have hardly seen a match this Season, where Celtic was engaged, that disgraceful scenes did not occur.'[50]

Unsurprisingly, the committee ruled that the disturbance was the fault of the Celtic supporters, resulting in the disqualification of Celtic from the Irish Cup competition. As both Glentoran and Celtic were disqualified, the victors of the other semi-final, Shelbourne were declared the winners of the Irish Cup without having to play in a final.[51] A mock final was played between Shelbourne and Glentoran at Shelbourne's ground in Ringsend, Dublin. Glentoran won by three goals to one. This match also did not pass without incident. The referee was badly assaulted by a small section of the 8,000-strong crowd as he was leaving the field.[52]

The Celtic directors were disgruntled with the decision of the IFA Protests and Appeals Committee to disqualify the club from the Irish Cup, and were even more perturbed by the decision of the IFA Emergency Committee to suspend the club from taking part in Association Football until further consideration as well as threatening the deduction of gate receipts owed to Celtic for damage caused by the riot. The club decided to threaten legal action against the IFA. In a letter sent to the IFA Council, the club stated:

> Your drastic decisions which hold our club responsible for the conduct of spectators over whom they have no control, and who were admitted by your officials to a ground over which my Directors had no control, seek to impose on our club a liability which we must repudiate and to identify our club and officials with conduct of spectators which we have always endeavoured by every means in our power to suppress . . . your decisions are of such far reaching character, and appear to us so contrary to the ordinary principles of justice which we feel certain you would desire to animate your resolutions, that my Directors cannot in the interests of the good name of our club and officials allow them to pass unchallenged.[53]

It was claimed in the letter that the IFA's

> removal of our club from the Challenge Cup Competition is entirely unauthorized by any rules or regulations of either the Competition or the IFA, that your suspension of our club until further notice is equally unjustifiable and further that your Association has no power to deduct all or any of the expenses for making good the damage to Cliftonville ground from the proportion of the receipts payable to our club.[54]

The club vowed to take legal action unless the decisions made by the IFA were rescinded. The tone at the IFA Council meeting was anything but conciliatory with most members roundly condemning Celtic and calling for the decisions taken to be upheld.

At the IFA Annual Meeting, in what would transpire to be the last all-Ireland IFA Annual Meeting, just over a month later, the IFA defended its actions: 'It will have been observed that the Association are defending a Law Action, and on this point your Council desire to say nothing further than that every decision given by them was in the best interests of the Game.'[55] Cliftonville furnished the IFA Council with a bill for the repairs required to the club's ground following the riot in March, amounting to £154 – a bill the IFA was expecting Celtic to pay.[56] Celtic and the IFA were deadlocked in a battle. Celtic brought its case to the Chancery Court in June, claiming the decisions made by the defendant, the IFA, 'were ultra vires, and for an injunction restraining defendant Association from so acting.'[57]

Over the following months, efforts were made to resolve the dispute. Called into action once again were the sister associations in Britain who once again obliged. T. White, president of the Scottish FA, was requested by the English FA 'in the interests of the Game generally, to intervene to obtain a settlement.'[58] By October a settlement was agreed upon, with the IFA agreeing to cover the legal costs of Celtic; it refused to rescind the decisions made in March, though.[59] *Sport* was in no doubt as to who was to blame for the saga. It was the IFA:

> Autocratic blundering legislation, which costs £584 to rectify. They rushed into it, suspended and fined Celtic, and also ousted them out of the Irish Cup, and when called to account couldn't stand over their decision. Instead, they go practically on their knees and pay Celtic's law costs and incidentally their own to settle the matter.[60]

The directors of Celtic had made a decision earlier in the year: 'In view of recent events they would not undertake the responsibility of reviving a team next season.'[61] Celtic would not field a team for another four years, it being felt it was too unsafe to do so until then.[62] Considering the violence that existed in Belfast, particularly from 1920 to 1922, with much of it perpetrated against the

Catholic community, it is easy to see why the club made this decision. According to Robert Lynch:

> Between the years 1920 and 1922, Belfast experienced the most intense and brutal period of violence in its history. This conflict, waged against the backdrop of partition and the carnage of the Irish Revolution, was by far the most violent in Ireland during the whole revolutionary period . . . Unlike in the rest of Ireland, however, the violence in Belfast consisted largely of urban rioting; almost 80 percent of the victims were civilians.[63]

It is estimated that over 450 people were killed and over 1,100 were wounded in Belfast from 1920 to 1922, a higher per capita death rate than in any other part of the country during the same period.[64] The catalyst for the violence was the expulsion of many Catholic workers from the Belfast shipyards in July 1920, leading many to describe the events as a pogrom.[65] This was followed by the wide-scale burnings of family dwellings, resulting in thousands of people being evicted from their homes.[66]

Given the violence that was engulfing Belfast at the time, more widespread than in Dublin, the IFA Protests and Appeal Committee made a fateful decision in January 1921. It ruled that both of the semi-finals and the final of the Irish Cup should be played in Belfast that season for safety reasons, much to the chagrin of the Leinster delegates at the meeting.[67] *Sport* claimed:

> The IFA are living in a fool's paradise if they fancy any Dublin club will travel to Belfast for the semi-final of the Irish Cup. They will travel there for the final if they qualify for it, but not for the semi-final. They will insist on their rights in this matter, and nothing that the IFA can say will alter their determination.[68]

One Dublin club, Shelbourne, would travel to Belfast for an Irish Cup semi-final tie that season against Glenavon, even though it was rumoured the club wouldn't.[69] Breaking point was reached, however, when the club was asked to return to Belfast for the replay of that fixture, having secured a draw in Belfast on the first occasion. It would ultimately lead to the Leinster Football Association seceding from the IFA, no longer the 'useless tail of an inept and moribund organization.'[70]

CHAPTER 9

'Cut the Painter'

The Leinster Football Association had felt aggrieved by a number of decisions made by the IFA since the First World War had ended, most relating to venues for matches. A motion put forward by the Leinster delegates to host the international match against Wales for the 1920 season was defeated by twelve votes to six; it was held in Belfast instead.[1] Months later another attempt to host an amateur international in Dublin was also thwarted, Belfast again being chosen as the venue.[2] The last senior international held in Dublin under the governance of the IFA was in 1913; none was held after the First World War. The IFA may have been reluctant to grant another international match to Dublin considering the political climate in the capital and the unsavoury incidents that had accompanied the last match in Dublin in 1913 against Scotland. It was attended by the Lord Lieutenant of Ireland, the Earl of Aberdeen, who received a lukewarm reception from the crowd and the Ireland's Own band refused to play 'God Save the King' before the match.[3] The GAA mouthpiece, the *Gaelic Athlete*, lauded the band, calling them the 'Irish-Ireland's Own Band' for their 'creditable' action in not playing the British national anthem.[4] There was also crowd trouble at the end of the match, fomented by a clergyman, according to the Scottish FA, where the window of the referee's room was broken and one of the Scottish players was assaulted.[5]

The decision of the IFA Protests and Appeals Committee at a meeting of January 1921 to host both semi-finals and the final in Belfast for 1921 was seen as yet another example of a Belfast bias within the association. The make-up of the IFA sub-committees, such as the Protests and Appeals, Finance, Emergency and International Committees, revealed a heavy bias towards the North-East division and other divisional associations within the northern region. Every IFA committee was dominated by Ulster delegates, particularly from the North-East division of Antrim, incorporating Belfast. In contrast, Leinster, Munster and Fermanagh and Western had limited representation on any committee. In fact, some of the delegates representing Munster and Fermanagh and Western were not even from those regions: it was seen as too impractical to travel to Belfast for meetings. Thomas Moles, editor of the *Belfast Telegraph* and a Belfast Ulster Unionist MP, served on the IFA Council and some of its sub-committees as a delegate for both Munster and Fermanagh and Western at different junctures.[6] Appendix A lists all the IFA sub-committees from the 1909–10 to the 1920–21 seasons, with each committee membership broken down by divisional association.[7] In many instances, membership of sub-committees consisted of over half the delegates hailing from the North-East region.

The composition of practically every sub-committee of the IFA had the bulk of its members coming from the North-East, the North-West and the Mid-Ulster regions, with just a smattering of delegates, if any, from the other regions. Leinster had overtaken the North-East as the largest divisional association in 1913 and yet its representation on the parent body's sub-committees did not reflect this. In 1913, the Protests and Appeals and Reinstatements Committee was composed of seven members, with three from the North-East, and just one from Leinster. The International Committee, a vital one, due to its choosing of the national team, was also composed of seven members in 1913, with just one from Leinster and three from the North-East. The other three delegates were from the North-West, Mid-Ulster and Fermanagh and Western, making it very difficult for one solitary Leinster delegate to ask for more Dublin-based players on the international team. Leinster had one member out of six on the Advisory Committee that same year and had no representation on the Finance, Emergency, Senior League Clubs Protests and Appeals, and Rules Revision Committees. The Munster Football Association had no representation on any sub-committee in

1913. The dominant North-East region, as well as having three members on the Protests and Appeals and Reinstatements and International Committees, had four out of eight members on the Finance Committee, three out of six on the Emergency Committee, five out of five on the Senior League Clubs Protests and Appeals Committee, two out of three on the Rules Revision Committee and two out of six on the Advisory Committee.[8]

By 1921, very little had changed. All committees were dominated by North-East representatives, including the Senior League Clubs Protests and Appeals Committee, which had five out of eight members compared to two from Leinster.[9] There was very little the Leinster delegates could do to halt the decision of that committee to hold the semi-final and final ties in Belfast for 1921, considering their numerical disadvantage. The one thing they could have done more of was attend the meetings of the committees of which they were members. The attendance record of Leinster delegates from 1910 to 1921 for IFA Council and sub-committee meetings was very poor, with the exception of the International Committee, where the Leinster representatives attended the bulk of the meetings. (see Appendix B.) It could be argued that the meetings were held in Belfast, making it considerably more difficult for people located elsewhere to attend; and, given the make-up of each committee, Leinster representatives could be forgiven for feeling like token representatives with little opportunities available to effect any meaningful changes. The paltry attendance record did not help Leinster's case, though, in attempting to gain more representation. Larry Sheridan was Leinster representative on the Protests and Appeals Committee from 1910 to 1913. In that period, forty-six meetings were held by that committee; Sheridan attended just three. There were two representatives from Leinster, J. Walsh and G.P. Fleming, on that same committee in 1921, where the decision was made to grant Belfast the semi-final and final Irish Cup ties for 1921. At that meeting on 13 January, Walsh was in attendance, Fleming not. Walsh argued for a Dublin semi-final. This was defeated by three votes to two.[10] Fleming's presence could have made a difference and Shelbourne may not have been forced to travel to Belfast to play Glenavon in one of the Irish Cup semi-final ties on 5 March.

A BRITISH SOLDIER LYING DEAD

whilst a crowd in Dublin look on in 1921. Safety concerns were the main reason cited by the IFA Protests and Appeals Committee for not scheduling the Irish Cup semi-final replay tie between Shelbourne and Glenavon in Dublin in March 1921.

Courtesy of the National Library of Ireland

The IFA Protests and Appeals Committee believed it was too unsafe for teams from Belfast to travel to Dublin in 1921. Despite this, both Linfield and Distillery declared their intention to play friendly matches in Dublin in the off-season.[11] As well as dictating that the key Irish Cup ties be played in Belfast, the IFA reneged on a promise to grant Dublin an Intermediate Cup semi-final tie: both semi-finals were played in Belfast.[12] St James' Gate, the holders of the Intermediate Cup, withdrew from the competition as a result, refusing to travel to Belfast to meet Forth River.[13] The Junior Cup semi-final ties were also awarded to Belfast.[14] In April 1921, just hours before Dublin United were due to meet St James' Gate in the Leinster Cup Final, the match was called off by the Leinster Football Association due to 'the prevailing conditions of the city.'[15] The IFA claimed that Shelbourne had stated it was unwise to host matches in Dublin due to the conflict taking place, also citing the violence between Glenavon and Shelbourne in Dublin a year earlier. This claim was not confirmed by Shelbourne.[16] The Northern Cricket Union and the Irish Women's Hockey Union had cancelled trips to Dublin for

A CROWD GATHERS OUTSIDE MOUNTJOY PRISON

in Dublin as six men are executed on 14 March 1921 for activities against the British Crown. Heightened tensions were experienced in Dublin that day, the same day the Shelbourne-Glenavon Irish Cup semi-final replay tie was scheduled to take place.

Courtesy of the National Library of Ireland

inter-provincial matches due to safety concerns.[17] On the other hand rugby circles were not overly concerned by the violence in Dublin where 'several Belfast sides played in Dublin and were well received.'[18] The Belfast media were quick to report on atrocities being committed against civilians in the metropolis and there were many to report in early 1921.[19] Instead of highlighting the regular unsavoury incidents occurring in Belfast, the *Belfast Telegraph*'s headlines focused more on atrocities in Southern Ireland such as 'Criminal Methods of the IRA', 'Terrorism in Cork', 'Murderer's Escape in Dublin' and 'Inevitable Weekend in Dublin.'[20] A bomb aimed at the Royal Irish Constabulary (RIC) killed a twenty-two-year-old woman in Westmoreland Street,[21] a porter was killed at Wicklow Hotel and a milkman was shot in Rathmines in January.[22] In February, a boy was wounded when a bomb exploded in Aungier Street,[23] two RIC members were shot

DUBLIN'S CUSTOM HOUSE ON FIRE
Another graphic example of the violence that engulfed Dublin in 1921.
Courtesy of the National Library of Ireland

dead in Parliament Street,[24] an exchange in Camden Street led to the death of a three-year-old boy[25] and a clerk was seriously wounded during a robbery.[26] March was witness to many bombing incidents in Dublin with three children injured in Bolton Street[27] and a man's leg blown off after an explosion in Great Brunswick Street.[28] One street clash led to the deaths of three and the wounding of four or five more.[29] Reading of such incidents, it is not surprising that people in Belfast would feel that Dublin was unsafe. There was, though, little thought from the IFA given to those travelling to Belfast from Dublin where the violence against civilians was on a wider scale (see Chapter Eight). Incidents involving Belfast Celtic, leading to its temporary withdrawal from all competitions, had highlighted the potential for violence in Belfast. There had been other incidents in Belfast directly linked to soccer matches. Immediately after a match at the Cliftonville football ground in August 1920, a riot broke out in the surrounding areas, leading to the deaths of five men and one woman.[30] Two months later a crowd of 3,000 loyalists who had attended a match at the same ground attacked a Catholic church. The ensuing altercation led to the deaths of three men.[31] Despite such incidents, *Sport* believed there was little to worry about:

> The conditions are now as favourable to their observance as they ever were. Fears to the contrary exist only in the per-fervid imaginations of people who mistake shadows for substances. Talk of danger to a Belfast team at Dublin, or to a Dublin team at Belfast, is not only a baseless libel on the football public of both cities but is highly discreditable to the people who indulge it.[32]

Shelbourne also believed it was not too unsafe to travel to Belfast and played Glenavon at Linfield's home ground, Windsor Park, on 5 March. Shelbourne was without three of its players and was only able to find two deputies. In a stroke of fortune, a Shamrock Rovers player, McVeagh, was travelling on the same train to Belfast as the Shelbourne team, to attend the match as a spectator. He was convinced to play for Shelbourne and helped the club's scratch team earn a nil-nil draw in Belfast.[33] It was almost universally believed that the replay would be played in Dublin. This would not be the case. Shelbourne would have to travel again to Belfast. At a meeting of the IFA Protests and Appeals Committee held on 7 March, it was moved to have the replay of the Shelbourne versus Glenavon match played in Dublin. An objection was raised:

> On the grounds that the previous resolution dealing with the semi finals stated that both semi finals were to be played in Belfast this year and on a vote being taken the motion was defeated by 3 votes to 2 and it was decided to replay the match at Belfast on Wednesday 16th March.[34]

Sport in a number of hard-hitting articles was aghast at the IFA's decision:

> **No greater insult has been known in the annals of Irish football** (printed in bold by the newspaper), considering that the **Shelbourne team had worthily earned the right to a re-play in the Capital** ... This most recent and cruelly unfair edict of the rulers of Irish football, **Is nothing other than a death-dealing blow to the Dublin team, as far as their connection with the North is concerned, and a direct challenge to the sport-loving public of the Irish Capital.** Word fails one at the

moment to convey adequately **the monstrous injustice of the IFA and their decision** to make Shelbourne travel for the second time to Belfast . . . is enough to make the Dublin sports agitate for the immediate overthrow of the Dublin teams' connection with the autocratic bosses of the Irish football world. It is understood up here that the Shels fulfilled their fixture in Belfast with Glenavon much against the wishes of the Dublin folk, and that rather than 'bow the knee' to the IFA for the second time, they will 'scratch' the tie with Glenavon. Shelbourne are foolish, indeed, if they decide to travel Northwards again.[35]

Another commentator of *Sport*, named Viator, expressed no surprise at the decision and believed the Leinster Football Association should look to the future as an independent body of the IFA:

That is all as I expected and predicted. Any of the Dublin clubs who for a moment imagine that they are upholding the interest of the IFA, by continuing their affiliation thereto are making a serious mistake, and the quicker they take steps to sever the connection the better. Belfast doesn't want them, and they are exposing themselves to contempt and humiliation by continuing their attachment, however weak and lukewarm thereto. It is quite practicable to establish a Leinster executive, from associations outside Ireland, to set up competitions of equal attractiveness to any in which Dublin clubs have been permitted to take part under the aegis of the IFA. This should certainly make for considerable Leinster improvement, extension, propagation and development generally. It would be far better to be a self contained and independent association unit within small confines than to be the useless tail of an inept and moribund organization.[36]

Sport was not the only newspaper to condemn the IFA. The *Evening Herald* claimed the decision had 'aroused the utmost indignation in Leinster circles' and called on the IFA Council to 'annul the decision.'[37] The *Irish Field* was also highly critical of the IFA Protests and Appeals Committee:

I cannot understand those club representatives who voted against the tie going to Dublin. A little while ago we heard a lot about Belfast clubs going to Dublin to play, and now that there is an opportunity it is not availed of. Rugby, hockey, and athletic clubs have gone to Dublin and were delighted to do so; now we have the dog in the manger policy ascribed to a little coterie of Association clubs.[38]

Belfast's *Irish News* saw the incident as:

> Against all canons of sport, fair play, and justice. I know of no other body who would perpetrate such a gross injustice on a club. It is indefensible . . . This is what our legislators work for: to put back the hands of the clock three decades. It looks as if they are out to kill the game they are supposed to govern.[39]

Writing a number of years after the incident, *Football Sports Weekly* remarked: 'An Association for all Ireland, who should hold the scales of justice impartially towards all within its ambit, reeked of religious and political bias, and were incapable of doing justice towards one of Ireland's oldest and best clubs.'[40] The *Northern Whig and Belfast Post*, although sympathising with Shelbourne, understood the predicament the Glenavon players were in: 'I have yet to find a northern player with any wild desire to play in Dublin under present circumstances . . . How many of those advocating that Glenavon should have travelled would play in Dublin at present?'[41]

Both Shelbourne and the Leinster Football Association soon made their feelings known to the IFA. Basil Mainey, secretary of Shelbourne, wrote to the Protests and Appeals Committee, stating:

> My Club decline to travel to Belfast to replay our Semi Final tie V Glenavon Club. My committee consider it grossly unfair to our Club and to football in Leinster generally that such a decision of your Committee should have been arrived at, and one contrary to all precedents hitherto observed. I herewith beg to return you the 25 admission tickets received.[42]

On a vote being taken, the Protests and Appeals Committee, at a meeting held on St Patrick's Day, 17 March, dismissed Shelbourne from the Irish Cup Competition and granted the tie to Glenavon. The committee also decided to refer the matter to the IFA Emergency Committee.[43] At a Leinster Football Association meeting called specifically to discuss the replay venue, the following resolution was proposed:

> The Council of the LFA strongly condemn the unsportsman-like action of a majority of the members of the Irish Senior

Clubs Protests and Appeals Committee in ordering Shelbourne to replay in Belfast their drawn Irish Cup tie with
Glenavon FC and we regard the decision to be against the best
interests of the game. We furthermore deprecate the action of
the Glenavon club in its refusal to come to Dublin more especially since the votes and influence of Leinster delegates were
always generously given in the past to support the claims
made by Glenavon FC to the IFA when their existence as a
football club was threatened.[44]

This was in reference to Leinster supporting the financial assistance for Glenavon, who had almost disbanded during the First
World War. It was decided to have the last paragraph referring to
Glenavon's perceived 'ingratitude' deleted, though.[45] *Sport*
claimed that thirteen out of fifteen of Glenavon's committee had
voted in favour of the club travelling to Dublin for the replay, it
was the players who refused to travel.[46] The same paper had highlighted previously that not all of Leinster were in support of
helping Glenavon during the First World War, with delegates
such as Harry Wigoder, voting against offering Glenavon a grant
of £50 in 1915.[47] In leaving the matter to the team to decide
whether to travel to Dublin or not, the Glenavon committee had
allowed 'the tail to wag the dog', according to the *Irish Field*.[48]

The Emergency Committee met immediately after the Protests
and Appeals Committee meeting was over on 17 March in Belfast.
Even though there were two Leinster representatives on the
Emergency Committee for the 1920–21 season, G.P. Fleming and J.
Walsh, neither was in attendance at that meeting to discuss the
Irish Cup semi-final replay. Out of eight Emergency Committee
meetings held that season, Walsh and Fleming attended none of
the meetings.[49] Eight people were present at the meeting, six from
the North-East and two from the North-West. Upon discussing
'the matter fully and after careful consideration', the committee
resolved, that 'the Emergency Committee are very sympathetic
and in accord with the resolution passed by the LFA but having
regard to the fact that the Senior Clubs Protest and Appeals
Committee have Council powers they are unable to take any
action in the matter.'[50] The matter was referred to the next full IFA
Council meeting, which took place on 22 March.

It was rumoured in many media outlets that the IFA chairman, James McElmunn Wilton, had resigned over the matter.[51] The rumours were unfounded. He was in the chair for the fractious IFA Council meeting of 22 March, a meeting with many Leinster representatives in attendance. A number of incidents were brought up by the Dublin contingent. The meeting had to conclude no later than 9:30pm that night due to curfew restrictions in Belfast at the time. Firstly, the decision to host both Intermediate Cup semi-final ties in Belfast that season was questioned. Larry Sheridan also brought up his failed attempt to have the amateur international between England and Ireland played in Dublin that year. James MacBride from the North-West region responded that matches in Dublin 'did not pay for the dinner'; if the match was scheduled to be held in Dublin, the English team would not have travelled.[52] Clearly, safety concerns were not the only factors affecting the IFA's decision to travel to Dublin, with finances also coming to the fore.

A number of Leinster representatives next brought up an incident that had occurred in February at an amateur international match between Ireland and France in Paris, which became known as the 'flag incident.'[53] At the match that Ireland won by two goals to one,[54] an attempt was made by a section of the crowd to have the Irish team walk behind Sinn Féin flags on taking the pitch.[55] It was believed that those responsible for waving the flags were overenthusiastic African students from the Royal College of Surgeons in Dublin.[56] The IFA officials at the match, in conjunction with the French authorities, prevented this from happening and had the people responsible removed from the ground. The four Leinster members of the team were unaware of the incident until the return ship to Ireland and 'expressed themselves greatly upset over the incident. They felt that a slur had been cast on them as being silent participants in an affair of which they had no knowledge whatever at the time . . . everybody should be entitled to carry whatever flags they liked without interference.'[57] At the IFA Council meeting, 'several Dublin representatives pointed out that politics had never been introduced into football in Dublin, and much damage had been done as a result of the incident.'[58] It was claimed that:

In Dublin Soccer was not favoured by some of the community, and this incident had given rise to much criticism. The incident might have been the means of wiping Soccer out of Leinster . . . players were leaving Soccer in Dublin and going over to Rugby and other codes. The incident had placed the Soccer officials in a very awkward position.[59]

Wilton, the IFA chairman, replied that the flags and the people responsible were removed from the ground, as the IFA was 'a non-political, non-religious body.'[60] Some commentators in the South of Ireland did not agree. The *Catholic Bulletin* stated: 'The incident revealed the "bitter anti-Irish atmosphere of Association football" and the air of "slavery in which all important Association matches were played".'[61] The *Irish Field* described it as:

Another incident magnified to intensity that hatred of any-thing emanating from the North. It may be that pressure from certain quarters down South is proving too much for the Leinster Association and its clubs to withstand . . . I know the members of the body there have a hard time of it, in the face of the calumny of Northerners.[62]

Despite Wilton's claim that the IFA was a non-political, non-religious body, many of the leaders of the association were closely identified with Ulster Unionism, including Wilton. He was secretary of the Derry division of the Ulster Volunteer Force during the Home Rule Crisis before the First World War.[63] He was elected as an Ulster Unionist to the Derry Corporation in 1923 and in 1935 he became Lord Mayor of Ulster's second city, receiving the support of both unionists and nationalists.[64] On his election as mayor, he was described in one newspaper as an 'Apprentice Boy, Orangeman and Freemason.'[65] Considered popular by all involved in soccer, both North and South,[66] he was derided, being compared to Hitler by nationalists in 1938, the year he was knighted for refusing to support a motion congratu-lating the election of Douglas Hyde as President of Ireland.[67] Other prominent unionists who played a significant role in the IFA's governance were Thomas Moles and the Marquess of Londonderry.

At the IFA Council meeting of 22 March, the Leinster represen-tatives then brought up the issue of Shelbourne having to travel

111

twice to Belfast to play Glenavon. The decision was described by one committee member as 'a scandal.'[68] It was retorted that it was too unsafe to travel to Dublin, a letter being reproduced from a Dublin club not guaranteeing the safety of teams travelling from Belfast. The Leinster representatives responded by stating that Belfast was also considered unsafe, yet Shelbourne still travelled to Belfast.[69] The chairman 'pointed out that the Committee who dealt with this matter had full Council powers and that no action could be taken in regard to what had been done.'[70] On a more conciliatory note, Shelbourne was offered expenses for having to stay overnight for the first trip to Belfast and permission was granted by Wilton for Shelbourne to organise a testimonial match, with a subscription from the IFA, on behalf of Basil Mainey who was celebrating twenty-five years as secretary of the club. The meeting concluded with the Leinster representative Harry Wigoder mentioning 'that he thought the best thanks of the entire Association were due to the Chairman for the excellent manner in which he conducted the business. This was agreed upon unanimously.'[71]

Sport believed the warm way in which the Leinster delegates were treated at the meeting was due to the fear in Belfast that Leinster would secede:

> The IFA Council were all so sweet over the Shelbourne case at the meeting last week. When they put their hand in the fire they were in haste to withdraw. With the exception of the 3 gents who ordered the Shels back to Belfast all were apparently in denunciation of the decision thus when they guessed its sequel might be the secession of Leinster.[72]

The paper also took a swipe at the Irish team selected for the upcoming match against Wales:

> The Welsh International will be played on Monday. It holds little if any interest for Dublin footballers. Not one Dublin player has been included on the team chosen to represent this country, and I do not recollect ever having heard of so many bitter expressions of disgust at the actual team chosen . . . very few in Dublin have any illusions with respect to the method of selection favoured by the Belfast Association, and it is pretty generally known that the selectors do not care twopence who is chosen so long as players belonging to their own clubs find positions on these International teams . . . In any case, the

whole thing matters very little now, as in all probability we in Dublin next year will be running our own Association quite independent of Belfast.[73]

The paper concluded by claiming: 'Irish Selectors have beaten us oftener than England, Scotland or Wales.'[74] The paper was a strong advocate of Leinster leaving the IFA, believing soccer in Leinster would be all the stronger for it.

The Leinster Football Association was moving in that direction too. At a meeting held on 7 April, upon receipt of the IFA's resolution not to reverse the Protests and Appeals Committee decision, the Leinster body, after a discussion, decided to set up a committee to draw up a report on whether the Leinster Football Association should continue its connection with the IFA.[75] The task of this sub-committee was to ascertain the wishes of the various clubs through the secretaries of the different leagues in Leinster.[76] It was believed that the findings would strongly endorse secession from the IFA, although there were concerns about one senior club (undoubtedly Shelbourne), according to *Sport*:

> At the moment there is a grave doubt of the attitude of one Senior Club, and only one. Important as that club may be, it cannot afford to disassociate itself from the action of all the other Leinster clubs, much as it would seemingly desire to do so. If it persists in its pose of neutrality whilst secretly inclining towards the maintenance of the existing state of things, it will eventually stand alone.[77]

The paper, on a zealous mission against the IFA, squarely rounded on it, for the crisis:

> They (the IFA) will be well in the soup when Leinster cuts adrift. They know whom to thank for it – themselves. They have been in the habit of bouncing all their careers, and every-body took it lying down. They thought they'd still walk over all and sundry. A Leinster secession will be bad for all of us, but we can afford to smile when the IFA are taught that autoc-racy won't always pay, that the worm turns sometimes.[78]

The committee returned to the Leinster Football Association on 4 May with its conclusion that the Leinster Association 'should start on its own', with a recommendation 'to canvass the clubs as to their views.'[79] The committee's resolution was endorsed by the

Leinster Council who 'then proposed that a Special General Meeting of the LFA be called for the purpose of disbanding the LFA and putting into operation a new Association next season'. At this point the chairman, R.E.T. Richey, expressed his disagreement with the decision and vacated the chair.[80] Richey, originally from Antrim, had strong connections with Belfast, making it too difficult for him to sever connections with the IFA.[81] An attempt to convince Richey to withdraw his resignation failed; Wigoder became chairman of the Leinster Football Association for the remainder of the season.[82] The circular sent to all the clubs in Leinster was a very balanced one, highlighting reasons for leaving the IFA, and the likely pitfalls they would encounter if they did so:

- Is it in the best interests of football that the association should continue its connection with the IFA Ltd?
- This subject is purely for the clubs themselves.
- The council wish to draw your attention to the following points should you decide not to affiliate:

(1) The other association would not immediately give recognition to a new one
(2) your club would not be eligible to compete in the Irish Cup, Irish Intermediate Cup or Irish Junior Cup according to your status
(3) your players would not be considered for International honours next season.

- During the present season, the principal rounds of the Irish Cup and Intermediate Cup were forbidden to be played in Dublin and the Irish Junior Cup was not played. In fact no matches with Northern clubs took place, thus the IFA cut themselves adrift from our association.
- It is considered that if the association had a free hand a lot could be done to develop and popularise the game, rules being drawn up on lines suitable to clubs without any restrictions.
- As stated before, the matter is one for the clubs, it is for them to decide. The council would be glad if you would place this matter before your members for their decision and communicate same to me at the earliest opportunity.[83]

At the IFA Annual Meeting held in Derry on 14 May, a sparsely attended affair,[84] a motion that had been placed before the

Emergency Committee a month previously by Shelbourne, was put forward.[85] It proposed (and it was passed) that if a Dublin club was drawn in the Irish Cup semi-final, the match would be played in Dublin, and for final ties, the venue would alternate between Dublin and Belfast, provided a Dublin team was in the final.[86] This 'little sop to keep them in tune' would prove too little too late for Leinster, whose path was firmly set on secession, 'very like closing the stable door when the steed is stolen.'[87]

Other proposals put forward by Shelbourne at an Extraordinary General Meeting, held on the same day, were defeated. The proposals were for the IFA Council to 'take entire control of the Senior Challenge Cup Competition, and [shall] make all arrangements connected therewith, including the draws for all rounds of the Competition, such control to be exercised by the full Council only and not to be delegated to any Committee thereof' and for the Protests, Appeals and Reinstatement Committee to deal with any protests arising out of the Irish Cup instead of the Senior Clubs Protests and Appeals Committee.[88] Essentially Shelbourne was looking for the Senior Clubs Protests and Appeals Committee to be disbanded, as it and everyone else in Leinster had no faith in its impartiality. The committee was established as part of an overall agreement with the senior clubs, leading to a resolution of the split of 1912. From the outset, the committee was totally dominated by people from the North-East region (see Appendix A). It was just composed of representatives from the North-East in its first four years of existence from 1912 to 1916 and, thereafter, there was token representation from elsewhere, with the bulk of membership still coming from the North-East.

In a sombre report read out at the Annual Meeting, the IFA Council lamented the 'internal eruptions' and deeply regretted:

> The absence of prominent Dublin and Belfast Clubs from the ordinary Senior Competitive Football, but they are pleased to recognize the fact that the majority of the Senior Clubs took part in the Irish Cup Competition, and they hope, as all interested in Football do, that the entire Senior Clubs may be in a position next Season to participate in the game as they did in days gone by.[89]

Acknowledging the trouble in Irish soccer, the Council defended its actions:

> It could not be expected that the report of your Council would be of the most fulsome and glowing description, as facts are stubborn things to combat, but it must be admitted that your Council on your behalf have by legislation and all other sources at their command done everything to further the interest of Association Football all over the country; that they have made mistakes may be most apparent, but they would like to point out that in no instance was a mistake committed with a purpose of hurting any particular organization under the jurisdiction of the Association.[90]

The report continued on a positive note:

> Better days are in store for the popularity and progress of the game, and their great wish is that the domestic troubles which have prevented the usual inter-changes of Football between the big cities may be removed at a very early date and that we may once again come back to the period that we can meet each other, as we should always do, in that friendly and keen rivalry which tends to promote success and a better understanding between all parts of the country.[91]

To emphasis the IFA's innocence, the report again pleaded that every decision made was 'considered in the best interests of the game, and there was no studied attempt in any way to endanger or hurt the Game in any District'; the Council's action 'was prompted by the peculiar conditions pertaining to Football during the Season.'[92] The Junior Committee Report also commented on the state of the game in Ireland, regretting 'that the position of Football throughout Ireland is not what they would like to see, this to a great extent is to be attributed to the disturbed state of our beloved land'. Due to the troubles the country was experiencing and the financial liabilities of running the competition, the Junior Cup Competition had been abandoned for the season.[93] The Junior Cup Competition, given the geographical spread of the teams involved, was the most difficult competition to organise.[94]

There were some within Leinster who wished to stay with the IFA. As well as the former chairman of the Leinster Football

Association, R.E.T. Richey, the chairman of the Leinster Junior Association was also reluctant to break from the parent body. At the Leinster Junior Association Annual Meeting, he refused to put a proposition before the meeting calling on junior clubs of Leinster to cease affiliation to the IFA. He also manufactured a result calling on the body to defer making a decision for a few weeks; the result of that vote was challenged. Several delegates left the hall, in evident disgust at the chairman.[95]

Most were in favour of secession including, it was believed, the public, who were attending matches in higher numbers than before. This, according to *Sport*, was evidence of support for a breakaway:

> In the belief that the Dublin clubs are about to break with Belfast the populace have come to the support of the game in numbers hitherto unequalled. The attachment to Belfast has always been viewed unfavourably by the bulk of the people, and the game in Dublin has consequently never enjoyed their wholehearted support.[96]

The paper also put forward another reason to break links with the IFA: matches being played on Sundays:

> Sunday soccer is taboo in Belfast. In Dublin it is quite the reverse. A working understanding could be come to here between the Saturday and Sunday clubs. Soccer is rampant in France, where it is quite common on Sunday. We can have French teams here if English or Scottish teams won't come. We can send teams to France if we are refused games in England.[97]

These turned out to be prophetic comments that would transpire within a very short period.

The Leinster Football Association held its Annual Meeting on 1 June in Molesworth Street in Dublin. A resolution was put forward at the meeting:

> That the time has come when a new association should be formed independent of the Irish Football Association, Ltd. That the newly elected Council of the Leinster Football Association should constitute themselves for the purpose of establishing a new body and report to a full meeting of the clubs when the draft constitution and rules have been considered.[98]

Clubs supporting the breakaway included Chapelizod, Jacobs, Dublin United, Westbrook, St James' Gate, the Wasps, Freebooters, Midland Athletic, Beresford, Fairview Celtic, SPD, YMCA, Lourdes CYMS, Seafield, Aunally, Roseville and Dodderville. Dundalk GNR was the only club who objected to severance with the parent body. On being asked why they had not commented, both Shelbourne and Bohemians responded that they had made no decision as neither had conducted a meeting yet.[99] At the Irish Football League AGM held on 27 May, Shelbourne stated it was not in a position to definitely state its intentions.[100] However, it was reported in the *Irish News* that both Shelbourne and Bohemians had unofficially decided to re-enter the IFA-run Irish Football League in the new season.[101] The *Irish Independent* commented that Shelbourne 'had already thrown in their lot with the IFA.'[102] Committee members supporting a rupture believed, that because clubs like Shelbourne and St James' Gate were victimised by the IFA, Leinster would be better off going it alone. Others commented on the imbalance of Leinster representation on the IFA sub-committees, with particular emphasis placed on the International Committee, where Leinster representation was just one out of six.[103] Another believed a new association embracing all of Ireland should be set up, with the headquarters in Dublin.[104]

Opposing the motion, Ritchey acknowledged that Leinster had been treated unfairly by the IFA; however, 'he failed to see what Leinster stood to gain by breaking away, unless it was the satisfaction of managing our own affairs. He preferred that the Leinster Association should become the premier Association, whilst remaining in.'[105] Wigoder was in favour of leaving the IFA on the condition that there be a big improvement in the quality of officials and referees. On a vote being taken, the proposition was carried, with just Ritchey dissenting.[106] Leinster had decided to 'cut the painter' and sever connections with the IFA.[107]

At an IFA Council meeting held on 7 June 1921, the IFA appeared to be blissfully unaware of the decision made in Dublin days earlier. A lengthy discussion took place on the motion passed at the Annual Meeting in relation to venues for Irish Cup fixtures when Dublin clubs were involved. Dublin United was granted permission to play Shelbourne in a benefit match in aid of a player who had broken his leg, and Bohemians was allowed to organise a match in aid of the widow and children of Patrick Sax who was killed in Dublin.[108] It was at an IFA Emergency Committee meeting later in the month that it was revealed that Leinster was no longer affiliated to the IFA. At that meeting, a short letter written by Leinster secretary, Jack Ryder, was read out in which it was stated, 'that at a meeting of the Representatives of our Clubs it was decided to form an Association independent of the IFA Ltd.'[109]

It was decided to write a letter to Leinster regretting its decision as well as to all clubs affiliated through the Leinster Football Association warning officials and players against taking part in soccer under the jurisdiction of a new association. It was also agreed to write to the football associations of England, Scotland and Wales, whose support would need to be called upon again.[110]

The battle lines were now drawn; the battle for the supremacy of soccer governance in Ireland was about to begin.

CHAPTER 10

The Football Association of Ireland is Born

Once Leinster broke from Belfast, it established a new association, the Football Association of Ireland. The FAI came into
being in June 1921, officially ratified on 2 September.[1] The League
of Ireland was founded on 30 August.[2] Replacing the Irish
Football League was the Football League of Ireland. The administrative make-up of the FAI was to all intents and purposes the
administrative make-up of the Leinster Football Association. An
opponent of the split, R.E.T. Richey, was still elected as president
and the chairman of the FAI, Larry Sheridan as honorary secretary. P.H. Stewart was to be honorary treasurer, J.F. Harrison as
vice-chairman and Jack Ryder as secretary.[3] At the ratification
meeting of 2 September, where 'the attendance of representatives
was most disappointing', all of the Leinster Football Association
committee tendered their resignation and immediately 'offered
themselves for re-election under the auspices of the Football
Association of Ireland.'[4]

There was still hope in many quarters in Ulster that this split,
like the one in 1912, was a temporary setback and could be
resolved before the summer was over. The IFA issued an ultimatum to clubs in Leinster stating that unless notification of
loyalty to the IFA was received before 21 July, clubs would be
deemed no longer members and would be unable to play football
against clubs from England, Scotland, Wales or Ireland.[5] Rutland
FC and Brideville FC sent letters back proclaiming fealty to the
IFA.[6] This decision was soon reversed. Brideville never followed
up on its original letter and Rutland 'stated they wished to have
nothing more to do with this Association.'[7] Dundalk GNR, who

had opposed leaving the IFA at the Leinster Football Association's Annual Meeting in June, applied to the IFA for affiliation. As the Leinster division was no longer affiliated, the IFA forwarded the club's application to the nearest division to Dundalk, Mid-Ulster, with a recommendation of acceptance of affiliation.[8] The two clubs of most interest were the two biggest clubs in Leinster, Shelbourne and Bohemians. Neither club stated their intentions at the Leinster Annual Meeting and it was unclear for some time after, if either would join with the rest of their Leinster colleagues. There was more at stake for the two clubs than other less established ones. The prospect of international selection, albeit slight, would be totally removed and local competition would be of an inferior quality. 'Ralph the Rover' (who was the former Linfield secretary John Gordon)[9] from *Ireland's Saturday Night* (the sport paper of the *Belfast Telegraph*) highlighted the dilemma facing Shelbourne and Bohemians:

> The breakaway will not help the game where the new body will rule, as through time things will become monotonous with nothing to vary the ordinary weekly fixtures. Internationals with the three sister countries will be lost to them, and even the opposition of a cross-Channel eleven will not be within their scope. So far as the players are concerned they will be the losers.[10]

This gloomy prospect led to the exodus of players from Ireland. Four of Shelbourne's players left for Pontypridd in Wales in the summer of 1921,[11] followed soon after by another to Bradford in England.[12] Despite a degree of procrastination, both Shelbourne and Bohemians decided to throw their lot in with the new association, the FAI, by the autumn of 1921. The IFA received letters to this effect from Shelbourne in August[13] and Bohemians in October.[14]

The FAI also received a huge boost from the nationalist Falls and District League in Belfast, which asked to be affiliated to the new body. A match was organised between Bohemians and a team from the Falls and District League in early September in Dublin.[15] A return fixture was held in Shaun's Park in Belfast at the beginning of October.[16] *The Irish Times*, in an article in which it called the FAI, the 'All-Ireland Football Association (AIFA)', stated the ramifications for the IFA:

The intention of the new association is to take over control of 'soccer' in Leinster, Munster, and Connaught and to welcome to the fold any Northern clubs that may decide on 'joining up'. Among those who have done so are a number from Falls road and district, and the visit of the Belfast-men to Dalymount Park was thus invested with considerable interest. The formation of the new Association is a serious matter for the Irish Association, whose membership heretofore consisted largely of clubs affiliated from 'the South'. It would be idle to contend otherwise. It is also a serious business for the clubs which have thrown in their lot with the AIFA, for automatically they come under the ban of the governing body and those associations which recognise the IFA as the only governing body in this country.[17]

In total, twenty-three clubs from the Falls and League District affiliated to the FAI, including Alton United, a team that comprised of many players from Belfast Celtic, still absent from football.[18]

The FAI also received the support of Munster and Connacht. It was able to lay claim that it, unlike the IFA, was a truly all-Ireland body. It did so, in an application it made to FIFA for membership in March 1922, stating that it was the governing body of the Leinster Football Association, the Belfast and District Football Association, the Athlone and District Football Association and the Munster Football Association.[19]

On 8 September the new season began for the two bodies, both vying for control over soccer in Ireland.[20] The IFA-controlled Irish Football League consisted of just six teams, Linfield, Glentoran, Distillery, Glenavon, Queen's Island and Cliftonville.[21] In an effort to attract spectators, the IFA reduced entrance fees to matches, one shilling for reserved areas, nine pence for unreserved areas with ladies allowed free entry.[22] The IFA, witnessing a *fait accompli* with competitions taking place outside its jurisdiction in Ireland, refused a request from Queen's University, Belfast, to play a team from Trinity College, Dublin, who were affiliated to the new association.[23] The universities North and South would compete for the Collingwood Cup again, the inter-varsities annual competition that still exists today, with Queen's University re-joining the fold after a few years' lapse.[24] The

English FA was told that a Liverpool club, Narint FC, who wished to play Bohemians, Shelbourne and St James' Gate in Dublin the following Easter would be unable to do so as all three Dublin clubs were suspended from the IFA.[25] A similar request from a Welsh club to play Shelbourne and Bohemians was turned down in November 1922 by the Football Association of Wales as neither club was affiliated to the IFA.[26]

The FAI-controlled Football League of Ireland consisted of eight teams in its first year, Bohemians, Dublin United, Frankfort, Jacobs', Olympia, St James' Gate, Shelbourne and YMCA.[27] St James' Gate went on to win the first league as well as the new cup competition, the FAI Cup. The new cup consisted of teams from the league as well as winners from a cup qualifying competition that included Shamrock Rovers and Athlone Town.[28] St James' Gate played Shamrock Rovers in the first final of the FAI Cup, ending in a draw on St Patrick's Day, St James' Gate winning by a goal to nil in the replay. It was commented that a rugby international that took place in Lansdowne Road on the same day as the replayed match did not seriously affect the attendance at Dalymount Park, where another large crowd witnessed the match.[29] It is estimated that 15,000 people attended the first match and 10,000 the replay of the FAI Cup Final,[30] providing the FAI with gate receipts of £609 and £470 respectively.[31] By contrast, the Irish Cup final of 1922 between Linfield and Glenavon, a two-one win for Linfield, had a crowd of just 5,000 in attendance.[32]

The FAI Cup final replay did not pass off without incident. After the final whistle was blown, some Shamrock Rovers supporters climbed over the fencing and attacked the winning team. They were joined by some of the Rovers players who confronted the rival players in the St James' Gate dressing room. The Rovers captain, Bob Fullam, attacked one of the St James' Gate players, Charlie Dowdall. Dowdall's brother, Jack, who had been on active service with the IRA in the War of Independence, brandished his revolver and with that the dispute was over.[33]

The first season of the FAI was more successful than expected with a 33 per cent increase in membership of Leinster clubs,[34] and despite attempts by the GAA to halt its progress, a steady if not spectacular rise in clubs in Munster.[35] The publicity surrounding the 'Split' seemed to focus more public attention on association football and new clubs began to be formed once again. The first season:

> Was a record-breaking one . . . The names of new clubs which were to become synonymous with the Leinster Football Association and success were known for the first time like Brideville, Dolphin, St. Mary's United from Donnybrook, Edenville, Williamstown, Talbot United, St. Barnabas, Mullingar, Queens Park; along with the more established clubs like Olympia, Frankfort, Chapelizod and Adelaide.[36]

The IFA, who saw its efforts to retain clubs outside Ulster meet with almost no success, decided to change tack, adopting a more conciliatory tone with the FAI. In February 1922, at an IFA Council meeting, a letter from the English FA mentioning an application from the FAI asking for recognition, was discussed. A sub-committee of five members with full council powers was established to draft a response to the English FA with the caveat that 'nothing should be done that would be detrimental to or effect a reconciliation for the New Football Association with the parent body.'[37] It was also mentioned by a council member (Lyttle) that he had received overtures from people from the Falls League expressing interest in re-joining the IFA.[38] The Falls League overtures were red herrings: nothing further transpired from the initial conversations and the Fall League remained under the fold of the FAI.[39] Based on input from the IFA, the English FA responded to the FAI's request for recognition: 'Having regard to the unsettled condition of football management in Ireland, the Council are not in a position to deal with the matter referred to in the correspondence with Ireland, and that until such conditions are satisfactorily arranged, the arrangements for our Irish matches must remain in abeyance.'[40]

At the IFA Annual Meeting held in Belfast in May 1922, the IFA Council acknowledged the difficult times:

> Conditions obtaining all over Ireland were not calculated to help any sport, and perhaps Football, which carries the greatest support of the classes, has been hit worst of all by the unfortunate occurrences which have prevailed in our midst

. . . It has been a struggle for your Association, and its Clubs as well, to carry on.[41]

Referring to the split, the IFA Council stated they:

Regret having to report that one of the Divisional Associations – Leinster – have for some causes or other formed an Association on their own, but . . . are also hopeful that time and common sense will bring about a settlement and that there will be no conflicting parties so far as the government of Irish Football is concerned. They would further like to point out to you that nothing will be left undone by them to have this unfortunate crisis settled, as they readily recognize that it is not for the good of Football to have two separate bodies both seeking paramount powers . . . Your Council, so far as they know, have neither by act or deed done anything to prevent a settlement of the present trouble with their friends in Leinster, and they again express the wish and hope that before next season starts a satisfactory settlement may be arranged.[42]

Alexander Thompson, who had served as IFA president from 1909 to 1912, disagreed with the assertion that the IFA had done nothing to prevent a settlement. He complained:

That the ordering back of Shelbourne to replay their Irish Cup semi-final was a most unsporting decision. He had always a great respect for the Leinster people, and after Welsh people Dublin folk were the best sports he had ever met. The Council in their report said they did nothing to prevent a settlement. Does the chairman know anything as to what is being done about a reconciliation? The Council neglected a fine opportunity before it developed, as someone should have been sent to Dublin. They should at once take steps to heal the breach. There were many good sports in Dublin, and also many in Belfast.[43]

He continued by accusing the council of 'sitting still and watching football drifting. What had been done to stem the rot?'[44] He concluded by stating: 'The country was too small for two football associations. Senior football . . . was on a downward grade.'[45] Wilton replied: 'The association was prepared to heal it at any moment.'[46] An alteration in the rules deleting Dublin as a venue for annual meetings was, according to Wilton, 'only a provisional alteration, and that when the Leinster body again joined the Association the rule would be changed to what it originally was.'[47]

At the same meeting, the overall state of soccer was looked at with trepidation. The poor attendances at the international matches had shown there was 'diminution of interest as compared with pre-war days'. It was mentioned that just £800 was taken at the gates for the international match against Wales; £2,000 had been the gate receipts at the same fixture two years previously. A scheduled amateur international against France had also been cancelled by the French Football Association 'on account of the present political situation in Belfast and District.'[48] Wilton blamed the non-travelling of the French amateur team on the press who 'had told them it was not safe to put one's head out of doors in Belfast.'[49] Wilton may have been sarcastic, but one member of the IFA Council (B. Beggs) would be shot and severely wounded in the troubles just weeks later.[50] Membership had been reduced from 387 clubs affiliated in 1921 to 282 in 1922, the bulk of clubs leaving being from Leinster. The demise of the Irish Cup was also lamented: 'This Competition was seriously affected by the conditions prevailing throughout the Country, and interest manifested in same was far below the usual standard, and consequently the Clubs and the Association suffered as a result of circumstances over which they have no control.'[51]

At the Irish Football League Annual Meeting, also held in May 1922, Tom Chambers, chairman of Linfield, said 'that he hoped the day was not far distant when they would again be competing against their Dublin friends in the League. After all, they missed the Leinster clubs, and he believed that the Dublin men also missed them.'[52] Wilton reiterated his call for a settlement between North and South in July 1922.[53]

At an IFA Council meeting held in December 1922, a letter was received from Linfield seeking to play a charity match in Dublin to help bring about a reconciliation with the Dublin clubs:

> The time has now come when an attempt should be made, in the best interests of sport to re-establish the old competitive relations that once existed, and they also believe if this object was accomplished on honourable lines it would prove to be a mutual benefit to the sport-loving fraternity of both cities.[54]

Linfield, who won seven trophies in 1922, was perhaps concerned about the quality of opposition available at that juncture.[55] The reading of the letter led to a discussion on ways a settlement could be reached between the North and the South. It was decided by the IFA to send a letter to Dublin asking them 'if they would appoint a deputation from their association to meet a deputation from the Irish Football Association Ltd to discuss ways and means for a settlement of the present football dispute in Ireland.'[56]

The FAI, who had experienced a far more successful first season locally than expected, was more reluctant to engage with the IFA and to reach out with a view to obtaining a settlement. One major conciliatory gesture that was made by the FAI was its choice of president to replace R.E.T. Richey, who left his post just months after the formation of the FAI, unsurprising given his opposition to the breakaway in the first place. The FAI chose Sir Henry McLaughlin, a Northerner who was well known and respected in IFA circles.[57] McLaughlin had played for Cliftonville and was knighted for his efforts to get people to join the armed forces during the First World War.[58] He served as 'both Honorary Director of Recruitment in Ireland and a member of the Irish Recruiting Council.'[59] He was also involved in the campaign seeking clemency for the Irish Volunteer Kevin Barry, who was ultimately executed for his part in an ambush on British forces.[60] It would take over six weeks for the FAI to reply to the request from the IFA in December 1922 to organise a conference between the two associations, curtly agreeing to hear what proposals the IFA had regarding the dispute, and asking for the meeting to be held in Dublin.[61] The key factor that brought the FAI to the table was the lack of international competition available to the nascent body, seen by many as a necessity for the association to survive and thrive. The draw of, and finances from, international matches were of paramount importance, particularly the marquee fixture of Ireland versus England.

The FAI embarked on an extensive and lengthy campaign to gain international recognition. With the exception of the IFA, the FAI approached the members of the International Football Association Board, the English FA, the Scottish FA and the Football Association of Wales, seeking international recognition.[62] At the annual meeting of the International Board held in Llandudno, Wales, in June 1922, members of the football associations of England, Scotland, Wales and Ireland unanimously decided that, 'under the present constitution of the International Board it is not competent for this Board to admit as Members the new Football Association of Ireland'. It was also unanimously decided that no country could be represented by two associations.[63] *Ireland's Saturday Night* saw this as a big victory for the IFA: 'So it is now definitely settled, at least so far as England, Scotland and Wales are concerned, that the only governing body in Ireland is the IFA.'[64] The argument of no country being represented by two associations was no longer valid. Following the signing of the Anglo-Irish Treaty in December 1921, the Irish Free State was formed in 1922. The IFA's jurisdiction was limited to the six counties of Northern Ireland, established under the Government of Ireland Act of 1920. The FAI used this as the main argument to warrant international recognition, an argument that would lead to the international governing body, FIFA, after some persuasion, recognising its right to exist and granting the Irish Free State body membership.

Another sporting body that opposed the foundation of the FAI was the GAA. It opposed soccer in all its forms, considering it a 'foreign game'. At a GAA Central Council meeting soon after the formation of the FAI, a motion was passed:

> An association calling itself the Football Association of Ireland catering as it does for foreign games viz. soccer football is antagonistic to the national ideals of the GAA, and its members occupy the same position as those of soccer IFA being debarred from taking any part in hurling, football, or athletics under GAA laws.[65]

The GAA was a thirty-two county body that retained its structure after partition. Other sports maintained governance on an all-Ireland basis, others actually became united, whilst some sports, like soccer, saw the political divide detrimentally affect its ability to stay united. The next chapter will look at how many of the sports dealt with the new political climate confronting Irish society from the early 1920s.

CHAPTER 11

Sport in a Divided Island

Ireland's Saturday Night, in a weekly cartoon piece entitled 'The Doings of Larry O'Hooligan', included a cartoon of O'Hooligan refereeing an inter-league rugby match between Leinster and Ulster in 1922, with a caption below the picture stating:

> The present series of interesting inter-city rugby games has given Larry some food for thought. It is a real source of sorrow to him that while Belfast and Dublin rugbymen, hockeyites, boxers, cross-countrymen, swimmers and others can meet in healthy rivalry from time to time the Association men must remain estranged. 'Tis true,' pity, and pity 'tis 'tis true.[1]

The sports that remained or became unified after the formation of the Irish Free State and the Northern Ireland jurisdictions saw some issues caused by the creation of two political entities on the island, primarily centred around anthems, flags and other emblems. Most sporting bodies that governed on an all-Ireland basis were mindful of the changed political landscape, and looked to adopt policies that would appease all. Some sports were more successful in doing this than others. Soccer was in a unique position. It was a sport of nationalists and unionists, Protestants and Catholics. Although most popular in urban areas amongst the working classes, it had strong support from all classes in most locations. It was the one sport that covered the widest range of demographic in Irish society. The sport most similar to it was athletics. It too struggled with the new political landscape in Ireland.

The National Athletics and Cycling Association of Ireland (NACA), founded in 1923, governed athletics and cycling on an all-Ireland basis from 1924 to 1925 and was formally recognised

THE LORD LIEUTENANT INSPECTING TROOPS

outside Belfast City Hall on the day of the first meeting of the Ulster Parliament, 7 June 1921. The Government of Ireland Act led to the partition of Ireland.

Courtesy of the National Library of Ireland

by the International Amateur Athletics Federation (IAAF).[2] The NACA came about after an uneasy alliance was formed between the Athletics Council of the GAA and its former rival, the Irish Amateur Athletics Association (IAAA). The unification was not smooth. On the insistence of NACA (based on a previous GAA ruling) that British soldiers, sailors or policemen on active duty be excluded from the body, the northern branch of the IAAA opposed amalgamation in 1922.[3] There was also resentment that the North was not receiving appropriate acknowledgement, with northern delegates having to attend an annual meeting in Dublin to form a unified body, even though the North had predominance in number of affiliated clubs.[4] The NACA president, John J. Keane, who also served as Irish Olympic Council president, agreed to compromise on the rule boycotting members of the British armed forces becoming members of NACA, as well as on Sunday competitions and the northern clubs accepted unity.[5] In a case of roles reversed in soccer North and South, 'the Northern group (in athletics) ran the risk of losing international recognition if they restricted themselves to the North, and would put in jeopardy the all-important "triangular internationals" held annually between the traditional "home nations" of England, Scotland and Ireland', leaving the northern group with little alternative.[6] The unity was paper-thin from the very outset, with no Ulster delegates present at the NACA Annual Congress in May 1924 that ratified the merger.[7] Notably there was no Ulster representative included in the new executive either.

Open conflict broke out at Easter 1925 over an event organised at the home of the soccer club Belfast Celtic. The IAAA had organised fund-raising events previously for Celtic who had withdrawn from competitive soccer from 1920 to 1924. At the event in 1925, on top of athletics, the meeting included a 200-yards whippet and an open-trot handicap. Under the laws of NACA (one Belfast newspaper referred to the laws as 'By Leave of Dublin'),[8] animal events and the associated gambling that accompanied those events contravened the IAAF's rule on amateurism.[9] The Ulster Council of NACA ignored the parent body and proceeded with the auxiliary events on top of the athletic ones. Keane reacted by declaring that all associated with the event had suspended themselves from NACA. 'His stance succeeded only in uniting Northern nationalists and unionists in opposition to Dublin intervention.'[10] There were reports of similar practices at other meetings, including an incident of horse and pony racing accompanying an athletics meeting in Dundrum, County Down, months later.[11] Many in the North believed there was an element of hypocrisy in the South, where veiled gambling was taking place, just less overtly than the open gambling commonplace at athletic events held in the North.[12]

At the second NACA Annual Congress, unlike the previous one, six northern delegates were in attendance. One of them was Robert Barr from Belfast Celtic. Keane objected to Barr's presence due to Barr being involved with a soccer club: 'Those professional clubs do not belong to "our side of the house", they support a sport which Congress did not sanction. Professional sports should be kept out.'[13] He was still admitted but, along with the other northern delegates, walked out of the meeting once no compromise could be reached on the impasse over gambling. It would culminate in the formation of a new body for athletics in the North:

> In July 1925, at Celtic Park, a large representative meeting of the old IAAA, Irish Cycling Association (ICA) and Cross Country Association of Ireland (CCAI) organisations agreed unanimously to form a new body for athletics in Ulster, the Northern Ireland Amateur Athletics, Cycling and Cross-Country Association (the Northern Association). The NACA Ulster Council remained, but it was now without the majority of the important Belfast clubs.[14]

Thomas Moles, editor of the *Belfast Telegraph*, an Ulster Unionist MP and IFA Council member, was appointed the new body's president.[15] He championed a new identity for Northern Irish sport within a British framework. The Unionist members of the Northern Association deeply resented the Dublin control of NACA, the use of the tricolour for international competitions and the provincial and county structure of NACA, aping the GAA structure.[16]

NACA was not overly concerned by the secession of many of the northern clubs, believing its international standing would help ease the parent body through murky waters. With the British Amateur Athletics Association (AAA) forming a branch in Northern Ireland in 1928, a move not blocked by the IAAF, this safety valve was removed.[17] A number of conferences were held over the coming years but to no avail. Both sides remained intransigent, the Northern Association looking to eke out its future under the British umbrella, NACA immovable in relinquishing all-Ireland control. It ultimately was a battle lost by NACA, who in its quest to resist partition in a sporting sphere, failed to realise the political reality of partition, a reality even acknowledged by the different Free State governments despite their frequent posturing's to the contrary. After 1934, Ireland's right to compete in the Olympic Games as a thirty-two county entity was lost. It led to NACA being suspended from Olympic competition, a suspension that would span decades (see Chapter Sixteen).[18]

One sport that did achieve a lasting union after partition in Ireland was cricket. Despite cricket being the most popular sport in Ireland in the 1860s and 1870s, with an estimated five hundred cricket clubs established throughout the country, there was no national body overseeing the game until 1890.[19] An Irish Cricket Union of sorts was formed that year in Dublin, a union more in name than fact.[20] It was formed primarily to select the team to represent the Gentlemen of Ireland for matches against international opposition.[21] Receiving little support from the Northern Cricket Union, the national body stutteringly existed in the 1890s; in reality a 'Cold War' existed between the Northern and Dublin body.[22] A further attempt was made at union in 1901 when a conference was held between the North and Leinster Cricket Unions during a visit by Leinster to Belfast for an inter-provincial match. At the meeting, 'it was decided that it was advisable to organise an Irish Cricket Union, which, in addition to the existing branches in Leinster and Ulster, should also have branches in the other two provinces . . . a draft of rules was approved of . . . submitted to the various clubs over the country.'[23] A year later the Committee for Control of Irish Representative Cricket was founded in Dublin. The Northern Cricket Union rebuked efforts by the new body for affiliation as it was felt they were not privy to the discussions on the new body's formation.

The 1900s followed a similar pattern to the previous decade, North and South further away from union than ever before. The Northern Cricket Union declined to host a match between the Gentlemen of Ireland and an Indian eleven in 1905. Leinster responded by cancelling that year's inter-provincial against Ulster in Belfast. No inter-provincial would take place until 1909.[24] Efforts were made again by Leinster clubs to form a union that year.[25] At a meeting of the Northern Cricket Union it was decided to send three delegates to a conference in Dublin to place the views of the Northern Union before it.[26] At that meeting it was unanimously adopted, including by the northern delegates, 'that an Irish Cricket Union for the promotion and control of cricket in Ireland, with branches in Ulster, Leinster, Munster and Connaught, be and is hereby established.'[27] Despite this proclamation, divisions soon appeared between the northern and national bodies. The Northern Cricket Union believed that the new union would be dominated by Leinster and Munster, that Dublin would control the national team selection and venue locations, and that there was little appetite to financially contribute to a body where little representation for the North was envisaged. On the face of it from venues chosen and teams selected for Ireland from 1910 to 1914, it would appear the Northern Cricket Union had some justifiable concerns. Of the sixteen home matches played in Ireland during that period, thirteen were held in Dublin, two in Munster and one in Bray. Ulster players only featured in fifteen of the twenty-seven matches Ireland played in that period.[28] The increased political divide between North and South, fermented by the Third Home Rule Bill, also accounted for the northern body's reluctance to join an Irish Cricket Union. Many Ulster Unionists were cricketers who occasionally used cricket grounds for drilling purposes for the Ulster Volunteer Force (UVF), an armed body established to resist Home Rule.[29]

Immediately after the First World War, the Northern Cricket Union had little appetite for union. This all changed dramatically in 1922 when the northern body appeared considerably more open to the concept. The northern body felt it would have a far greater say than it was offered before on all issues relating to cricket on an all-Ireland basis. In 1923, it was agreed to have a small committee elected to be the governing body for cricket in Ireland. The committee consisting of four northern representatives, four southern representatives and a chairman was tasked with selecting and arranging the teams for all future Irish representative matches. Heralding the move, *The Irish Times* claimed:

> There can be no doubt that such a body, if it receives loyal support, will be of great benefit to Irish cricket . . . Everybody rejoices that in most forms of sport, at any rate, Ireland is unified. In golf, in Rugby football, in cricket, Ireland means Ireland; there is no distinction made between Northerner and Southerner. We welcome the birth of the Irish Representative Cricket Control Committee, which should provide a further bond in the realm of sport between the North and the South.[30]

Not everyone in the North was satisfied on how the new body was formed. At a meeting of the North-West Cricket Union, regret was expressed that its branch had not been invited to co-operate in the movement.[31]

The first decade after partition did see a vast improvement in relations between North and South in cricket, borne by equality in dealings never realised before. W.P. Hone, in his official book *Cricket in Ireland* remarked: 'It is a minor paradox of Irish Life that the division of our country has brought cricketers from the two separated states more closely together.'[32] A sign of closer co-operation was the choice of Belfast as a venue for the first time for an international representative game against Wales in 1924.[33] The union formed in 1923 would be cemented over the following years, leaving cricket as it is today, like sports such as rugby, golf and hockey, governed on an all-Ireland basis.

Hockey experienced relatively little turbulence with the partitioning of Ireland. The Irish Hockey Union (IHU) was formed in 1893 with provincial branches established in 1898–99.[34] The IHU was structured similarly to a federation with the provinces partially autonomous.[35] With the IHU primarily responsible only for selecting the international team, there were far fewer opportunities for conflict. It was decided soon after partition for an IHU flag with the crests of the four provinces to be used instead of the tricolour and the playing of the 'Londonderry Air' ('Danny Boy') as the team's anthem.[36]

The Golfing Union of Ireland was also established along similar lines to hockey and rugby, with the provincial councils managing all provincial affairs. The union's meetings also alternated between Belfast and Dublin, leaving little scope for disagreements.[37]

The sacrifices rugby in Ireland made for the First World War effort have been well documented. There were also some, fewer in number, who played rugby in Ireland and contributed towards the independence struggle against Britain. Most famously, Éamon de Valera, who would lead the Irish efforts in the War of Independence from 1919 to 1921, was an avowed follower of the game, playing it as a youth whilst studying at Blackrock College. In later life he claimed, 'For Irishmen there is no football game to match rugby and if all our young men played rugby, not only would we beat England and Wales, but France and the whole lot of them together.'[38] Ironically, he was directly involved in the shooting dead of the president of the IRFU in 1916, Frederick Browning. 'Browning was tragically killed when his unit of the Veterans' Corps, returning to Beggars' Bush Barracks after a route march on Easter Monday 1916, was fired upon by outposts from Commandant Éamon de Valera's garrison in Boland's Mills, under the mistaken impression that the advancing men were combat troops.'[39] Kevin Barry, who played rugby with UCD, was also a casualty of the War of Independence. Other rugby playing volunteers included Jim McInerney and Dan Gallagher from Limerick.[40]

Although some rugby players were committed nationalists, many others had more in common with rugby followers north of the new border that became Northern Ireland. Unlike those who administered soccer south of the border, most of the administrative layer of the IRFU comprised of men who were invariably middle class, Protestant in religion and unionist in outlook. Presidents of the IRFU during the years of the struggle for independence and beyond, such as Frederick Browning, Alf Tedford, Harry Thrift and W.P. Hinton, were all Protestant and from upper-middle-class backgrounds.[41] Although now governing on one island for two separate political entities, many of the decisions made by the IRFU during the 1920s and 1930s, cemented the relationship between rugby in the Irish Free State and in Northern Ireland.

In 1923, the IRFU commissioned the building of a new ground in Belfast, with a suitable field obtained in the district of Ravenhill, to accommodate a crowd of between 20,000 and 30,000 people, including 4,000 covered stand seats.[42] The field in Ravenhill cost the IRFU £2,300, with an additional £15,500 spent on building the stadium.[43] The chairman of the northern branch of the IRFU, Dr H. Emerson, commented that they 'had received the heartiest support from the parent body of the Union.'[44]

The IRFU, echoing sentiments more closely aligned with Protestantism than Catholicism,[45] actively discouraged the playing of rugby matches on Sundays. It sent a letter in 1929, banning the staging of league and cup matches on Sundays, where money was collected.[46] This met with the disapproval of Munster and Connacht rugby organisers, as well as from many in Leinster.[47] A Sunday rugby culture had existed in Munster from the mid-1880s onwards.[48] Unlike the perception of an anti-national bias within Dublin and Belfast, rugby in Munster was more fluid and localised.[49] The IRFU, after a special general meeting in January

1930, agreed on a compromise relating to Sunday rugby. Matches could be played on Sundays with the permission of the branches of competing clubs.[50] The Munster branch of the IRFU also disagreed with the principal toast at union dinners being offered to the King of Great Britain. It recommended in 1933 that the first toast should be offered to Ireland instead,[51] a recommendation that was ignored, with the IRFU still being criticised a year later for offering the first toast to the King at a banquet.[52]

An incident that sparked the biggest controversy related to the choice of flag for Irish rugby internationals in Lansdowne Road in Dublin. At the annual meeting of the IRFU in 1925, Harry Thrift's proposal to have a specially designed union flag flown at Lansdowne Road because 'the Union governed the game all over Ireland' was carried.[53] *Football Sports Weekly* remarked on the decision:

> The Union have ... decided to have a special flag designed, which will comprise the arms of the four provinces, to be used at all home Internationals, instead of the National Flag. That is an interesting compromise, which shall not escape notice in many quarters. All countries fly their National flags at their home Internationals, and the National flags of the visiting countries are those flown, out of compliment to the visitors.[54]

The Rugby Union flag was not flown at internationals held in Ravenhill: the Union Jack remained the home flag for those matches. The decision not to fly the Irish tricolour at Lansdowne Road saw the IRFU receive severe criticism from many quarters. The *Gaelic Athlete* condemned the IRFU's 'antipathy to the country' through their 'unanimous repudiation of the National flag.'[55] The University College Galway rugby club lobbied its sister colleges to 'lend their aid in ridding rugby of its anti-national bias.'[56] Once its senior clubs protested at the flying of the union flag, the Munster branch reversed its original decision of supporting the IRFU and recommended the flying of the tricolour.[57] The IRFU also received a stinging rebuke in Dáil Éireann from Richard Walsh, who condemned the IRFU for its slowness to embrace the new state by refusing to fly the tricolour at matches at Lansdowne Road. The IRFU had, he claimed, 'designed a bastard flag before they would agree to recognise the national flag.'[58] The

IRFU initially refused to alter its position, eventually compelled to do so after an intervention by the Irish Free State government. The Minister for External Affairs, Patrick McGilligan, sent a letter to the secretary of the IRFU in 1932 recognising that the IRFU was 'not an exclusively Irish Free State institution', but he could not 'see why the international practice of flying the flag of the country in which international matches are played should not be followed at Lansdowne Road'. He advised the union to fly the 'National flag on the principal flagstaff at Lansdowne Road' at the upcoming international match against England.[59] It resulted in the IRFU, at its next meeting, deciding to fly the tricolour alongside the union flag at all international matches at Lansdowne Road.[60] Given the incidents that occurred in the 1920s and 1930s and the profile of those who governed rugby in Ireland, it is little wonder union between North and South was never in jeopardy.

In the early 1920s 'the GAA had moved from being a focus of opposition to the British State in Ireland to being one of the most important structures of institutional support for the Irish Free State, and later the Irish Republic, outside of the Catholic Church.'[61] It remained a thirty-two county body vehemently opposed to partition and anyone who acknowledged or accepted its existence. It saw the FAI as one such body. Throughout the 1920s and beyond it embarked on a campaign to oppose all elements in Irish society it saw as foreign, and in particular British. The GAA believed an anglophile residue had remained in the country despite the British no longer being present in most of its territory.[62] According to Marcus de Búrca, 'in the civil service, in the National Army and at most official functions, it became fashionable to adopt British social habits and even to imitate British customs. Little or no effort was made to evolve or even to support distinctively Irish ways or customs.'[63] This was one of the main reasons the many efforts to remove the GAA's ban on 'foreign games' were defeated throughout the 1920s. Aside from a close vote in 1922, votes to defeat this ban were heavily defeated in 1923, 1924, 1925, 1926 and 1929.[64] Strongly supporting the GAA in retaining its ban, its mouthpiece, the *Gaelic Athlete*, described soccer and rugby as 'exotic imitations' of Britishness[65] and it described Irishmen who played those codes as 'blatant Imperialists for all Ireland to roll itself up in the Union Jack and sing and toast "Irish Nationality" with a leer on its lying lip.'[66]

Unlike the IFA, the FAI allowed the playing of soccer on Sundays. This led to increased antagonism with the GAA, whose games were primarily played on Sundays, both fighting for space and people at the same time.[67] The popularity of soccer in the Irish Free State in the 1920s was seen as a grave offence to many GAA followers. Some people left the GAA to switch to soccer, particularly in the border counties.[68]

Helping the GAA to curb the growth of soccer and other sports were many institutions of the Irish Free State, including the national army and the new police force, An Garda Síochána, where Gaelic games were exclusively played.[69] The first commissioner of the Garda Síochána, Eoin O'Duffy, was particularly opposed to soccer, calling it:

> The game of the British Garrison, the atmosphere surrounding it is anglicised, and no one can contradict me when I say that the enemies of Irish Freedom patronise and finance it. Ireland asks her sons to play and support our National games; the friends of the Empire ask you to play and support Soccer – make your choice, and for goodness sake do it at once. We welcome every Irishman to our fold who has a pride in the ancient traditions of our race and who, to preserve our individuality, is prepared to cast aside everything which means to make us slaves to the mannerisms of an alien race.[70]

Governments too would play their part in discriminating against 'foreign games' by introducing Entertainments Taxes to all sports except indigenous ones such as Gaelic games. Many believed the GAA was entitled to preferential treatment as it, unlike the FAI, could not earn income from international fixtures.[71] By seceding from the IFA, members of the FAI had relinquished the opportunity to play international fixtures against teams from the British associations. In the early years of its existence it looked to redress this, as well as seeking recognition from the international federation, FIFA.

CHAPTER 12

The Football Association of the
Irish Free State is Born

The IFA and FAI met for the first time in the Shelbourne Hotel in Dublin at the beginning of February 1923. It would be the first of many meetings held to try and reach a settlement. The IFA's wish to have the meeting closed to the press was granted: the media would be furnished only with the official report from both associations once proceedings had concluded.[1] The meeting which lasted for three hours was considered a frigid affair. At the outset it was agreed there would be no chairman.[2] Wilton kicked off proceedings by asking the Dublin delegates to state their grievances. This was met with a reply from the leader of the FAI delegation, J.F. Harrison, asking what new proposals the IFA had for the betterment of the game in Ireland, without attempting to answer Wilton's original question. Wilton also avoided Harrison's question and asked if the FAI delegation had full council powers. On receiving the reply that the delegation did not but was so representative that its recommendations would carry great weight, Wilton then proceeded to outline the IFA's proposals. The IFA was:

> Prepared to concede (1) the question of representation from the various associations to be adjusted so as to give the Southern portion of Ireland more representation on the Council; (2) Dublin should have a fair share of international matches; (3) Council meetings should be held alternately in Belfast and Dublin.[3]

One of the FAI delegates then responded stating the biggest obstacle to a settlement in his eyes was that the FAI:

> Would never agree to the entire control of football being run from Belfast, as they might as well give up altogether. He

140

would suggest dual control . . . We might as well be plain and straight in this business, and I wish to state that unless the headquarters be in Dublin, if there is one controlling body, we could not hold the clubs in the South we have got since leaving the IFA. They would go over at once to another game.[4]

Another remarked that 'the Leinster FA were not prepared to play second fiddle to the IFA'.[5] Larry Sheridan commented:

We can't get past the sentimental point of the office being in Dublin. There is a strong political bias in this matter, and if we send representatives up to Belfast, Munster would go out from under us, as the political feeling was such at the moment that they would not agree to be governed from Belfast.[6]

The 'strong political bias' Sheridan referred to was the ongoing boycott of Belfast organisations and goods by many in the South, caused by the Belfast Pogroms of 1920–22. Once the pogroms began in the summer of 1920, Dáil Éireann felt it could not stand idly by. It imposed a boycott on banks and insurance companies from Belfast. In reality the boycott soon extended to other businesses and farming too. The industries Catholics were primarily expelled from, engineering and shipbuilding, were practically immune from the boycott as they were reliant on export markets.[7] It led to many incidents enforcing the boycott in the coming years. Workers from Belfast firms in Louth were threatened by the IRA and given twenty-four hours to return to Belfast in March 1921.[8] Shots were fired into a shop not believed to be co-operating with the boycott in Carrick-on-Shannon in Leitrim a month later. One of the gunmen was accidently shot dead by his own gun whilst breaking a window.[9] A bread cart from Belfast was burned by masked men in Armagh.[10] The Great Northern Railway was forced to close its routes from Dundalk to Enniskillen due to the kidnapping of drivers who delivered Belfast goods.[11] A Dublin representative of a Belfast drapery was kidnapped by Irish Volunteers at his home in Dublin.[12]

Once the Anglo-Irish Treaty was signed in December 1921, with a provisional government being established in Dublin shortly afterwards, the leader of that government, Michael Collins, met with the leader of the newly created Northern Ireland government, James Craig, to harmonise relations between

North and South. Resulting from the meeting was the Collins-Craig Agreement with one provision being the discontinuance of the Belfast Boycott by the southern administration on the condition that religious and political discrimination be halted in the North.[13] Months later, there were still widespread reports of abuses against Catholics in Belfast. According to the North Eastern Boundary Bureau established by the provisional government, from 31 March to 24 May 1922, there were sixty-five Catholics killed, with 134 wounded; 221 Catholic families were evicted from their homes in the same period.[14] The appetite to halt the Belfast Boycott was slight amongst many in the South. All bodies associated with Belfast, such as the IFA, were looked upon with deep trepidation. It is little wonder the delegates from the FAI objected to being governed from Belfast, knowing it would lose many from its fold if it was.

On the question of dual control, Wilton pointed out that the International Football Association Board had ruled there could be only one body recognised in Ireland. On increased representation, Wilton said the IFA were open to the South getting more but he could not see how a divisional association such as Munster, with eight or ten clubs, could be entitled to the same representation as Antrim with over two hundred.

The FAI delegates asked the IFA delegates to leave the conference for a period to allow the FAI time to come up with proposals. The proposals put forward by the FAI were:

1 All clubs and organizations having their headquarters within the Irish Free State to be under the control of the Football Association of Ireland.
2 Any club or organization with its headquarters outside the Irish Free State to be eligible for membership of the Football Association of Ireland on the usual conditions.
3 The present Irish Football Association to become the North of Ireland Football Association, or some similarly named body.
4 The relations between the Football Association of Ireland and the North of Ireland Football Association to be, except as hereinafter provided, similar to the relations existing between the Football Association of England and the Army Football Association.

5 Except in competitions in which clubs from both Associations participate, the North of Ireland Football Association
to have full control over all clubs and other organizations
directly affiliated to it.

6 In competitions open to and participated in by clubs from
the two Associations, and in all international matters, the
controlling bodies to consist of representatives of the two
Associations on a scale to be arranged.

7 Suspension of clubs, organizations, players, officials, etc.,
by the Association to which they are affiliated to be recog-
nized and maintained by the other Association within its
jurisdiction.

8 All funds accruing to either Association by reason of membership or competitions entirely within its control to be the
property of that Association.

9 All funds accruing from competitions, etc., dually controlled to be shared by the two Associations on a scale to be
arranged.

10 The North of Ireland Football Association to have the right
to nominate members on all international selection committees on a scale to be arranged.[15]

On receiving the FAI terms, Wilton informed the southern
delegates that the proposals were impossible: there was no good
in continuing the conference. He felt 'that there was not even a
basis for discussion in them; and that, if in future any conference
was desired, the overtures must come from Dublin. The conference accordingly broke up.'[16]

Wilton was then accused by the FAI of a 'breach of faith',
through an article that appeared in a newspaper, for publishing a
report to the press on the conference ending prematurely. It had
been agreed that both the IFA and FAI would submit their
reports to the press simultaneously.[17] The IFA was also accused
of offering no terms to the FAI. Wilton, in an open letter published in *Ireland's Saturday Night*, commented that he could not
'allow such a reflection on my personal honour to go unchal-
lenged, particularly when it is without the slightest foundation'.
He was of the firm belief that it had been agreed at the conference that each association would conduct a council meeting on 7
February, with simultaneous press reports delivered after the
meetings, a course of action he subsequently took. On the issue
of terms not being offered to the FAI, he remarked:

You know that this is not so. As a basis for discussion I made certain suggestions involving radical changes in the government of the game, chiefly with regard to grievances which I thought you might have, and which might have been altered or extended in the course of an interchange of opinions, but this was made impossible by the dramatic presentation of an ultimatum bristling with sine qua non conditions.[18]

He concluded the letter by offering an olive branch, an attempt to keep lines of communication open:

I am confident all is not lost. I feel that when the prevailing conditions cease to exist, as they must; and when the present feeling changes, as it will, a way will be found out of the impasse to an honourable settlement which will show our fellow-countrymen that, at least in the realm of sport, Irishmen can agree to settle their own differences. Such a consummation is, I am sure, earnestly wished for by all parties, and by none more so than yours sincerely.[19]

In the same paper that day, another cartoon of Larry O'Hooligan appeared showing him looking on, covering his ears, as two players, representing Belfast and Dublin, rupture a ball entitled UNION with the caption below: 'The ball burst again. Larry looks on disconsolately while he sees the relations between the IFA and the FAI more ruptured than ever.'[20]

At a subsequent IFA Council meeting, Wilton was praised for the way he handled the conference. At the same meeting Linfield withdrew its offer requesting a match in Dublin for charity, given the outcome of the conference. However, Wilton, again showing his willingness to reach an agreement with the FAI, granted permission for Queen's University to play fixtures against Dublin University and University College Dublin, even though the latter two were affiliated to the FAI. He also granted 'Belfast Celtic FC permission to lend their ground to Alton United FC to play a match with Shelbourne United from Dublin in the New Football Association's Cup Competition.'[21]

At the IFA Annual Meeting of 1923, references were made to the efforts the IFA made in reaching out to the FAI:

Captain J.M. Wilton, in the interests of the game, made overtures to them to meet representatives from your Council, with

144

the object of discussing and adjusting any differences that might exist. After the lapse of six months, and no response having being received, your Council extended a further invitation, the result of which a conference was held, and your representatives perhaps erred in offering too favourable terms, with the result that they were asked to relegate your Association to that of an affiliated body and hand over the Government of Irish Football to the New Association. This they, even if so inclined, had no power to do, and the conference unfortunately proved abortive.[22]

One delegate commented that 'no effort should be spared to try and bring about reunion between North and South, to establish the old-time friendship that formerly existed.'[23] Wilton replied by saying:

There might be a development which might result in reunion. He could assure them all that . . . they would be the first to make every possible effort to bring together the North and South. He could not see why Irishmen could not settle their differences, at least in the realm of sport. They were too good sportsmen to allow anything to prevent the welfare of sport in the old country, and he had every hope that in the very near future their difference would be amicably settled. He assured them that the Council of the IFA would leave no stone unturned to have the reunion an accomplished fact before another annual meeting.[24]

To a loud applause, he concluded with the wish 'that before their next annual meeting they would have a "United Ireland".'[25]

At the same meeting, the prospects for the future of the game were looked on with a great deal more optimism than in 1922, the IFA believing 'a return is assured to those bright days heretofore existing'. The basis of this optimism came from a record gate at the Scottish international, with over 30,000 in attendance and a profit of £1,165 made from the match as well as a healthy increase in club membership, to 340. The one major blight was the fall in support for the Irish Cup: 'the interest manifested in this competition was again far below the usual standard, with the result that both the Clubs and the Association suffered.'[26] The improvement in fortunes of the IFA did allow the body to revisit its tactics with the FAI, allowing it more security in its dealings. The IFA had something the FAI didn't have: its trump card, international recognition and plum annual ties with the leading soccer countries in the world. There were also reports from 'the other side of the Boyne Bridge, and there are people optimistic enough to predict the return of Bohemians and Shelbourne to League football before another season starts on its way.'[27]

During the summer of 1923, persistent rumours appeared that there was discontent in the FAI camp, that the senior teams Bohemians and Shelbourne were unhappy and were looking to re-affiliate to the IFA. 'Ralph the Rover', in his weekly column with *Ireland's Saturday Night*, expressed the view gathering momentum that summer:

> There is hope that more than one further team will compete (in the League), as one cannot altogether close their ears to the rumblings of discontent amongst some Dublin teams with the Southern Association. It is reported that some thirty clubs on the other side of the Boyne had expressed the interest of returning to the fold. There are other people optimistic enough to say that both Bohemians and Shelbourne, and perhaps another Dublin side, will figure in League football next season; but the next week or two will tell a big tale. There is no doubt whatever that the old League teams would be delighted to be back, and to fight in a true sporting spirit with their old Northern foes, and there is also no doubt that the Southern opposition would be most welcome in the North. Let us hope all be well – that North and South will cement all their differences, at any rate on the sporting fields, and that the peace will be such as will prove unbreakable to the greatest extremists.[28]

The rumours were well founded. A number of clubs affiliated to the FAI did approach the IFA that summer looking to regain membership to the northern body. A new football association was also formed in Dublin, one of its representatives was Harry Wigoder, who had been one of the main people responsible for forming the FAI. Wigoder, as well as other delegates from the new body, travelled to Belfast to meet the IFA in June 1923. At the meeting, the new association from Leinster expressed their views on the state of soccer in Dublin and put forward their reasons for looking to affiliate to the IFA:

> After a long discussion, the Chairman ... informed the
> Deputation of the necessary steps they would require to
> enable them to take up the position of the Leinster Football
> Association in accordance with the terms of the Articles of
> Association, and the Deputation agreed to immediately call
> together a meeting of the clubs, with a view to carrying out the
> suggestions of the Committee so that they may be in a posi-
> tion to constitutionally take the place of the late Leinster
> Football Association.[29]

The new association subsequently sent out letters to two
hundred clubs in Leinster, claiming it was the new Leinster
Football Association affiliated to the IFA and looking for those
clubs to affiliate to the new body and the IFA. Linton FC, the
Wasps FC and the biggest coup for the new body, Dublin
Freebooters, immediately submitted applications to the IFA for
reinstatement, applications that were granted.[30] An even bigger
prize than Freebooters started to look like a distinct possibility:
Bohemians sent a deputation to Belfast to meet the IFA and the
Irish Football League with the purpose 'of Bohemians once more
returning to the Association.'[31] There was a belief in the press that
Shelbourne was also seeking to re-join the IFA, Freebooters being
likely to drop out of the league if that was to transpire.[32] It was
reported that Bohemians was looking for guaranteed gates of
about £40 per game if the club was to re-join the Irish Football
League, a bone of contention for the IFA who believed this figure
was too high. Bohemians had more to gain in having northern
opposition visiting Dublin as there was more of an interest from
the Dublin crowds to see northern teams than there was of Belfast
crowds viewing the southern teams.[33] The IFA could have looked
at it another way too. The capture of Bohemians from the clutches
of the FAI would have undermined the new association severely,
potentially fatally.

The primary reason for clubs in Leinster seeking to settle their
differences with the IFA was the issue of international recognition.
Once the conference between the FAI and the IFA failed in
February 1923, many in the South believed the prospect of interna-
tional competition had evaporated, as summed up by *Ireland's
Saturday Night*, which compared the future of the game for both
North and South:

Surely the time has now arrived when those with an interest
in football south of the Boyne will realise that they have no
chance of securing International recognition, and that their
best plan for the sake of the game in Dublin and district, is to
sink all their differences with the parent body, and get on with
the sport. Unless there is an outlet somewhere I'm afraid the
good old game will go from bad to worse in the Free State.
Visits from Northern clubs and occasional representative fixtures are really the only things that will help and improve
interest in the game. We in the North admit the standard of
play would be improved locally by Southern opposition, but
where we are better off is that variety is added to our programme by English, Scottish and Welsh visits.[34]

In the early summer of 1923, the IFA believed it was only a
matter of time before the FAI folded and soccer in Ireland would
be re-united. This hope was soon dashed. By July most of the clubs
looking to re-affiliate were dithering. It was reported at an IFA
Emergency Committee meeting in early July that Bohemians 'had
adjourned their decision re again affiliating with the IFA for a few
weeks'. The new association in Dublin stated 'that they would not
be able to make proper headway until the end of August.'[35] The
rumours of Shelbourne returning to the IFA fold were quashed at
the club's annual meeting in July: a decision was made to enter a
team to the FAI league the following season.[36] Freebooters withdrew its application to the IFA and decided not to enter a team to
the FAI either.[37] In a letter to the IFA, the new association
explained its reasons for its change of heart: 'in the event of the
Free State FA being recognised by the Football Association, they
would be compelled to dissolve their Association.'[38] The FAI's
campaign to gain international recognition was finally beginning
to bear fruit, a campaign that required the help of the fledgling
Free State government as well as allies who were key players in
the French Football Federation.

When the FAI was formed, letters were sent to football associations all over the world informing them of the FAI's birth.[39] Little
progress was made prior to the Irish Free State being formed in
1922. Before then, it could be argued that the FAI was a rebel
organisation and the IFA, the fourth oldest association in the
world, had jurisdiction over all of Ireland. Once the Free State was

established, the key tenet of the FAI's argument for recognition lay in its claim that it had jurisdiction in the Irish Free State and the IFA held sway just in the six counties of Northern Ireland.

The FAI's first overtures were to the associations of England, Scotland and Wales. Because they supported the IFA, as had been the case for many years before, the FAI found little joy with those associations. Rebuffed by the British associations, the FAI's best opportunity for recognition lay with the international governing body, FIFA.

FIFA was founded in Paris in 1904. The first president of FIFA, the Frenchman Robert Guérin, strived to bring the English and British associations into the FIFA fold from the beginning. Initially he was rebuffed. He claimed that dealing with the British was 'like slicing water with a knife'.[40] On suggesting an international federation to the English FA, Guérin was met with the response from Frederick Wall, English FA secretary, 'The Council of the Football Association cannot see the advantages of such a Federation, but on all such matters upon which joint action was desirable they would be prepared to confer.'[41] Guérin commented in the 1920s, 'Tiring of the struggle and recognizing that the Englishmen, true to tradition, wanted to wait and watch, I undertook to invite the delegates from various nations myself.'[42] Seven nations attended the first FIFA meeting in Paris: Belgium, Denmark, France, the Netherlands, Spain, Sweden and Switzerland.

Once FIFA was formed, the English FA decided it was prudent to join, doing so with the other home associations in 1905. With his efforts to organise an international competition thwarted, Guérin resigned as president in 1906. He was succeeded by Englishman Daniel Woolfall, whose primary aim was to ensure the pre-eminence of the English FA. It was understandable that the English FA would take a leadership role. Before FIFA was founded in 1904, some of the founding member countries of FIFA had never played a match; others had no football federation.[43] On being elected FIFA president, he stated:

> It is important to the FA and other European Associations that a properly constituted Federation should be established and the Football Association should use its influence to regulate football on the Continent as a pure sport and give all

Continental Associations the full benefit of the many years' experience of the FA.[44]

By 1914 the federation had grown to twenty-four members, including non-European countries such as South Africa, Argentina, Chile and the United States. Despite opposition from the IFA,[45] FIFA was admitted to the International Football Association Board in 1913.[46] After the First World War, Woolfall was succeeded as president by another Frenchman, Jules Rimet. Rimet's reign would see FIFA become a truly global organisation.[47] Under his presidency, FIFA went from a membership of twenty to eighty-five. He internationalised football.[48] Its status was hampered straight after the war, though, by the decision of the British associations to withdraw their membership from FIFA. They did so because of FIFA's inclusion as members, the defeated nations from the First World War, the Central Powers.[49]

The FAI's first efforts to become a member of FIFA met with limited success. The international governing body was unclear of the Irish Free State's status as a national entity and was reluctant to do anything that might upset the English FA, even though the English FA was no longer a member of FIFA. It, like all other football associations, had a tendency to fawn over the English FA, seen as not only the first association but also the primary authority in global football. The English FA and its committee members were regularly in receipt of gifts and titles bestowed upon them by associations around the world for 'numerous services rendered' by the 'great Federation' to the game of soccer around the globe.[50] A leading soccer official in France, Achille Duchenne, claimed in 1923 that the entire board of the French Football Federation was 'at the English entire devotion . . . [a] fact which I personally lament.'[51]

In its first application for membership to FIFA on St Patrick's Day 1922, the FAI claimed it was applying for membership on the grounds that it was the only governing body of all clubs in the Irish Free State as well as thirty-two clubs in Northern Ireland; it had spread the game to parts of Ireland where it was never played before, and it had increased the popularity of the game in other areas. The application concluded by stating:

The FAI maintain, and it cannot with truth be denied, that, so long as they have inalienable and undivided support of all the clubs and Divisional Associations of the Irish Free State, they are equally entitled with all other Associations to all the rights, privileges and prerogatives enjoyed by them.[52]

Membership to FIFA was not forthcoming at that stage. Months later, though, FIFA, in conjunction with the French Football Federation, did grant permission to the Parisian club, Gallia, to visit Dublin and play clubs affiliated to the FAI 'in recognition of the fact that the Irish Federation is seeking affiliation.'[53] Writing to Ryder, Duchenne, from Gallia, commented: 'Our Club feels greatly honoured and pleased to be the very first French club to be invited to visit Ireland.'[54] It was agreed that Gallia would play Bohemians and Pioneers on 31 March and 1 April 1923. The two matches, played in front of representatives from the Irish and French governments, were a financial success.[55] More importantly, it was the first real example granted internationally, of the FAI's right to exist. Concerned at the development, the visit of Gallia was raised at an IFA Council meeting, where it was decided to bring it up at the next International Football Association Board meeting.[56] In Achilles Duchenne, the FAI had a strong ally. The FAI visited Duchenne and the secretary of the French Football Federation, Henri Delaunay, in April 1923 to seek guidance on the best line of policy to pursue at the FIFA Annual Congress, due to be held in Geneva the following month.[57] An early pioneer of European football, Delaunay would become the first General Secretary of the Union of European Football Associations (UEFA). The UEFA European Championship trophy is named in his honour. Duchenne and Delaunay made it

quite clear that while France could not understand the existence of two Associations claiming to govern football in the same area, she could having regard to the National position, thoroughly support two Associations in Ireland, one governing exclusively in the Irish Free State and the other in Northern Ireland.[58]

Duchenne in particular was very helpful to the FAI, advising the association to claim:

The application for membership by the FAI does not mean to affect in any way the actual membership of the IFA, this Body

151

governing all clubs situated inside the Ulster province, a fact
... which I believe will help to show that you do not intend to
bring the International Federation into a quarrel but simply
want recognition equal to that given to a less powerful body.[59]

He also believed it was important to mention that General
Reginald Kentish of the British Olympic Committee had stated to
the press that the Irish Free State was entitled to take part in the
Olympic Games, seeing as it was a dominion body similar to countries such as Canada and South Africa.[60] Kentish had been
convinced by John J. Keane, president of the Irish Olympic Council,
of the merits of admitting the Irish Free State to the 1924 Olympics
in Paris.[61]

The FAI received the support of the Irish Free State government, who, in a letter to the FIFA Annual Congress, wished the
FAI good fortune; the minister (Desmond FitzGerald) 'sincerely
hopes that their mission will be successful, and that Ireland will
be enabled to take her proper place in the world of International
Association Football, a game which is to-day such a powerful
means of renewing and strengthening International friendships.'[62]
In the letter to FIFA, Osmonde Grattan Esmonde, on behalf of the
Minster for External Affairs, stated:

> This is to certify that the Football Association of Ireland, estab-
> lished in the year 1921, with its Headquarters in the City of
> Dublin, is acting with the consent of the Government of
> Saorstat Eireann, and in that capacity is entitled to all the
> rights and privileges appertaining to and enjoyed by each and
> every separate National Association, in accordance with Rule
> 1, of the Articles of the Federation Internationale De Football
> Association, instituted in Paris, on the 21st of May, 1904.[63]

A diplomat and future TD, Grattan Esmonde would also
become president of the FAI and the Leinster Football Association.[64]
In the FAI's application to FIFA, it claimed to be the only body
governing soccer in the Irish Free State, covering an area of 27,128
square miles, compared with the 5,456 square miles of Northern
Ireland. It was asserted that the Irish Free State possessed the same
national status as Canada and South Africa, both members of
FIFA, and was not governed in any respect by the British
Parliament at Westminster. The FAI also stated it controlled more

clubs than had ever been governed in the whole of Ireland: 'the very existence of the game in the Irish Free State is, in the opinion of my Council, dependent on the maintenance of the Football Association of Ireland, since that body alone can satisfy the national aspirations of the clubs.'[65]

The FIFA Annual Congress held in Geneva in 1923 was the first in nine years, the First World War and its aftermath putting paid to a congress before then. Commenting on the last congress, held in Christiania (present-day Oslo) in 1914, the FIFA general secretary, Cornelis August Wilhelm Hirschman, stated:

> At the last Congress the delegates agreed unanimously ...
> 'assembled at Christiania on 27th and 28th June 1914 declares
> itself willing to support any action, which tends to bring the
> nations nearer to each other and to substitute arbitration for
> violence in the settlement of all the conflicts which arise
> between them'. A few hours later it was reported that ARCH-
> DUKE FRANCIS FERDINAND of Austria was murdered, and
> nobody will have had any idea, that this fact would give rise
> that within six weeks the greater part of Europe would be set
> in fire and flame by a war which continued for more than four
> terrible years.[66]

New members to FIFA could only be admitted at Annual Congress. As this was the first congress in nine years, there were many applications. Nine countries were granted membership of FIFA. The most contentious decision related to Ireland. Frederick Wall, secretary of the English FA, had a letter read out at the FIFA congress, stating the English FA believed the FAI should not be considered for membership as the dispute between the FAI and the IFA was a domestic matter; the English FA would continue to recognise the IFA and would not allow its clubs to play against those of the Dublin body, and a serious situation would arise between the English FA and FIFA if the FAI was granted membership.[67] Bob Murphy, who was an FAI delegate at the congress, wrote to the Ministry of External Affairs, stating the effect the English FA letter had on proceedings:

> This letter was the death knell of our hopes of immediate
> admission to the Federation. The position of the FA of
> England in relation to the Federation is a peculiar one. The

Associations in the British Isles are not now members of the Federation, have seceded on the pretext of the Federation's refusal to exclude the Central Powers from membership. The British Associations retain, however, a friendly connection with the Continental bodies, which are still engaged in developing the game throughout Europe and are greatly assisted in that direction by visits from English and Scottish clubs. France and Belgium are particularly dependent on English goodwill in this way and the attitude of their representatives showed it. Switzerland and Italy contended that England should not be allowed a dominating influence in the proceedings of a Federation from membership of which she had withdrawn. These two countries strove to have the Free State Association admitted to membership without further delay. Norway, Finland and Sweden, while advocating enquiry to an end within the shortest possible space of time, suggesting various time limits and finally securing the 1st September. We found the representatives of those countries most sympathetic in their remarks about the application.[68]

Many of the delegates from other countries asked questions about the Irish Free State's political status, its relations to Westminster and the nature of the boundary between the six counties of Northern Ireland and the rest of Ireland. The FAI asked the Free State government to intervene and contact the British Foreign Office, which had the capacity to 'destroy our chance of recognition' and with it 'the fate of all the international sporting organisations in the Free State.'[69] After a debate, it was agreed that the FAI would be granted membership based on the following principles:

1 If the Irish Free State possessed the political status claimed by the delegates, the Federation would grant membership to its national association.
2 The Federation would not allow the Football Association of Ireland to claim any membership within the six-county area, nor would it permit the Irish Football Association, Ltd., to encroach on the Irish Free State territory.
3 Subject to satisfactory assurances on the first two points, the Federation would continue its relationship with the Irish Football Association, Ltd., and would admit the Football Association of Ireland to membership as the national association of the Irish Free State.[70]

It was decided that the FIFA Emergency Committee should confer on the FAI case and reach a decision on the membership application later in the summer. The FAI immediately took on board the recommendations made at the FIFA Annual Congress. Firstly, it changed its name from the Football Association of Ireland to the Football Association of the Irish Free State (FAIFS). Secondly, it decided to allow only clubs based in the Irish Free State as members of its association. Clubs from the Falls and District League as well as all other clubs in Northern Ireland had their membership cancelled.[71] One of those clubs, Alton United, had caused a sensation earlier in the year by winning the FAI Cup in just the second year of the competition. The junior club from Belfast beat the senior star-studded Shelbourne in the final on St Patrick's Day in Dalymount Park. The Alton United team was escorted from Amiens Street train station to Dalymount Park by an armed guard provided by the IRA. The club was also unable to bring the trophy back to Belfast due to the troubles in Belfast at the time.[72] The victory for Alton United was a humiliation for the FAI, demonstrating, as some commentated, 'the superiority of the North over the South'.[73]

The FAIFS applied to the International Football Association Board for recognition again in June 1923. The basis of its application rested on its right to govern solely for the territory of the Irish Free State:

> In view . . . of the altered condition of affairs in this country, I am to ask you to be good enough to receive our application for membership to your Board, as an entirely separate national entity, controlling Association Football in the territory of the Irish Free State; or, in the alternative, to grant such recognition as will enable the clubs of this Association to meet the clubs of the Associations comprising your Board.[74]

At the annual meeting of that body, held at the Causeway Hotel, Giant's Causeway on 9 June, it was resolved: 'That application for membership from the Football Association of Ireland or the Football Association of the Irish Free State cannot be received.'[75] The main opponents were the IFA delegates, who claimed the position was unchanged since the last meeting of the International Board, and referred to the failed conference between the two bodies.[76]

The FAIFS contacted FIFA a month later enquiring about the efforts being made by the international federation to contact the British Foreign Office. Hirschman responded by saying efforts had been made to make contact but no answer had been received. He also stated a letter had been sent by the IFA to FIFA stating it:

> Recognises the national status of the Irish Free State and defends the view that it does not necessarily follow that Football in Ireland should be divided into two separate organisations, as it would injure existing competitions, hitherto open to all clubs in Ireland; National Cup, Irish Football League, and International Matches. It informs me that a number of clubs within the Free State, with full regard for the fact that the Irish Free State has separate political status, are desirous of remaining members of the I.F.A.[77]

Ryder, who was not aware or pretended to be unaware of some senior clubs threatening disaffiliation at the time, commented:

> The IFA's statement that members of the Free State Association wish to join the Belfast body in order to compete in the Irish League and Irish Cup is an impudent effort to confuse the issue. It is true that a couple of Junior clubs at one time contemplated application for affiliation to the IFA, Ltd., but they have since abandoned that idea and have renewed their membership of my Association. Since the signing of the Treaty between Ireland and England on the 6th December, 1921, no Free State club has competed in the so-called Irish League or Irish Cup despite the hardship inflicted on the clubs and players of the Free State in being denied recognition by other National Associations. With this most practical proof of the loyalty of the Free State clubs to their own Association in mind it is unnecessary to offer any other refutation of the Belfast body's statement. I am, however, to point out that the latter Association's expressed desire to acquire membership within the Irish Free State is in direct contravention of the principle laid down at the Congress by the representatives of Belgium and endorsed by the Federation, that, with the independence of the Irish Free State defined, the Federation would neither allow the Free State Association to hold membership within the area controlled by the Belfast Parliament nor permit the IFA, Ltd., to interfere in the football affairs of the Irish Free State.[78]

FIFA came to a decision on the Free State body's application for membership: it granted the FAIFS provisional membership status on 10 August, the same day Uruguay was granted full member-ship.[79] Also, on the same day, the FIFA secretary, Hirschman, wrote to the English FA justifying its decision to accept the Free State body as a member:

> It was stated that the actual situation is, that Ireland consists at present of two countries with two nationalities: the Free State of Ireland (27,128 square miles), recognized by the League of Nations, and being in the same position to Great Britain as Canada and South Africa, and the remainder of Ireland (5,458 square miles). The Free State representing a separate nation claims to govern its own sports, and its Government recognizes the Football Association of Ireland as the national authority for football. The old Irish Football Association having only jurisdiction over the remainder of Ireland, both Associations are not overlapping each other. From a sporting point of view, it was stated that the Free State of Ireland was recognized by the International Olympic Committee and enti-tled to send competitors to the Olympic Games. The Football Association of Ireland does not wish to interfere in any way with the Irish Football Association, which is operative only outside the Irish Free State. The Congress considered that it was not right to withhold membership of the Federation to an Association who had fulfilled all required formalities according to the Articles of the Federation, and that it was no more than a matter of justice to admit such an Association. Moreover, it was of opinion that it was even their duty to the interests of football to have a recognized controlling body in a new State.[80]

Hirschman concluded by appealing to the reasonableness of the English body: 'The Congress, fully appreciating the loyal attitude of The Football Association towards the Federation, expressed its confidence that, after taking knowledge of the stand-point of the Federation, The Football Association would recognise it as quite reasonable.'[81]

Although accession to the International Board was again snubbed, the Irish Free State government's efforts with the British Foreign Office as well as FIFA's decision to grant the FAIFS provi-sional membership soon started to pay dividends with the English FA. The Governor-General of Ireland, Tim Healy, it was believed, also intervened to influence the English FA.[82] In the summer of 1923, the English body started to show signs of being more open to recognition of the Free State association. On receiving notification that the FAI had changed its name to the FAIFS and had restricted its membership to clubs within the territory of the Irish Free State, instead of dismissing the development out of hand, the English FA appeared to be open to recognising the Free State body.[83] It was claimed in *Ireland's Saturday Night* that the English body had informed FIFA it also believed the FAIFS should be recognised:

> At the last meeting of the English Association that body gave it as their opinion that the Free State Association should be recognised, but that they were not entitled to representation on the International Board. I should state, to make myself more clear, that the English Association has not really yet decided to recognise the Free State as a governing body, but has merely given an opinion to the Federation. Of course that is practically equivalent to them looking on the Free State Association as the ruling authority outside Ulster.[84]

The paper believed that:

> England's expressed opinion has, so far as that is concerned, done more harm than good. It has made it more difficult for the parties to find a solution to the problem. No one wants to see the game hampered, as it may be, by two governing bodies, and something will have to be done to heal the sore and thereby find a means of running the sport as a sport, and by one ruling authority.[85]

At an IFA Council meeting, Wilton claimed that the English FA had not recognised the Free State Association,[86] that it had merely decided to call a conference of the British associations and the two Irish bodies with the objective of reaching an agreement on the governance of soccer in Ireland.[87]

This conference took place in Liverpool on 18 October 1923. Presiding was the chairman of the English FA, John Charles Clegg. In attendance were representatives from the English, Scottish and Welsh associations as well as from both of the Irish bodies. Clegg stated he had called the conference to see if anything 'could be done to straighten out matters in regard to Football in Ireland'; he then asked the Free State Association representatives to make their case. Five points were made:

1 The Free State Football Association recognises the Northern Ireland Football Association as the sole governing body of football in that portion of Ireland which is outside the Irish Free State, and, in exchange, expects to be recognised as the sole governing body of Football within the Irish Free State.

2 The Free State Football Association will, on reciprocal terms, recognise and enforce within the Irish Free State all suspensions imposed by the Northern Association on clubs, players, etc., under control of the Northern Association.

3 In order that the whole of Ireland may be represented in International Matches with England, Scotland, and Wales, the Free State Football Association is prepared to join with the Northern Association in setting up a Selection Committee, with equal representation from the two Irish Associations, to control the game. It will also agree as regards Ireland's home International matches with the countries of Great Britain that they should be played alternately in Northern Ireland and the Irish Free State.

4 The Free State Football Association will facilitate intercourse between its clubs and the clubs of the Northern Association, and it is prepared, should any desire for competitive games between the two sets of clubs manifest itself, to confer with the Northern Association with the object of fixing regulations to govern such Competition.

5 The Free State Football Association, having altered its title – 'Football Association of Ireland' – in order to define clearly the limits of its jurisdiction, expects that the Irish Football Association, Ltd., will, in its turn, substitute for its present name some title which will indicate precisely the extent of its control. In the opinion of the Free State Football Association the title 'Irish Football Association' is not appropriate in existing circumstances.[88]

Having heard the Free State proposals, the other delegates at the conference responded by stating that:

No objection was made – (1) To the Football Association of Ireland having changed its name to the Football Association of the Irish Free State; (2) To the Irish Football Association, and the Football Association of the Irish Free State, exercising full jurisdiction within their own area; (3) To the mutual recognition of suspensions.[89]

The conference concluded by recommending:

1 That the Football Association of the Irish Free State be recognised as an Association with Dominion Status; the Association, Clubs and Players of the Football Association, the Scottish Football Association, and the Football Association of Wales, be eligible to play matches with the Football Association of the Irish Free State and its clubs and players.
2 That the present suspensions by the Irish Football Association be removed.[90]

Commenting on the conference, J.F. Harrison, the FAIFS chairman, stated:

> Their association had achieved a great victory and . . . their international status was now fully secured. Even should they fail to come to an agreement with the IFA they were on an equal footing with the other countries affiliated to the International Board. He could hold out no hope of agreement with the Northern body except on grounds of equal representation on an All-Ireland Executive Council.[91]

The *Freeman's Journal* was not as optimistic on the outcome of the conference, commenting that only the first two proposals by the FAIFS were agreed to. The IFA refused point blank on the proposal surrounding international matches and did nothing to change its name from the Irish Football Association to a name more reflective of its political status; and a lukewarm commitment was made to meet to discuss competitions between clubs of both bodies. The paper also believed the status received by the FAIFS as an association with dominion status as opposed to a full association was significant and detracted 'from the completeness of the recommendation and minimises the concession considerably.'[92] The FAIFS had achieved a victory in finally gaining recognition from the British associations. It was hoped this would lead to international fixtures against its neighbours, providing financial security to the fledgling association. It was also felt there would be closer co-operation between the North and South bodies: many believed it was only a matter of time before reunion was achieved.[93] An agreement for Bohemians to travel to Belfast to play Linfield on the same day, 27 December, that Glentoran travelled to Dublin to play Shelbourne stoked this belief.[94]

Such perceptions were to be deceptive. The 'victory' achieved by the Free State body was of a very limited scale. Although recognised, it was only on a dominion basis. It would be a further twenty-three years before England would play a team from the South, and it would take thirty-seven years for Wales to do so and thirty-eight years for Scotland to meet a Dublin team.[95] The IFA was the true victor of the conference, conceding nothing.[96] It suited the IFA for the Free State association to have dominion status, thus allowing it to pick players from the Free State for its 'Ireland' team without sanction, something it would do regularly until 1950. Both bodies would meet after the Liverpool conference to seek common ground, a meeting that took place in March 1924. At one point it looked as if reunion was on the cards: it became tantalisingly close. But the talks would become undone again because of a dispute over one point.

CHAPTER 13

False Dawn

The FAIFS contacted the British associations to arrange international matches immediately after the decision was made at the Liverpool conference in October 1923 to officially recognise the Free State body. The Scottish FA replied two months later that it was unable to send a representative team.[1] The FA of Wales was also unable to send a team: 'In view of the fact that we are due in Belfast in March, and also that our Welsh League Southern Division are playing the Free State League in February, we cannot clear this Season to come over on another occasion to Ireland.'[2] The Welsh League Southern Division did visit Dublin in 1924, playing against an Irish Free State selection in Dalymount Park: 'Thirteen thousand people, paying £850, roared a welcome. The match, which became a forerunner of many between the two Leagues, ended in a draw.'[3] According to *Football Sports Weekly*, the meetings between the Welsh and the Free State League came about because the Irish Football League in Belfast was forced by the English and Scottish Leagues to discontinue its annual bout with the Welsh League.[4] The Welshmen were followed a few weeks later by Glasgow Celtic.[5] Most of the players who had won the Scottish Cup for Celtic the previous year came to Ireland, where a crowd of 22,000, providing a gate of £1,232, saw Celtic defeat a selection of Irish Football League players by three goals to nil. Providing such opposition as the FA of Wales did was helpful and was appreciated by the FAIFS. The letter from the FA of Wales was disingenuous, though, as it gave the impression the Welsh association was open to an international fixture with a team from the Free State. In reality it had no intention to do so, 1960 being the first year both countries would meet. An attempt by the FAIFS to have an international with England was also thwarted in late 1923.[6]

Following the Liverpool conference, the FAIFS also aimed to secure an agreement with the IFA on all outstanding issues from the conference. At an IFA Council meeting where it was agreed that 'all suspensions passed on players and officials in connection with the forming of the New Football Association were now removed, and that clubs of this Association could now play matches of a friendly nature with the clubs of the Free State FA', a letter was read from the FAIFS asking what the IFA intended to do on the issues of the international team, competitions between the two bodies and the name most suitable for the Belfast body. The IFA decided to adjourn the matter until the council's meeting in December.[7]

At that meeting it was agreed to send the reply to the 'Free State FA':

> That there was nothing left in abeyance from the Conference in Liverpool, but if you consider that a Conference with my Association would be of any assistance, we should be pleased to meet now if you so desire, to discuss any matters that would be of benefit to the game in Ireland.[8]

The FAIFS wrote back claiming the control of international matches was in abeyance and again sought a conference. Wilton remarked:

> The most extraordinary thing about the Free State FA letter was that the latter body had now confined themselves to asking for a share in the control of the international matches. He held that this contention was impossible, as the Free State Association was now a separate entity with Dominion status, and the IFA were in the position of a nation in the national control of football. He was afraid that if any agreement were come to regarding the playing of Free State players in international matches the other countries would ask some time, if not immediately, what right the IFA had to play players who were not under their control.[9]

This led to a long discussion on the eligibility of players for international matches. Some believed people were eligible who were born anywhere in Ireland or born abroad of Irish parentage. Several believed that Free State players were eligible in the same way in which Irish players assisting cross-Channel clubs were eligible. There was also a discussion on the Dublin clubs becoming associate members, allowing them to compete in the Irish League, similar to the arrangement between English and Welsh clubs, as 'it was the desire of most of the senior representatives that some means should be found to renew intercourse with the Southern clubs.'[10]

At the same meeting, a letter was also received from Frederick Wall, secretary of the English FA, which stated:

> The Conference at Liverpool in October last, as I understand completed the duties for which it was convened. There were certain matters referred to, domestic to the Irish Football Association and the Football Association of the Irish Free State, but these were matters with which the Conference could not deal – They may only be dealt with by friendly conversations between the two Associations.[11]

It was eventually agreed to hold a conference, open to the press, in Belfast on 8 March 1924, with the Free State delegates invited as guests for tea beforehand.[12]

The conference was held at the IFA offices in Wellington Place. It lasted for over three hours and it appeared the solution was amicable to both parties. The FAIFS delegates asked the IFA delegates what they were prepared to offer the Free State body in order for them to agree to one governing body for soccer in Ireland again. The IFA proposed six main points:

1 The selection and control of International Matches to be vested in a Committee of equal representation from the Free State FA and the IFA, with the existing Chairman of the IFA as Chairman of the Committee.
2 The control of the Irish Senior Cup, to be dealt with by a Management Committee of equal representation from the Free State Association and the IFA.
3 The control of the Irish Junior Cup, to be dealt with by a Committee of Management consisting of equal representation from both bodies.
4 The Free State FA to deal entirely with their own internal affairs, that is, with offences by their clubs, and all matters which might best be described by the word internal.

5 Divisional Associations from the North and South, to have
equal representation on the Council of the new body.
6 Meetings of the Council to be held alternately in the North
and South.[13]

It was reported in different media outlets that point five on divisional representation on the IFA Council was dependent on the game progressing in southern Ireland. Southern Ireland would have more representatives on the council if there were more clubs in the South than in the North.[14] *The Irish Times* reported that:

> Representatives of the Free State Football Association and the Irish Football Association arrived at a provisional settlement of the dispute that has split Irish Association football for several years. Certain definite proposals were agreed upon, and will have to be ratified by the Councils of both Associations. There is, however, little doubt but that a complete healing of the breach will be announced in a very short time.[15]

A reporter from *Sport*, present at the meeting, commented that 'when the IFA delegates announced their offer it more or less took the breath away of the Free State delegates', who were so pleased and surprised with the terms.[16] J.F. Harrison, the chairman of the FAIFS, believed the principal issue was control of the internationals. To ensure all of Ireland might be represented in internationals with England, Scotland and Wales, he was 'prepared to join with the Northern Association in setting up a selection committee, with equal representation from the two Irish Associations, to control the games. They would also agree that internationals in Ireland be played in the North and South alternately'. He concluded by intimating 'that the Southern delegates regarded the majority of the proposals as entirely satisfactory, and expressed appreciation of the sporting spirit in which they had been met.'[17] *Sport* remarked: 'I take it the Free State FA has no wish to lose its identity or to merge itself in another Association. It desires unity on equal terms with the IFA as regards Internationals with the countries of Great Britain whilst retaining its recognised right to Internationals with other countries.'[18] Both delegations left the conference with the task of reporting back to their respective councils and reaching a decision on the proposals. Confident of an agreement, the proposed settlement was unanimously ratified at the subsequent IFA Council meeting. A communication was also sent to the FAIFS, 'asking them to be good enough to get their end settled up, in order to facilitate the meeting with regard to alterations to the Articles, which were necessary to comply with the terms of the settlement.'[19]

The FAIFS received some congratulatory notifications on an agreement being reached, with one correspondent calling it a 'wise and farseeing decision which will be hailed with the greatest gratification by all Footballers, not to speak of the General Public, and will further tend to promote the good fellowship that formerly did exist between North and South.'[20]

Alas, it was to be a false dawn. At an FAIFS Council meeting, the proposed settlement was not ratified. The primary objection was that the northern chairman would be the permanent chairman of the joint body on selecting the international team.[21] It did agree to 'proceed with the discussions if granted alternate Chairmanship of that Committee'. The IFA replied that they would not continue with the conference, as an agreement had already been entered into between the IFA and the Free State Council.[22] The discussions ended; soccer was still split on its post-1921 lines. The IFA was adamant about who was responsible for the impasse. At its annual meeting in May, the council reported:

> That notwithstanding the efforts made to effect a settlement of the trouble which brought about the secession of the clubs in the South of Ireland, they have been unable to report a satisfactory conclusion, but they desire to assure the members that any delay in this direction is not due to the Council of the IFA Ltd as they at all times met the Southern people in a fair, generous and sportsmanlike manner. They were always imbued with the one thought, and that thought was peace, in order that the game might be conducted all over the whole of Ireland by one governing body . . . at the request of the Free State Association, your Council appointed a deputation to meet them in Conference, and the result was that a satisfactory conclusion seemed to be secured, but, unfortunately, for the hopes of peace, the Council of the Free State turned down the Agreement entered into between their Delegates and those of the IFA . . . They still hope for a happy ending to this unfortunate impasse which has divided the Country in the sport of Football.[23]

False Dawn

The IFA could be forgiven for being disappointed at the FAIFS' decision. The parent body, established in 1880, the fourth oldest football association in the world, had conceded a great deal of control to the southern body, a body that was less than three years old. It was essentially offering to share governance of soccer in Ireland, with the one caveat. The agreement that looked to all intents and purposes secured broke down on that one point, the choice of chairman for the International Selection Committee. Considering the large emphasis the southern body had always placed on the international team selection, it is not that surprising. As a constituent part of the IFA fold before 1921, the Leinster Football Association representatives attended International Selection Committee meetings more regularly than any of the meetings of the other sub-committee they were on, by a considerable margin (see Appendix B). Attendance at those meetings still had little impact: players from Leinster clubs were invariably left out in the cold on being called up for international duty.

Appendix C lists all the Irish international caps won from 1882 to 1921, with the exception of an international friendly between Ireland and Scotland in 1902 in aid of the Ibrox Disaster Fund, and of the victory internationals held after the First World War. The caps are broken down based on the location of each player's club at the time of each international. Overall, 1,144 caps were awarded by the IFA over that time period, the vast majority of the caps going to players who played for clubs based in Ulster (798). The IFA did not allow Irish players playing for overseas clubs to play for Ireland until 1899. Such players won 271 caps between 1899 and 1921. Players playing for Dublin clubs received seventy-five caps in total from 1882 to 1921, averaging at just two caps per year. Although soccer was more developed in Ulster at an earlier stage, professionalism was brought in sooner, and there were more senior clubs in Ulster to choose from, the discrepancy between Ulster and Leinster representation was huge. Once Dublin clubs became more competitive and started to win Irish Cups and compete in the Irish Football League, their representation on the international team did increase. It was not commensurate with their achievements, though. In 1908 the two Irish Cup finalists were Bohemians and Shelbourne. Five international caps were won between the two clubs that year, and three the following year. The same clubs reached the final again in 1911, and again just five people from those clubs were called up for international duty. After the First World War, just one cap was won by a player playing for a Dublin club before the split of 1921: Ned Brooks from Shelbourne played against Scotland in 1920. Shelbourne won the Irish Cup in 1920. In that same period twenty-three caps were won by players playing for Ulster-based clubs.

The IFA may have believed, with some justification, that the offer made to the FAIFS in 1924 was a generous one. The FAIFS was in a very different situation, though, to the organisation it spawned from, the Leinster Football Association. It was the governing body of a new political entity, not a divisional association of a parent body. It also governed for a significantly larger portion of Ireland than the IFA, something it was at pains to emphasise in its campaign to gain international recognition. Given the history of southern-based players being selected for Ireland, it would be galling for the new body to revisit past times, co-operating with an Ulster-controlled body that could demonstrate an Ulster bias yet again.

The FAIFS' efforts to play internationals against England, Scotland and Wales was, for the time being, put on hold. For players affiliated to the Free State Association to obtain international competition they would have to look elsewhere. The Olympic Games in Paris in 1924 provided a solution, granting the association its first taste of international competition.

CHAPTER 14

First Olympians

The Paris Olympics were the first chance for the fledgling association to show itself to the world. It was also the first Olympic Games the Irish Free State competed in as a separate country, the International Olympic Committee (IOC) ruling that the Irish Free State was entitled to do so in 1922.[1] Irish people had competed in previous Olympic Games, the modern games coming into being in 1896, primarily under the British umbrella, most notably at the London Olympic Games of 1908, where 'native-born Irishmen, collected as many as eight gold, seventeen silver and eight bronze medals in fifteen different disciplines.'[2] Although representing Great Britain, the men's Irish hockey team did win a silver medal at the 1908 Olympic Games competing as Ireland, losing to England in the final.[3] The year 1924 would be the first occasion Irish athletes could compete solely under the Irish banner.

As FIFA organised the soccer tournament in the Olympic Games, and with the FAIFS becoming a provisional member of FIFA in 1923, the path for the Free State association to compete in the games seemed secure. One big obstacle appeared in the way. John J. Keane, Irish Olympic Council president, objected to the FAIFS sending a team. Keane, a fervent GAA supporter, opposed the FAIFS, as it seceded from the IFA and in so doing accepted partition according to him. The Irish Olympic Council was run on a thirty-two county basis.[4] It sent a letter and a telegram to the IFA requesting the northern body 'to co-operate with the Irish Free State in sending a team to Paris to represent Ireland in the Olympic Games'. The IFA replied it was unable to do so, 'that as our Colleagues on the International Board, England, Scotland and

Wales were not competing in these games', it wished to 'inform the Olympic Council that they were adopting a similar attitude.'[5] The British associations, led by the English FA, were not happy with the definition of an amateur as outlined by the IOC and had decided not to send a soccer team to the Olympics.[6] The home associations who had re-joined FIFA in 1924 would leave the international federation again later in the decade on precisely this issue, the definition of an amateur, and on whether the receipt of 'broken time' payment should be considered in the realm of amateurism or professionalism.[7] 'Broken time' payments were paid in lieu of salaries by different sporting bodies whilst the sporting participants were away from their jobs competing in sporting activities. Despite Keane's opposition, the FAIFS did have allies in the IOC, with one representative who wrote to Harrison stating:

> Keane applied to French Olympic Committee yesterday. His very lame excuse in refusing signature for Foot-Ball Team has left the Gentlemen of Committee here rather perplexed. The excuse he puts forward is that your Federation does not represent a united Ireland so far as soccer is concerned. I may tell you at once that even if you do not choose any players from Ulster or North, Olympic Committee will accept entry.[8]

He continued by stating it was not understood:

> Why politics should be brought in where your Federation is concerned notwithstanding fact that your Association is recognised by International Board. I have arranged for your team to be put into the Draw which takes place to-morrow evening. I have been invited to be present during proceedings. The Olympic Committee is with you heart and soul, only they would not like any scandal to take place with Irish Olympic Committee. Please let me know per return if you have been able to get any players from north.[9]

The FAIFS did manage to find one player who was born in the North of Ireland: the crisis was averted.[10]

As only amateur players were allowed to compete in the Olympic Games, the FAIFS could only choose from its amateur clubs to represent Ireland. It underwent an intensive search to select the strongest possible team to go to Paris, including taking out advertisements in the national newspapers calling for people interested to apply. Inundated with applications, mostly from amateur players based in Dublin,[11] the FAIFS eventually settled on a squad of sixteen players consisting of five players each from Athlone Town, Bohemians and St James' Gate and one player from Brooklyn.[12] Two trial matches had led to the selection of the final sixteen. Ryder wrote a letter to the ones chosen, outlining the itinerary and costs covered for the trip:

> The team and reserves will leave Dublin (Westland Row) at 8:10pm on Saturday, 24th May, 1924 and will arrive at Paris on the afternoon of Sunday, 25th . . . Hotel and travelling expenses, from the moment of leaving Dublin until the return there, will be defrayed by my Committee but no payment will be made to any member of the party in respect of loss of wages, etc., occasioned on the trip. If you accept the invitation you must provide yourself with a passport valid for travel in France.[13]

The trip was a huge financial undertaking for the FAIFS. The FAIFS created a fund for the Olympic trip, asking all footballers and ex-footballers to contribute. It was estimated that the cost of sending a squad to Paris would be over £800.[14] The visit of Glasgow Celtic to Dalymount Park brought a gate of over £1,200 to the FAIFS coffers. The FAIFS Cup Final between Athlone Town and Fordson's from Cork saw a gate of over £1,000. This was the first occasion that two 'provincial' teams contested the FAIFS Cup Final.[15] These matches did help somewhat in improving the finances of the association.[16] For the Celtic game, it was believed that once expenses, Celtic's share of the gate and money owed to the state for entertainment tax, were taken into account, the profit was only £250. There was a suggestion that the team would not be able to continue on in the Olympic tournament were they to advance to the later rounds.[17]

The party did leave for Paris on 24 May. It was a long arduous journey. Leaving Dublin at 8:10pm that night, the group arrived in London at 5:30am the following morning. They then left London for Folkestone, and from Folkestone to Boulogne at 9:15am, finally reaching their destination of Paris at 4:30pm on 25 May.[18] A day later in an official ceremony, the Irish team and their officials laid a wreath at the Tomb of the Unknown Soldier at the

Arc de Triomphe. Inscribed on the wreath was the message, 'For the French heroes who died for their country.'[19] In attendance at the ceremony were representatives from the French and Irish Free State governments.[20] This possibly marked the first time the Irish Tricolour was unfurled in an official capacity in Paris.[21]

Twenty-two teams took part in the football tournament of the Olympic Games. Ireland received a bye in the first round and was drawn against Bulgaria in the second round, the winner guaranteed a berth in the quarter-finals.[22] This was the first occasion an Irish Free State international soccer team competed. The match took place on 28 May. Ireland wore blue jerseys and white shorts, and black stockings with blue tops. A green shamrock was embroidered on a white shield on the breast of the jerseys. The team consisted of four players from Athlone Town (including the captain, Denis Hannon), three players from Bohemians and St James' Gate and one from Brooklyn. With the tricolour flying in the ground, the team ran onto the field to the tune of 'Let Erin Remember'.

The team of the Philippines, a dominion of the United States, also participating in the Olympic Games for the first time, took issue with the Irish team being allowed to fly its own flag without being accompanied by the Union Jack. The Philippines had to fly its flag alongside the American flag.[23]

The choice of anthem for the Irish team was also a source of some contention. The directors of the IOC had asked the Free State government to supply them with copies of the Free State national anthem months before the Olympic Games commenced.[24] The Free State had no official anthem by 1924. 'The Soldier's Song' was generally played at national functions. The Department of External Affairs believed 'that while it was excellent as a revolutionary song, both words and music are unsuitable for a National Anthem.'[25] It was believed 'A Nation Once Again' was also inappropriate, so the Thomas Moore melody 'Let Erin Remember' was opted for instead for the Olympic Games.[26] It soon became common practice to play 'A Soldier's Song' at functions within the Irish Free State and 'Let Erin Remember' at functions abroad. The Executive Council of the government ruled in 1926 that there should be uniformity: it directed for the 'The Soldier's Song' to be used at home and abroad.[27] Chief amongst the song's supporters was the President of the Executive Council, W.T. Cosgrave.[28] Many were opposed to the adoption of 'The Soldier's Song' as the national anthem. The *Irish Statesman* believed it to be:

> Most lugubrious and commonplace. We find it impossible to decide whether the air is duller than the words, or the words are duller than the air. We do not believe there is a musician of repute or a poet who would defend with a good conscience either air or words.[29]

Others believed it to be too long. At the Dublin Horse Show held in the Royal Dublin Society (RDS) in Ballsbridge, in 1928, where both 'God Save the King' and 'The Soldier's Song' were recited, the crowd sang to the former and not to the latter, the brevity of the first song over the other cited as the main reason, and not the political affiliation of the clientele.[30] The playing of 'God Save the King' at Trinity College Dublin, was questioned the same year by the Governor-General, James McNeill, who believed 'The Soldier's Song' should have been played on his arrival instead. It was not played he felt 'due to ignorance as well as prejudice. If it were known that it was not an expression of loyalty to the King but an act of discourtesy to the Government of the Saorstat, including the King's representative, the National Anthem would be played.'[31]

'The Soldier's Song' was adopted as the national anthem without any fanfare or publicity, perhaps through no great love or desire for the song. The Irish-language version, 'Amhrán na bhFiann', that is recited almost exclusively now, only became common from the 1930s.[32]

At the match against Bulgaria, the referee noted he had never encountered a more nervous bunch of players than the Irish. Playing in front of the 45,000-seater Stade de Colombes stadium, the attendance was a paltry 1,659. That figure included 1,137 complimentary tickets.[33] Of the twenty-four soccer matches at the 1924 Olympic Games, the Irish matches were the least well attended.[34] Contributory factors for such a small crowd may have been that the football tournament was being played at the start of the Olympics, as well as that the Irish media focused its attention on the upcoming Tailteann Games. The Tailteann Games, due to be

THE GOVERNOR-GENERAL OF THE IRISH FREE STATE, JAMES McNEILL
with World Boxing Heavyweight Champion, Gene Tunney, at the Viceregal
Lodge, 1928. That same year McNeill took umbrage with Trinity College,
Dublin for playing 'God Save the King' on his arrival at a function instead of
'The Soldier's Song'.

Courtesy of the National Library of Ireland

played in Ireland in August 1924 for the first time since ancient
times, was a sporting and artistic festival used by the Free State
government as a method to project a positive image of the fledgling
state.[35] One paper that did recognise the significance of the
Olympic event was *Sport*, which reported:

> To be the first Irishmen to compete in the Olympiad is great
> ... They must not think of themselves. Their uppermost and
> inseparable thought must be of their country. Their country
> expects them to do their duty to play as Irishmen, to win as

174

Irishmen and, if the worst comes to the worst, to lose as Irishmen fighting unflinchingly to the last.[36]

For most of the game the Bulgarians staved off attack after attack from the Irish. The breakthrough finally came for the Irishmen in the seventy-fifth minute when Paddy Duncan scored a goal from what looked to be an offside position.[37] It would be the only goal of the game; Ireland won its first international encounter and advanced to the quarter-finals.

The next opponents were the Dutch who Ireland met on 2 June. Again the attendance was dismal, 893 as well as 613 complimentary tickets making up the crowd. The Netherlands ran out winners by two goals to one after extra time, ending Ireland's interest in the competition. The official Olympic Report described the game as an uninteresting match played by two primitive teams.[38] It was another creditable performance by Ireland, though.

The following day Ireland played a friendly against Estonia, a game that was won by the Irish by three goals to one. Ireland's adventure in Paris was concluded with a formal dinner for the Irish delegation hosted by the Parisian club Cercle Athlétique de Paris on 4 June. In attendance was the FIFA president, Jules Rimet.[39]

Ireland could hold its head up high on its first international outing, going out in extra time at the quarter-final stage. In an article condemning the GAA's insular ban on 'foreign games', *The Irish Times* praised the efforts of the Irish team:

> Where other countries are adopting games which they can play in international contests, Ireland is reverting to the games of the ancient Gael, to the exclusion of those Saxon sports that have become the inheritance of the whole civilised world. The Free State Association football team, however, competed at the Olympic tests with some credit, and survived two rounds before it lost a close game to Holland. Free State athletes are making their first international appearance in the Olympic Games, and the fact that the country is represented at all is a subject for congratulation.[40]

The Irish Free State team did play another match on their return home from Paris. The United States Olympic team, returning to America, stopped over in Dublin and played against Ireland in Dalymount Park on 14 June. Watched by a poor crowd

THE IRISH FREE STATE SOCCER TEAM

who played against the USA in a friendly match on the latter's return home from the 1924 Paris Olympics in Dublin on 14 June 1924. This was the first FAI-selected Irish international team to play on Irish soil, three years after the birth of the association.

Courtesy of the National Library of Ireland

of only 3,700, it generated just £240 in gate receipts, 'a financial failure', as acknowledged by Jack Ryder.[41] The US team, who on entering the pitch carried the Irish Tricolour and the Stars and Stripes, were warmly welcomed by the crowd. The FAIFS chose 'The Soldier's Song' over 'Let Erin Remember' for the encounter.[42] After amusingly chanting their battle cry in the centre of the field before the match, the US team was well beaten by the Irish team. Ireland ran out three to one winners, with all Irish goals scored by Ned Brooks from Bohemians.[43]

CHAPTER 15

Monopolising the Name 'Ireland'

The conference held in March 1924 between the IFA and the FAIFS had ended in failure on one point, the chairman of the International Selection Committee hailing permanently from the IFA. Following the Olympic trip to Paris in the summer of 1924, the FAIFS lobbied the football associations of England, Scotland and Wales, attempting to overcome the impasse between both Irish bodies. In its correspondence with the British associations, it placed particular emphasis on the IFA using the name 'Ireland'. The FAIFS called it a 'travesty that a body whose activities have been restricted to an area representing one-sixth of Ireland should be allowed to usurp the rights of the remaining five-sixths' and formally protested 'against the monopoly of the name "Ireland" in football affairs by the Association in Belfast.'[1] The FAIFS concluded by saying it was open to reaching an agreement along the lines discussed at the Liverpool conference the previous October.

It prompted the secretary of the English FA, Frederick Wall, to write to the IFA stating 'that the only outstanding question between you (the Irish bodies) is that of an alternative Chairman and that if this question is cleared out of the way there may be a possibility of an arrangement.'[2] A further letter from the English FA informed the IFA that it had 'no desire to interfere with either Association as to their internal affairs' but was not in a position to make arrangements with two Irish associations and would agree to play international matches with Ireland on the condition that Ireland acted as one body. The English FA offered the opinion that both Irish associations should agree to alternate chairmanship and international matches being played alternately in Dublin and

Belfast. It concluded by stating it was not in a position to offer a view on the financial arrangements for those matches.[3]

It was agreed by the IFA Council to concede to the two suggestions from the English FA, but would not be 'prepared to make any further concessions.'[4] The one stumbling block from the conference in Belfast of March 1924 was now overcome. It was felt the FAIFS should now have no further objections. But the FAIFS would have one more objection that would derail the prospect of union again. It related to financial entitlement for international matches played. The FAIFS offered two proposals: 'That the receipts of the games played in Ireland should be either (1) retained by the Association within whose area the game is played, or (2) pooled.'[5] The IFA was not open to either proposal: it wished to retain the receipts from all the matches. The IFA, in offering concessions to the FAIFS did so, in many respects, to bring it back under its fold, the prodigal son returning to its parent. It did not see the FAIFS as an association with equal standing: it would be a division yet again of the IFA. The FAIFS felt that as the representative soccer body of the Irish Free State, it was entitled to equality with the IFA. Given its geographical remit, many in the southern body felt the FAIFS was entitled to more say than its northern brother.

The new cleavage in the relationship between the two Irish associations formed the basis of a conference again held in Liverpool in March 1925. In attendance were representatives from the English, Scottish and Welsh associations as well as members of the IFA. No one was invited from the FAIFS. The FAIFS was forced to write a letter to the English FA (also asking that it distribute the same letter to the representatives from the Scottish and Welsh FAs) to state its claims. In the letter, the FAIFS stated it was:

> Determined to secure that the use of the name 'Ireland' shall not be monopolised in football matters by the body in Northern Ireland, and are equally determined not to surrender to that body, in exchange for a nominal permission to participate in Irish international matters, the Free State' Association's rightful share in the proceeds of the home games.[6]

It further contended that the decision reached in Liverpool in October 1923 recognising the FAIFS as the sole governing body for soccer in the Irish Free State and the IFA's control confined to Northern Ireland had, eighteen months later, still not been realised on a practical level. At the conference itself held on 14 March, without FAIFS representation, unsurprisingly, the IFA emerged the victors. Following the conference, the English FA released a statement:

> It was with much regret that they had learned that the two Irish Associations had not come to a mutual agreement for united action in respect of International Matches as no consideration will be given to any suggestion to play more than one International Match and that in the meantime the status quo will continue.[7]

Commenting on the decision, *The Times* of London, stated:

> The effect of the decision, which will be confirmed in due course by the national associations of England, Scotland, and Wales, is that international games with the Irish FA will be continued and that the Free State FA must accept the terms already offered by the Irish FA unless the latter modify them, if they are to be directly concerned in those games. It is evident from the decision of the conference that the view taken was that the Irish FA is not to blame for the present impasse.[8]

At the IFA Annual Meeting in May 1925, the IFA Council reported:

> In connection with this unfortunate dispute the Free State Association this year made an additional demand to the effect that they desire in addition to the terms already offered they should share the receipts of the International Matches. This your Council were unable to concede ... Your Council however still hope for a happy solution of this unfortunate impasse which has divided the Country in the Sport of Football.[9]

Writing a comprehensive article on the split in the newly published *Football Sports Weekly*, Robert Murphy, vice-chairman of the FAIFS, contended that finance was the most vital point to the dispute. He could not accept that the IFA should receive all of the money from proceeds in Northern Ireland and also the Irish Free State. He disputed the claim by northern advocates that the game in the North could not exist without proceeds from the international matches, pointing to the remarkable growth the game was experiencing in the Free State and with it financial security for the first time. He also stated the FAIFS, in seeking its share of the profits, did so, 'not from need of the money, but with the object of securing its due share of recognition'. Unity on paper, he claimed, looked feasible, but in practice, not so. 'The political division of the country has not tended to make the inhabitants of the respective areas more reliant on each other's good faith (a vivid example is presented by the athletic trouble), and a rapprochement, while probably certain, will not be speedy'. Advocating union, he believed that, without it, the quality of football in the Irish Free State was falling behind that of its competitors, a natural consequence of limitation of competition. Referring to rogue bodies such as the National Football Association, he also contended unaffiliated football was in vogue and widely prevalent in Dublin and Belfast, mainly attributable to the dispute between the two Irish governing bodies. He concluded by hoping an agreement could be achieved:

> What the future holds I do not know, but with harmony restored between North and South, and the game spreading, as it is in every part of the Irish Free State, Ireland's position would, for the first time in football, be really strong. A final decision in the dispute will be taken some day. There will either be a settlement by force (the threat to suspend international games) or an agreed settlement which would really make for harmonious working. All whose aims are to place Ireland first and sectional interests after will hope for that agreement.[10]

Further antagonism between the IFA and the FAIFS had been averted in late 1924 when the northern body rejected an application from the National Football Association, a body from the South dissatisfied with the FAIFS, which looked to affiliate to the IFA. It rejected the body's application as it would be in contravention to the rulings of the Liverpool conference the previous year.[11] Despite this, the IFA and members of the press in the UK did attempt to gain political capital from what appeared to be significant dissent in the South, by exaggerating its problem and claiming that over sixty clubs had disaffiliated from the FAIFS.[12]

180

Football Sports Weekly called the actions of the National Football Association 'deplorable and futile': no football association in the world would recognise the rebel association's status. The paper appealed to the FAIFS to let bygones be bygones, to bring the clubs and players back into the fold and unify soccer in the Free State.[13] The National Football Association, realising it had no secure footing as a viable entity, disbanded in October 1925, and sought re-affiliation with the FAIFS.[14]

Another conference held in Liverpool in 1925 between the home associations would drive a further wedge between the two Irish bodies. Ryder had received a telegram from the English FA saying it was unable to consent to a match between Liverpool and Shelbourne in May of that year.[15] At an English FA Council meeting two months later, Liverpool asked again to play matches against clubs from the Free State during the close season. The Council deferred making a decision pending the outcome of a conference between the four associations of the United Kingdom.[16]

The English FA invited the other associations to a conference in Liverpool in September to consider 'the whole question of playing matches during the close season, in the UK, the Irish Free State and on the Continent, and also to consider a request from the South African FA for a British team to tour South Africa next year.'[17] At the conference, held on 5 September, it was decided that all clubs from the four home associations must not play matches in the Irish Free State during the close season. No action was taken against clubs for playing matches on the Continent during the close season, a clear affront to the FAIFS.[18] Commenting on the outcome of the conference, the FAIFS-friendly newspaper, *Football Sports Weekly*, was particularly scathing of the IFA delegates:

> Messrs. McBride, Small and Watson represented Ireland at the Liverpool Conference. I would like to know the reason for allowing clubs to go to Australia in the close season and refusing them the right to play in the Free State. The Free State Association is reckoned a State with Dominion status. Why, then, are they boycotted as compared with the other Dominions? At the conference which decided no matches for the Free State in the close season, it was decided that a team would likely be sent to South Africa after 1926.[19]

The paper went further by calling the decision a 'flagrant and highly discreditable breach of the agreement reached in October, 1923, at the previous Liverpool conference',[20] seeing it as a further attempt by the IFA to starve the FAIFS of money, a means of forcing the southern body to agree to its terms.[21]

The FAIFS may have been deprived of international fixtures and with it, increased competition and income. The game in the South did provide solace for the fledgling body, though, being more popular than it had ever been before. Signs of increased popularity of the game were noted soon after the formation of the FAI in 1921. During the House of Commons debate in 1922 on the Anglo-Irish Treaty signed in December 1921, Winston Churchill looked to paint a picture of Ireland not 'rapidly lapsing into a condition of Bolshevist anarchy,' that it was in a position to govern itself and daily life was returning to normal. To illustrate his point he researched the sporting activity in Ireland at the time:

> The 'Sunday Independent' of the 26th of last month, which is a paper I have examined, contained reports of no fewer than 26 important football matches in Southern Ireland, and announcements of no fewer than 29 Gaelic football fixtures for that Sunday ... The attendance at the semi-final of the Irish football cup is said to have surpassed all recent records ... The 'Irish Independent' contained reports of a meeting in Cork on the 24th February — Cork is a very bad place — for the purpose of forming a divisional association of the Football Association of Ireland in Munster.[22]

Soccer all over the Free State experienced strong growth throughout the 1920s, including in locations such as Munster and Connacht, where it had never flourished historically. The newly formed FAI visited Cork in 1922 to set up a branch in Munster. According to *Football Sports Weekly*, 'one of the greatest difficulties they encountered was the fear that the Dublin people would treat the handful of local enthusiasts as callously as Belfast had done in the past. However, these difficulties were overcome.'[23] The FAI, perhaps mindful of how regional divisions had been treated by the IFA previously, did contribute largely to helping soccer grow in Munster. The Free State body assumed liability for the rent of Victoria Cross Grounds for fifteen years and allowed the Munster FA to retain its affiliation fees until it was on a sound financial footing.[24] Inter-provincial matches between Leinster and Munster were also re-instated. By 1925, clubs affiliated to Munster had mushroomed from half a dozen clubs in 1922 to over one hundred.[25] The embodiment of the growth of soccer in Munster was the Cork club Fordsons. With winning the FAIFS Cup in 1926, the first Munster club to do so, the popularity of the club and game in Cork was cemented. Fordsons win was also a major boost to soccer in Waterford, where the game had been growing from strength to strength since 1923.[26]

The west also saw a significant increase in activity with the game taking an 'ineradicable root in Galway town, and a club has sprung into being at Tuam and another as far away as Clifden.'[27] A club from Sligo, Sligo Celtic, contested the FAI Cup in 1923, the second year after the cup's formation.[28] In the same year, the Leinster FA played a team from Sligo in what was deemed the first inter-provincial match after the split.[29] Straddling the east and the west, Athlone Town won the premier Free State cup trophy in 1924, beating Fordsons in the final, with what was a record attendance of 21,000.[30] In fact, the first five years of the cup competition would see the attendance at the final increase annually from 10,000 to 25,000.[31]The gates had to be closed fifteen minutes before the start of the 1925 final between Shamrock Rovers and Shelbourne due to the size of the crowds.[32] By comparison, only marginally more people attended the All-Ireland hurling final of 1926 than the 25,000 who attended the FAIFS Cup Final of 1926, Cork winning the Hurling Final for the first time since 1919 and Fordson's of Cork winning the FAIFS Cup final.[33] Looking back on the 1925–26 season, *Football Sports Weekly* commented on the popularity of the game in the Free State:

> Association football is booming, and is the coming game amongst the youths. It is extraordinary the wonderful progress the game is making in the provinces. New clubs are springing up in many towns and already the game has extended to Wexford, Waterford, and Longford. There is also to be seen new teams in Drogheda, Tullamore and Navan, and several other towns.[34]

By contrast, the IFA was not experiencing as big an interest north of the border and particularly bemoaned the lack of interest shown in the IFA Irish Cup for the first few years after the split, to the detriment of clubs and the association.[35]

In 1925 Shamrock Rovers travelled to Belfast to play the Irish League champions, Glentoran, a game the Dublin team won by two goals to nil.[36] It was seen as a major boost to the game in the South. The 1924–25 season was an extraordinary one for Shamrock Rovers, 'winning all three premier trophies. The performance was enhanced by the fact that they were never defeated in 32 games, embracing League, Shield and Cup competitions. Rovers' record in the League was eighteen played, won thirteen, drew five; Shield – played nine, won seven, drew two.'[37] The meeting of Shamrock Rovers and Glentoran in Belfast and a meeting of intermediate teams from Leinster and Ulster in 1925 were foretastes of the first representative fixture between the two leagues in Ireland; teams from the Irish Football League and the Irish Free State League met in March 1926.[38]

The Irish Football League in Belfast was open to playing an inter-league match against a team from the Free State on the con-dition that the English and Scottish leagues would not object to such a match. Always quick to criticise the authorities north of the border, *Football Sports Weekly* remarked: 'How comes it that one body of Irish footballers should feel it incumbent on them to ask permission from both a Scottish and English group of clubs to play a football match with another body of Irish footballers?'[39] With the English and Scottish leagues having no objections to such a fixture, at an Irish Football League meeting it was decided on a vote of nine to eight, to meet a team from the Free State in March 1926.[40] The match took place in Dalymount Park and was won convincingly by the Free State League team by a score line of three goals to one. Commenting on the result, *Football Sports Weekly* remarked: 'It showed us that we have nothing to learn from our Northern brethren.'[41] In the corresponding fixture in Belfast the following season, the match ended in a one-one draw.[42] The match in Dublin was attended by James Wilton and many other officials from the IFA. *The Irish Times* believed it was a significant moment for soccer in Ireland:

184

How far the match will be successful in bringing the two bodies together again in an effort to form one governing authority in this country . . . remains to be seen; but this much is certain – that the revival of friendly relations between the footballers of the Free State and Ulster . . . proves very conclusively that the time is ripe for a business-like attempt to settle the dispute on the basis of give-and-take, which is apparently the only lines on which that most desirable consummation can possibly be reached.[43]

At a dinner in Jury's Hotel following the match, the FAIFS president, Sir Henry McLaughlin, expressed the hope 'that that day they had joined a link which, he trusted, would never be broken again' and 'that the match would do something extraordinary for Irish football'. The president of the Irish Football League (Booth) looked forward to a time when their team would mix more freely with the Free State League and when there would be 'one competition common to the whole of Ireland'. The match in Dublin netted the Northern League a profit of £414, which was £65 more than the combined amount earned from the English and Scottish league encounters.[44] Bringing the proceedings to a close, McLaughlin remarked, 'that a famous Englishman had said that the battle of Waterloo was won on the playing-fields of Eton. He would now say that Ireland was going to find her unity on the playing-fields of Ireland.'[45] The match would lead to some commentators proposing an All-Ireland League of clubs from North and South, with teams participating from the principal cities of Belfast, Cork and Dublin.[46]

The FAIFS would have another significant match just days later, a match considered 'the first genuinely orthodox football international in history between the Free State of Ireland and another country.'[47] Since the Olympic Games of 1924, the southern body had tried unsuccessfully to obtain more international fixtures. The secretary of the French Football Federation, Henri Delaunay, wrote to Ryder in April 1925 saying France could not commit to an international match against Ireland as the French fixture list was fixed and 'the question of the high rate of exchange in the British countries has not failed to influence once more the Board's decision.'[48] The Belgian FA also cited the financial burden of a trip to Ireland as their reason for not accepting an invitation from the FAIFS.[49] The Italians, who had been one of the Free State's main supporters in the latter's campaign for FIFA membership, told the FAIFS they were not in a position to send a team to Ireland but proposed an initial match in Italy to be followed by a return fixture to Ireland at a later date, a proposal that was accepted by the FAIFS.[50] *Football Sports Weekly* optimistically remarked the fixture between Italy and the Irish Free State would become an established annual fixture.[51] The same paper also reported that the IFA subsequently contacted the Italian football authorities to arrange a fixture between the Northern Irish and Italian bodies; the paper believed 'they would not have dreamt of such a match had not the Free State first moved in the matter.'[52]

A letter was sent to all clubs in December 1925 by the FAIFS stating that players would be needed for seven to eight days during March in Italy, and for clubs to provide a list of players available for selection. The letter stipulated that 'only those players who were born in the Irish Free State are eligible for selection on International Matches.'[53] To finance the trip, the FAIFS contacted Glasgow Celtic and Rangers, Manchester United, Everton and Aston Villa to arrange matches. None were available.[54] The association also asked for the match in Italy to be played in the north of the country, somewhere like Milan or Turin, to help reduce the costs.[55] Initially the match was scheduled to be played in Milan, but it was decided eight days before the match to switch the venue to Turin.[56] As the match took place during the middle of the season and players were required to travel for upwards of a week, none of the Irish players who played for cross-channel teams were available for selection. The FAIFS was reliant on only local players to meet the Italians on 21 March 1926.[57] One of the players due to play, Ned Brooks from Athlone Town, was forced to withdraw due to the death of his son in a motoring accident.[58] The team arrived in Turin less than twenty-four hours before kick-off. Five of the team had played in the Free State Cup Final the day of the departure, at which Fordsons beat Shamrock Rovers by three goals to two.[59] Due to heavy rain, just 12,000 people were in attendance at the Irish Free State's first full international. The Italian authorities unsurprisingly had to enquire from the Irish about the colours of their shirts and the flag to be used.[60] The Italians raced into a three to nil lead by

half-time, a lead they sat on for the second half. An Italian correspondent wrote, 'A huge difference in class divided the two teams
... our goal was never seriously in danger through the merits of
the Irish.'[61] There was no reporter from Ireland at 'the most
momentous event in the short history of Free State soccer.'[62] *Football
Sports Weekly* cited the long journey to Italy without any rest as a
contributory factor to the Irish Free State's poor showing.[63] The
trip, which included a stop-over match against Cercle Athlétique
de Paris (CAP) in Paris, cost the FAIFS just under £700.[64] CAP
returned the favour and visited Ireland two months later in May,
playing matches in Cork and Dublin. The Leinster Council treated
the French visitors to 'an audience with the Governor-General, a
dinner dance and cabaret, a visit to the Theatre Royal, an excursion
to Wicklow via Glendalough and Greystones, and a meeting with
the President of the Irish Free State.'[65]

In late 1926, a journalist from *The Irish Times*, J.P. Rooney,
started a campaign to effect a settlement to the dispute in Irish
soccer. In an article he wrote, he sided very heavily with the IFA:

> It must be realised that Free State players cannot be included
> in Irish International teams, that Ireland is the only country in
> the world in which two Football Associations are necessary
> for the management of the game, and that the Free State
> Association owes its glorious isolation to its reluctance to
> agree to the condition that the receipts for the International
> matches should go into the common exchequer of the
> Association, with which we were willing, according to the
> agreement entered into by our accredited representatives at
> the 1924 conference, to resume friendly relations.[66]

Mocking the level of international fixture enjoyed by the Free State
Association, Rooney remarked:

> Free State footballers, under the Dominion status conferred on
> the Free State Association by the International Board, can
> enjoy trips to Italy, France, Spain, Russia or Belgium, and our
> legislators can take continental holidays to demonstrate the
> strength and vitality of Association football in the Free State.
> The necessity for these propagandist tours would, however,
> disappear if the split was healed, and the superfluous funds
> might more profitably be devoted to a more intensive devel-
> opment of the amateur game and of the amateur clubs.[67]

He concluded by suggesting:

> All that is necessary to bring about the settlement is for each party to accept the conditions which were agreed to by the Free State delegates to the conference in Belfast on March 8, 1924. They were then rejected on the question whether the proceeds of the international matches played in Dublin should go to the FSA or to the Association which the FSA delegates were willing their Association should rejoin. Even on the basis of fifty-fifty in relation to the international 'gates', a claim by the FSA cannot hold water, for if there is to be one association for the government of football in Ireland there must be a common exchequer where internationals are concerned.[68]

Encouraged by the reaction his articles received, Rooney subsequently wrote to the FAIFS and the IFA, suggesting a new conference between the two Irish associations in Dundalk to be chaired by the English FA chairman.[69] The IFA sent the lukewarm reply stating it was 'at all times prepared and willing to consider any proposals that may be placed before them by the Irish Free State Football Association for the settlement of the difference that at present exist in Irish Association Football, so that football in Ireland will be controlled by one Association.'[70] The FAIFS was less forthcoming to Rooney's overtures, probably due to the heavy bias he showed towards the IFA in his articles.

The *Irish Independent* believed Rooney had conducted his campaign in the wrong way by being so closely aligned with the IFA position: 'Press propaganda inspired from one side only will not tend to create the atmosphere essential for even a consideration of the matter by the other side.'[71] The *Evening Herald* also took umbrage with some of Rooney's ascertains, namely that the IFA did not consent to alternate chairmanship at the conference of March 1924. It was only pressure exerted from the English FA that forced the northern body to do so. The paper also believed the headquarters of the reunified association should be in Dublin: 'The Northern body also intimated that Belfast should be the headquarters of the Central Association to be set up, but no one has come along to explain why these should not be situated in Dublin, just like those of every other branch of sport in Ireland.'[72] Writing for *Football Sports Weekly*, the former Irish international before the split, Charlie O'Hagan believed that Rooney's intervention was a ploy by the IFA to re-open the debate, brought on by desperation. He believed the game in the North was 'doomed', as 'a competitive keenness' could not be maintained. He stated:

> These football 'Die-Hards' of the North imagined, not so long ago, they could hold themselves aloof from Southern Ireland and still maintain their prestige in International warfare. Now that the dream is passed they have suddenly awakened to the fact that they are slipping back perceptibly, and if something be not done (and that speedily) 'the old Football House in Belfast' must crumble and decay.

He warned the FAIFS against listening to the IFA's latest attempts, advising the Free State body to 'prepare in a way that will not even permit the wolf to approach the door – they must slay him before he gets within striking distance.'[73] Given the bias Rooney demonstrated towards the IFA and the perception that he was a stooge of the northern body, his efforts to forge a solution to the split met with no success. A campaign undertaken by the FAIFS the following year would also see the prospects of a healing of the division greatly diminished, the campaign to force the northern body to use the name 'Northern Ireland' instead of 'Ireland'.

In February 1927, the FAIFS wrote to the IFA asking the latter body to alter its Article of Association to reflect 'the present conditions of football jurisdiction in Northern Ireland and in the Irish Free State'. In the letter it was stated that certain articles within the IFA rule book were in contravention of the terms of the Liverpool Agreement of 1923:

> Which gives to the Irish Football Association and the Football Association of the Irish Free State sole authority to exercise jurisdiction in their respective areas. My Council deem it their exclusive right to select for International purposes players who were born in territory which is now known as the Irish Free State.[74]

In reply, the IFA stated: 'We fully recognise that there are Articles in existence in our Articles of Association which are not now applicable, but having regard to our repeated attempts for an amicable settlement of the present dispute in Irish Football, we

189

had no desire to remove any of the Articles referred to'. The northern body also took exception to the FAIFS' claim that it and it alone could select players for international matches born in the Free State:

> My Committee are surprised that your Association claim the right to select players for International Matches, as in accordance with the terms of the Liverpool Agreement, you are an Association with Dominion Status, and therefore cannot select players for International Matches. The Irish Football Association are the only body who have the right to select for International Matches any players born in Ireland, this right we intend to exercise provided we consider the players fit to represent their Country in these Contests.[75]

This correspondence between the two Irish associations was a far cry from the atmosphere at the Inter-League match between the Irish Football and Free State Leagues held in Belfast in March 1927, a game that ended as a one-all draw. It was commented that:

> Everyone present was in joyful spirit and animated with a feeling of truer friendship between North and South. A huge crowd and a splendid gate, all for the betterment of the game itself, and it is hoped for a greater understanding between the two Associations and officials of management. There was nothing more appropriate than the song, 'The more we are together'. It was sung merrily and gleefully by all, Northerners and Southerners.[76]

Football Sports Weekly believed the southern body was perfectly in its rights to 'have several "misleading references" in the rules' of the IFA deleted.[77] 'Trefoil', writing for the *Sunday Chronicle*, questioned: 'What control have the Free State over players who come from clubs under the International Board?'[78] Replying to Trefoil, *Football Sports Weekly* maintained that the IFA had 'no more claim upon those men than they have upon the defunct Niggers of Tasmania, and I would go further and say, to use a slang term, they have a "hard neck" to poach and encroach upon the rights of the Free State.'[79]

In a series of articles on the split written at the same time as this latest episode, 'PROGRESSIVE', in *Football Sports Weekly*, believed that the administrators were to blame for the continuation of the

impasse between North and South, calling them 'a group of irrec-
oncilables, who don't possess as much brains as would whitewash
a back-yard' and who 'can hold up the prosperity and progress of
the whole of football in Ireland with impunity.'[80] He further stated
it was little wonder many southerners would have no faith in the
IFA, considering the injustice meted out to Shelbourne in 1921,
who were forced to travel twice to Belfast to play Glenavon. He did
give the IFA credit, though, 'for being genuinely desirous of a settlement, that would fully meet the aspirations of the Free State,
giving them such safeguards as would make a repetition of what
happened to Shelbourne in the future an impossibility', and he
ascertained many in the South did not want reunion as 'some clubs
would automatically, as a result, revert to a lower grade of football'
and would have less influence over an all-Ireland body's finances.
He believed it was 'the clubs' apathy and lack of moral courage
that is responsible for the present sorry state of affairs.'[81]

A similar letter received by the IFA from the FAIFS on the IFA's
right to select players born in the Free State was sent to the football
associations of England, Scotland and Wales. With this avenue,
again bearing no fruit, the FAIFS turned to a source it had received
support from in the past, FIFA. It put forward a motion at the
Annual Congress of FIFA, held in Helsinki from 3 to 5 June 1927,
'to designate the Irish FA in the list of Associations as "Northern
Ireland".'[82] Italy seconded the motion.[83] Twenty-one national
associations were in attendance at the Congress, including representatives from the English and Scottish FAs. It was unanimously
decided by all associations present that the IFA should be recognised as the Football Association of Northern Ireland.[84]
Commenting on the decision, *Football Sports Weekly* remarked:

> The outcome of this will provide interesting developments in
> the near future as the English Association (as well as the
> Scottish) was represented; and now to put the matter plain and
> blunt so that the most unintelligent can hardly misunderstand
> the position, the English Football Association must either
> honour the International Federation's ruling in the letter and
> the spirit, or else bring about disruption by turning it down.[85]

Despite agreeing to the FAIFS motion, England and Scotland
still recognised Northern Ireland as Ireland and refused to play an

international team from the Free State. The FAIFS, in a memorandum to the Free State government, highlighted the implications the abuse of the name Ireland was having: 'We submit that in recognising Northern Ireland in sport as "Ireland", and in excluding from the benefits accruing from the use of the name "Ireland", the FAIFS, the British Associations are committing an unwarrantable aggression on the rights of the citizens of the Saorstat.'[86]

The issue was brought up again at the FIFA Annual Congress of 1929, held in Barcelona, where it was decided to refer the matter to the International Football Association Board.[87] Praising FIFA for its support, James Brennan, FAIFS chairman, stated: 'The advance in the interest in, and in the skill of the game in the Irish Free State has . . . been contributed to in no small measure by the helpful and progressive attitude of the FIFA.'[88] Without the support of the British associations, FIFA was powerless to have any impact with the international rules body.[89] Hirschman did provide the FAIFS with some hope for the future by claiming that no one on the FIFA board agreed with the IFA position of selecting players on its international teams who were born in the Irish Free State. He concluded optimistically by stating that the wishes of the FAIFS would be fulfilled in the future.

This hope would not be realised in the years ahead. Instead the animosity between the two Irish associations, one that looked likely to be resolved on a number of occasion throughout the 1920s, deepened in the 1930s and beyond, to a state of open conflict.

CHAPTER 16

Towards Antipathy

By 1930 both Irish associations were experiencing different fortunes. The Free State body had overseen the growth of the game to unparalleled levels since its foundation nine years previously. The game had not only grown to new levels in its established centre of Dublin but it had spread to areas where it had never experienced any semblance of support previously. By 1930 there were almost 350 clubs affiliated to the Leinster Football Association.[1] By 1932, the FAIFS could boast an affiliated membership of 470 clubs, 369 from Leinster, eighty-five from Munster, fifteen from Connacht and two from Ulster.[2] The first inter-provincial match between Leinster and Connacht was held in 1931, demonstrating the growth of the game in Connacht since the foundation of the Irish Free State.[3] Amplifying the growth in the Free State was the state of soccer in Northern Ireland which was experiencing very different results. The IFA, which had 325 clubs affiliated to its fold in 1926,[4] saw this reduce drastically to 234 just two years later, 'due to the serious unemployment which prevailed at the commencement of the season.'[5] By 1930 there were just 226 clubs affiliated; the following two years would see a further reduction.[6]

The FAIFS could also boast of some promising results in inter-league matches with the Northern Irish and Welsh leagues. Other than a humiliating six goals to one defeat against the Irish Football League in 1930,[7] the Free State League's results against the northern league were favourable. The Free State League also defeated the Welsh league by three goals to one in 1931.[8] The Northern Irish League body had the more lucrative annual

fixtures against teams representing the English and Scottish
leagues. These fixtures were seen as a chore by the latter two
bodies, though. One Scottish official remarked that the fixture,
instead of being a competitive match, was more akin to 'keeping
an appointment'.[9] Commenting on the dispute in Irish soccer and
the inter-league match the English League XI won by six goals to
one in October 1926, an English official remarked:

> The only thing about your North and South trouble that is
> worrying us . . . is the fact that certain representative games in
> Ireland, in which we are interested, are absolutely farcical. The
> games are no contest affairs. Take, for instance, the Inter-
> League game in October. It was a walk-over, and the gate
> hardly more than £300. We lost money on the fixture.[10]

The Irish Football League's record against the English League
from 1894 to 1926 demonstrated the lack of competitiveness in the
annual fixtures. Of the twenty-five matches played, the Irish Football League won none, drew two and lost the other twenty-three.[11]

Football Sports Weekly, in an article entitled 'Is Northern
Football Declining?', believed that senior football in Northern
Ireland had become a 'wash-out'. During the pre-split days,
there were six senior clubs from the northern region: Linfield,
Belfast Celtic, Cliftonville, Distillery, Glentoran and Glenavon.
After the split, six more clubs joined the senior ranks: Larne,
Ards, Newry, Barn from Carrickfergus, Portadown and Queen's
Island, 'none of which has a following which, at the most gen-
erous estimate, can be reckoned as worth more than £30 from a
financial point of view'. Without Belfast Celtic, who rejoined the
Irish Football League in 1924, senior football in Northern Ireland
'was as dead as the proverbial door-nail.'[12] The only two clubs
who attracted large crowds in the North were the two rival
clubs, Celtic and Linfield.

The FAIFS, by 1930, had finally been invited to the table of
international football. Losing twice to Italy in 1926 and 1927, the
Irish Free State team played Belgium in each of the following
years, winning on all three occasions.[13] There was still no prospect
of a fixture against any of the British associations, who stood by
the IFA and only countenanced one fixture annually against

'Ireland', an Irish team selected by the IFA. Much to the chagrin of the FAIFS, the IFA wantonly selected players born in the Free State, a direct contravention of the agreement reached in Liverpool in October 1923, according to the FAIFS. Commenting on the 'misuse' of the name 'Ireland' in 1929, the FAIFS chairman, James Brennan, remarked that the FAIFS:

> Has more clubs in affiliation and the quality of the play within its jurisdiction does not suffer in comparison. It is therefore not logical that the IFA should continue to be allowed to designate their representative teams as 'Ireland', a circumstance that leaves the promotion of the annual games between the Northern Ireland body and the Associations of England, Scotland and Wales open to the charge of misrepresentation. Protest on this ground made to the Football Associations of England, Scotland, Wales and Northern Ireland have had no effect; and it is difficult to resist the conclusion that the International Board is not entirely free from political influences in its treatment of the matter.[14]

To complicate matters further, FIFA, whose membership supported bids by the FAIFS in 1927 and 1929 for the IFA to change its name to reflect its political status, no longer had in its fold as members all the British associations. FIFA had ruled that amateur players should be paid for 'broken time' at the Olympic Games, the football competition being organised by FIFA at the Games. At a meeting of the four home associations it was ruled 'that Article 4 of the FIFA, permitting payment for broken time, cannot be admitted, and reiterates its determination to adhere to the British Association's definition of an amateur', and 'that each association represented here to-day gives notice to the Olympic Committee that we cannot deviate from our definition of an amateur.'[15] At a further meeting of the home associations, it was decided by all of them to withdraw their membership from FIFA.[16] FIFA did retain its two seats on the International Board. A letter was sent by the English FA stating its reasons for withdrawing from FIFA yet again. In the letter, the home association's vast experience compared to most of the associations who were members of FIFA was condescendingly referred to: 'The great majority of the Associations affiliated with La Féderation de Football Association are of comparatively recent formation, and as a consequence cannot have knowledge which only experience can bring.'[17]

Realising FIFA's support alone would not suffice, the FAIFS called for the assistance of the Free State government in 1930 to bring pressure on the English FA to eliminate 'the absurdity of the north-east team masquerading as Ireland', it being believed that the English FA was the most sympathetic of all the British associations to the FAIFS' stance.[18] In lobbying the Irish government, the FAIFS cited the international matches its association had overseen, where Ireland's reputation abroad was enhanced by the playing of the national anthem and the flying of the tri-colour. The IFA was derided for playing 'God Save the King' and flying the Union Jack at an 'Irish' international fixture against France.[19] In a memorandum sent to the government, the FAIFS listed the key events that had occurred between the two Irish associations since the split in 1921 asserting that the 'aggression [of the IFA] should be prevented by the Government of the Irish Free State'. It also commented on the recent split in Irish athletics, stating that 'a separate governing body has come into existence in Northern Ireland and has recently had its right to recognition as the sole governing body of athletics in Northern Ireland recognised by the world's governing bodies corresponding to the FIFA'. It questioned the anomaly of the governing bodies in Great Britain recognising the Northern Ireland athletics body and yet in soccer the British bodies recognised the Northern Irish body, the IFA, as the soccer body for all of Ireland.[20] With the Northern Ireland body being accepted as the primary Irish association, it appeared to the world that the twenty-six counties had seceded from Ireland instead of the actuality of the six counties doing so under the Government of Ireland Act of 1920. The FAIFS assured the Free State government:

> We wish to re-affirm our willingness to share the internationals with the Association in Northern Ireland on the conditions already suggested, that is, that Ireland's home games should be played alternately in Northern Ireland and the Irish Free State; (2) That the gate receipts accruing from international matches in either area should be appropriated by the Association controlling in that area; and (3) that the

expenses of Ireland's international matches in Great Britain should be jointly defrayed.[21]

The High Commissioner of the Irish Free State, on behalf of the Minister for External Affairs, subsequently contacted the English FA, complaining of the IFA acting for the whole of Ireland in its selection policy for international matches and suggesting that a committee of equal representation should be set up between the two Irish associations to choose an all-Ireland international team, with matches to be played alternately in Dublin and Belfast and gate receipts shared in proportion. The IFA replied that there was nothing new in the High Commissioner's proposals – the issues had only been discussed at the last International Board meeting in June 1929 – and as the FAIFS had accepted dominion status in 1923, the IFA had every right to play as 'Ireland' in international matches. The IFA also expressed regret that the matter had now entered into the arena of politics.[22]

One key element that did not help the Free State's campaign to prevent people born in the Free State from playing for IFA international teams, was the players themselves As Peter Byrne points out in his book, *Green is the Colour*:

> For the next twenty years, Northern Ireland would continue to play southern players at their discretion, and while there were some notable exceptions, these individuals mostly welcomed the opportunity of additional international football, not to mention the match fees. Officials in Dublin continued to campaign against the system which allowed them to do so, but for all the protestations, the reality was that the majority of players were loath to surrender these extra perks until they were eventually forced to in 1950.[23]

Over twenty players played for both 'Irelands' up to 1950, representing teams from the Free State and Northern Ireland. Included in this list were players such as Patsy Gallagher, Tommy Breen, Jimmy Dunne, Billy Lacey, Paddy Moore and Tom Farquharson.[24] Farquharson, the Cardiff City goalkeeper, decided he would no longer play for an IFA-selected team in 1925. A man of republican sympathies, he had been apparently arrested with his friend, future Taoiseach Seán Lemass, for tearing down British army recruiting posters in St Stephen's

Green.[25] Speaking in 1931 on his decision not to play for an IFA-selected team, he stated:

> I feel it an honour to play for my country, but I contend that it is wrong that the selection of the national side should be left to the Irish Football Association, which is representative of the North of Ireland only. A big principle is involved, and I believe this is the first time that the grievance which many Free State players hold has been ventilated in this way. I hope my action will have the result of the Irish FA and the Free State FA coming together, and ensuring that in future Ireland teams shall be selected by a body that is really representative of both the North and the South.[26]

Farquharson was capped four times for the Free State international team, memorably captaining the team and saving a penalty against Spain in a one-all draw in Barcelona in April 1931.[27]

Not sharing Farquharson's sentiments, three players from Bohemians declared themselves eligible for an amateur international in November 1930 between an IFA-selected Irish team and England. This resulted in the FAIFS suspending the players indefinitely.[28] The Lord Mayor of Dublin, Alfie Byrne, decided to intervene in the matter. At a meeting of the IFA Council in December 1930, a meeting that focused on celebrating the fiftieth anniversary of the IFA, it was revealed that Byrne had visited Belfast stating that he was acting on behalf of the Free State association, to discuss football matters in Ireland. The Lord Mayor also suggested the FAIFS should send the following telegram to the IFA: 'That the Lord Mayor of Dublin, having interested himself in the matter, we, the Free State Association, hereby raise the suspensions pending completion of negotiations.'[29] On receiving no correspondence from the FAIFS, the IFA chairman, Wilton, concluded 'that they [the FAIFS] . . . had repudiated the Lord Mayor of Dublin's interference, as they had done in several other instances in similar circumstances.'[30] At the same IFA Council meeting, correspondence was read from the Scottish FA, supporting the IFA in not recognising the suspensions of the three Bohemians players.[31] At the subsequent International Board meeting held in Gleneagles in Scotland, it was decided that no action should be taken on the issue.[32]

A sign of the ever-increasing souring of relations between the FAIFS and the IFA was the former body's decision to cancel the now annual inter-league match between the two leagues in 1931 due to the IFA not recognising the suspensions of the three Bohemians players.[33] Reacting to the decision of the FAIFS, one senior official within the IFA angrily remarked:

> With the existing dispute the Irish League or its clubs have nothing whatever to do; that these clubs strongly resent the attitude of the Southern body, and that it means the complete severance of the painter. As long as these friendly matches were arranged between the clubs of the Free State and those down here . . . there was always the hope of an amicable settlement being reached; but even that hope has now completely vanished, as our clubs will certainly at the next meeting of the League decide to have nothing further to do with any of the Free State League clubs. It is a great pity; but the Free State people, who obviously do not desire a settlement of any kind except on their own terms, which they will never get, will ere long realise their song [sic].[34]

The IFA official also claimed that:

> At the next meeting of the International Board the Irish Football Association will insist on the Board more clearly defining the position of the IFA in relation to international matches. We know our position, but evidently the Free State people do not. It is our intention to make things pretty clear for them, to leave not the slightest doubt as to our right to manage the international matches in the name of Ireland, and to select the team for them from any club we think has eligible players . . . the Irish Football Association has full control of all international matches in which Ireland is concerned. It will be for the Board to see that the International Federation, with which the FAIFS is in membership, compels its members to conform to the decisions of the Board, or in the alternative for the Board to inform the Federation that if it is unable to control its members it must cease to have any relations with it. That is the position at the moment, and that is exactly what will occur.[35]

The International Board meeting did not exactly transpire as the IFA envisaged. The English FA, under pressure from the Free State government, did change its mind on the rights of players representing associations in international fixtures outside the territory they were born in. It proposed a motion to delete an agreement made at the International Board meeting of 1895, to be substituted with: 'In International matches the qualification of players shall be birth within the area of the National Association. In the case of British subjects born abroad, their qualification shall be decided by the nationality of their fathers.'[36] This motion was supported by FIFA but rejected by the IFA and by the Scottish and Welsh FAs and, therefore, defeated. Although the IFA did achieve a victory of sorts at the International Board meeting, it was coming under increased pressure from the English FA, the association still with the most power in global football, to resolve the impasse with the Southern body. This pressure led to another conference in 1932 between the two Irish associations, a conference that would turn out to be the last meaningful attempt for decades by both bodies to re-unify.

At an IFA Council meeting in January 1932 with 'an unusually large attendance' present, it was unanimously decided to enter into a conference with the FAIFS with the aim of bringing about a possible settlement of the international question.[37] At the first day of the conference, held in Dublin, it was agreed: 'That a joint committee be formed of equal representation from the IFA and the Free State FA with alternate chairmen, to control international matches, the profits and losses to be equally divided between the two Associations each year.'[38] Although some IFA delegates believed it would be difficult to convince many on the IFA Council to share funds from the lucrative British fixtures versus the continental ones of the Free State, both sides eventually agreed on shared finances.[39] With the obstacle of profit-sharing finally agreed upon, it looked as if a settlement was likely. The IFA readied itself to sign an agreement to be inserted in its rule book,[40] with Wilton commenting that 'he considered it a matter for gratification that the resolution had been passed.'[41]

The second day of the conference was held in Belfast and what was hoped to be a rubber-stamping affair turned out quite differently. The FAIFS asked for equal representation on the International Board, taking one of the IFA's two seats. This was the first occasion this had been requested by the FAIFS. The IFA flatly refused the request, instead asking why the matter was not brought up in Dublin. The FAIFS responded by saying there was no need to bring it up as 'the international agreement was to be on a fifty-fifty basis, that basis was to hold good in everything appertaining to international football.'[42] During the debate one IFA delegate referred to the International Board as a 'glorified picnic party'. It was argued that the FAIFS already had a seat on the International Board through its membership of FIFA and should not be entitled to two seats. The FAIFS countered by stating the IFA had previously been a member of FIFA too and also had two seats. One IFA representative claimed: '"The Free Staters wanted to be either a Dominion or a Republic", and that was the reason they (the IFA) would not agree.'[43] *The Irish Times* believed the IFA would not cede one of its seats on the International Board as it wished to retain 'its position as the principal ruling body, with the FAIFS occupying a secondary place in Irish football'[44]. The debate ended acrimoniously. The FAIFS secretary, Jack Ryder, tried to get the talks back on track, but to no avail. He justified the FAIFS stance by stating that anywhere the name 'Ireland' was being used, the FAIFS must have representation. He was hopeful that negotiations could be resumed 'in order that the friction which has retarded the game's full development in Ireland may be removed.'[45] The IFA decided there was no further point in continuing the discussions.

At the Annual Meeting of the IFA two months later, the IFA Council reported:

> In order to have Peace in Irish Football your Council agreed, at the request of the Football Association of the Irish Free State, to give them equal share in the formation of an International Committee to select teams, and carry out all arrangements in connection with International Matches, and to play these matches alternately North and South, and to give them equal share in all profits accruing from these matches, but they regret to state that these terms were not accepted by the Football Association of the Irish Free State, they made a further demand for representation on the International Football Association Board. Your Council unanimously decided they could not agree, as this was an impossible request.[46]

It was also pointed out that this was not the first time the FAIFS had introduced an additional claim close to an agreement, pointing out 'that in 1924, when the dispute was almost settled, the Free State FA did then as they did in this case, make a further claim, which could not be granted, and the Conference broke down owing to this additional demand by the Football Association of the Irish Free State.'[47]

At the FAIFS Annual Meeting the same year a motion was passed not to play Northern Ireland clubs as long as the IFA used the name 'Ireland'.[48] For a conference that had promised so much at the half-way stage, it was a bitter blow for many to see it end so acrimoniously the next day.

Both associations would go their separate paths, there would be no more conferences on a settlement for many years to come. The 1932 conference would be the closest they would ever come to union again.

The FAIFS remained reliant for fixtures on FIFA, competing in the second outing of the fledgling FIFA World Cup in 1934, whilst the IFA followed the English FA's policy of splendid isolation until the end of the Second World War, by associating itself primarily with the British fixtures.

An interesting postscript to the split was the case of Shelbourne being fined £500 and suspended from the FAIFS in 1934.[49] The club had received the punishment for refusing to play the remainder of its fixtures towards the end of the 1933–34 season because of not being compensated adequately for an international match that had clashed with one of Shelbourne's matches.[50] It wrote a letter to the Free State League claiming:

> My Committee have had under consideration the unfair fine and subsequent suspension inflicted upon my club . . . and have arrived at the conclusion that the action of that body has been actuated by a desire to prevent my club from participating further in serious football. Under these circumstances my club has no alternative but to apply for admission to membership of the Irish Football Association.[51]

The IFA Council referred the club's application to its Emergency Committee.[52] At an FAIFS meeting, the IFA was warned that it had no jurisdiction over any club in the Free State and the matter was referred to the English FA and FIFA. At the same meeting, the Dundalk football club was reprimanded for playing in a five-a-side tournament in Belfast.[53] The IFA Emergency Committee decided that, due to 'the existing agreement', Shelbourne's application for membership 'could not be considered'.[54] The matter was soon dropped and Shelbourne would re-appear two years later in the southern League.[55]

A thawing in the relationship between the two Irish associations occurred as the 1930s progressed. This may have been prompted by the decline of fortunes the sport was experiencing in the Irish Free State because of rising costs and increased taxes, leading to falling crowds.[56] It was mooted at an FAIFS Council meeting in 1935 to contact the IFA to see if circumstances warranted another meeting between the two bodies.[57] On hearing from the FAIFS, the IFA asked 'what matters you desire to confer upon?'[58] Ryder responded with a lengthy letter saying he wanted the relationship between the FAIFS and the IFA to 'be of the friendliest character, and are moreover anxious that in all international matches the country should be represented to the fullest extent by the best talent available in the thirty-two counties.'[59] On the primary reason for the negotiations breakdown in 1932, FAIFS representation on the International Board, he stated:

> In seeking equal representation on the International Board, we are primarily concerned with being represented in all matters appertaining to the affairs of Ireland in International connections . . . The fact that circumstances have since placed 26 out of 32 counties in Ireland outside the control of the IFA must surely warrant an alteration . . . either to the effect that the IFA can only use the name of Northern Ireland, or, and preferable, that one of the two members from Ireland should be representative of the FAIFS.[60]

Ryder received a short reply from the IFA a day later stating 'no good purpose would be served by further negotiations.'[61] No meeting took place. Ryder, who had served the Leinster Football Association and the FAIFS for over forty years, would die only weeks later after a short illness.[62]

A reflection of a move towards a thawing in the relationship between North and South was the clamouring of calls from clubs in the South to reignite the inter-league matches against a representative team from the northern clubs.[63] In 1938, at a special meeting of the FAI (it reverted to its original name; see below), the ban on playing clubs from Northern Ireland and representative inter-league matches was rescinded by a vote of 110 to 17 against. At the same meeting hopes were expressed that there could be a healing with the IFA, leading to one association in Ireland.[64] A letter was subsequently sent to the IFA by the FAI requesting a conference to discuss the differences between the two associations.[65] Despite a more cordial atmosphere between the associations, there were a number of incidents that led to heightened tensions. In 1937, the IFA had taken issue with the southern body selecting three players from Northern Ireland to play against France and Switzerland, even though players born in the South had been selected regularly for IFA international teams since the split. It sought to bring the issue up at the subsequent International Board meeting, seeking 'a ruling as to the right of the Football Association of the Irish Free State to play as Ireland in matches against Continental Nations, and selecting players born outside their own area.'[66]

The FAI went further months later by sending a number of officials to Belfast to scout on players representing the IFA in an international fixture, as potential players for the FAI international team.[67] This backdrop to the request for a new conference did not augur well for its hopes. The FAI formally asked for a conference in May 1938 'to amicably compose the differences existing between our two Associations.'[68] The IFA requested, as in 1935, the matters the FAI wished to discuss. It was also pointed out to the FAI that the IFA was 'bound by contract to play all their home internationals at Windsor Park ... for a period of twenty years.'[69] The FAI secretary, Joe Wickham who had succeeded Ryder after the latter's death, replied that they were aware of the arrangement with Linfield but felt the conference should still go ahead.[70] This did not sway the IFA who responded: 'That while at all times desirous of working in harmony with the Football Association of the Irish Free State, this Committee, taking into consideration all the circumstances, consider no good purpose could be served by further Conferences with that Association.'[71]

A factor that contributed significantly to scuppering any chances of a conference between the associations was the renaming of the southern association to the Football Association of Ireland.

> In accordance with the new Constitution (Bunreacht na hÉireann of 1937), the Association changed its title back to that of 'The Football Association of Ireland', as known prior to the 1923 International Board Conference at Liverpool. Notification of this was sent to the Football Associations of the world and accepted by all except the Scottish FA, who dropped all titles and the Irish FA (Belfast) who have refused to accept the new title and have continued to designate us 'Football Association of the IFS'.[72]

The FAI wrote to the IFA reminding the northern body of its name change following 'the enactment of the new Constitution under which the Title of this State was changed to "Ireland".'[73] The IFA replied: 'We cannot recognise your Association using the word "Ireland" in your new designation.'[74] Under Article 4 of the new constitution, the name of the state was changed to Éire, or Ireland in the English language. 'This was regarded in Britain and Northern Ireland ... as exercising a claim over the entire island.'[75] The IFA wrote to all the British associations explaining why it could not use the new designation, the Football Association of Ireland.[76] The IFA had the support of the British government on its stance, which refused to use the term 'Ireland' in any official document until the Good Friday Agreement of 1998, with the Irish Government undertaking to forgo its constitutional claim to Northern Ireland through the removal of Articles 2 and 3 from the constitution.[77] Once Ireland had changed its name from the 'Irish Free State' to 'Ireland' in 1937, Britain embarked on a worldwide diplomatic campaign to have the territory encompassing the twenty-six counties to be known as 'Éire', as it believed only the whole island should be called 'Ireland'. For agricultural produce such as eggs that were exported, an agreement was reached to use the term Éire (Irish) on products.[78] The Irish Government wanted the word 'Irish' to be included on produce it exported, as it had 'a certain trade value in relation to our exports of agricultural produce, and it is felt that every effort should be made to avoid the loss of whatever goodwill attaches to its use.'[79] Internationally, there followed a considerable amount of confusion on what to call the country. When Spain was asked to use 'Ireland' instead of 'Éire' it was pointed out that 'France was France with or without Alsace-Lorraine, and that Spain was Spain with or without Gibraltar.'[80] The *Manchester Guardian* wrote in 1946 of the confusion surrounding the 'correct and diplomatic way of referring to the country known variously as Éire, Southern Ireland, the Free State, and "Dev's Republic".'[81]

The Irish Government too had issues with the name for Northern Ireland, for years preferring to use the terms the 'Six Counties' or the 'North of Ireland', instead of Northern Ireland, as the use of the latter name denoted acceptance of partition.[82] The Northern Ireland government did contemplate changing the name of the territory it governed from 'Northern Ireland' to 'Ulster' in 1937. The business community, fearful that 'exports of linen to the United States would be seriously affected if we dropped the term "Irish" and substituted "Ulster"', swayed the Stormont government to retain the name 'Northern Ireland'.[83]

The IFA was not the only sporting body that refused to use the name 'Ireland' for teams representing the twenty-six counties. The International Olympic Committee rejected the Irish Olympic Council's claim that its team should carry the name 'Ireland', on the grounds that athletes from the six counties of Northern Ireland were not under the Irish Olympic Council's jurisdiction. The Olympic Committee wrote to the Irish Olympic body saying the name 'Éire' should be used. To illustrate its point, an Irish postage stamp inscribed 'Éire' was included in the letter. The Irish Council retorted: 'As regards the Irish postage stamp enclosed with your letter, it does not appear to be material to the point at issue'. It enclosed a Swiss stamp inscribed 'Helvetia' and a British stamp inscribed 'Postage Revenue'.[84]

At the 1948 London Olympics, the Irish officials were informed by the IOC that the Irish team were required to march as 'Éire', between Egypt and Finland, and not as 'Ireland', during the Opening Ceremony.[85] The confusion that existed for more than a decade was only effectively resolved when Ireland became a republic in 1949. The British Prime Minister, Clement Attlee, in a memorandum to his Cabinet, laid out the most appropriate titles he believed should be used:

The Ireland Bill formally recognises the title 'Republic of Ireland' as the name attributed to Southern Ireland by the law there in force . . . The term 'Ireland' should never be used in official documents or correspondence to the South: it should be reserved for use where a reference to the island as a whole is intended. Similarly, the adjective 'Irish' should not normally be used except in relation to the island as a whole . . . The use of the term 'Éire' should be discontinued. As a geographical description of the South, 'Southern Ireland' may be used as an alternative to 'the Irish Republic'.[86]

The FAI international team would soon after be called the 'Republic of Ireland' too, the name still in use today.

The Second World War did see both Irish associations co-operate more closely. In 1941 the FAI called for a charity match in aid of Belfast refugees affected by the war, between the winners of the IFA and FAI Challenge Cup competitions, on Sunday 4 May. *The Irish Times* considered it 'remarkable that a Saturday match was not suggested', considering the IFA's prohibition of matches on the Sabbath day.[87] Peter McKennan, a Linfield player, had been suspended from the IFA for playing a Scottish league side against an FAI league side on a Sunday the previous year.[88] Despite reservations by the International Committee of the IFA, the Irish Cup winners, Belfast Celtic, did travel to Dublin to play the winners of the FAI Cup, Cork United.[89] After an invitation from Wilton, Dr Willie Hooper, the president of the FAI, had presented the Irish Cup to Belfast Celtic after their defeating of Linfield in the final in 1941.[90]

A year later the IFA granted permission to five Belfast clubs and Derry Celtic to take part in matches against FAI teams, leading to the inauguration of an inter-city competition.[91] In 1943 it was mooted that the twelve clubs from the inter-city competition would secede from the IFA and the FAI and form their own league; this was vehemently denied by the clubs.[92]

Both associations met the same year to arrange a junior match between the leagues from both the IFA and FAI. It was the first meeting between the bodies for many years, leading to hope for eventual union.[93] Many in the South believed union could only be possible if the IFA allowed matches to be played on Sundays.[94] Others felt it was a necessity that they unify, as the number of senior clubs grew less and less in both jurisdictions.[95] The IFA even granted permission to the FAI to choose players from the IFA's territory for matches against Spain and Portugal in 1946. The FAI offered to 'reciprocate in like manner if ever your Association should require players from clubs under our jurisdiction.'[96] A month earlier representatives from the IFA had attended a dinner in Dublin to celebrate the silver jubilee of the FAI, the Leinster Football Association having seceded from the IFA twenty-five years earlier.[97] These were to be high points in the relationship between both bodies as old animosities reared their head soon after. The catalyst was, ironically, the British associations' decision to re-join FIFA.

The campaign for British re-entry into FIFA was led by the English FA secretary, Stanley Rous, who believed that the loss of prestige Britain had suffered through its collapsing empire could be softened by a greater role in world football.[98] He would become FIFA president in 1961. To appease FIFA, Rous and the English FA believed both Irish associations should only choose players born in their own territories. He wrote a letter to the IFA seeking an 'assurance that the players selected to take part will be only players whose birthplace is Northern Ireland' for the match between England and the IFA-selected Irish team on 28 September 1946.[99] The IFA could offer no such assurance, as the 'International team will be selected as heretofore in accordance with the Rules of the International Board and the Agreements of same.'[100] A similar letter was sent by Rous to the FAI secretary, Wickham, asking that the FAI choose only 'Éire-born players' for the forthcoming match between England and an FAI-selected Irish team,[101] a request the FAI consented to.[102] The Irish President, Seán T. O'Kelly, sought the advice of his former Cabinet colleague Oscar Traynor on whether he should attend the match or not. Traynor had previously been a professional footballer, including a period as goalkeeper for Belfast Celtic from 1910 to 1912.[103] Traynor recommended O'Kelly should attend, 'as it will be the first occasion since the foundation of the State that an English International Team has accepted an invitation to play in the twenty-six counties.'[104] It was, in fact, the first time any association from Britain agreed to play an FAI international team. O'Kelly did attend, although he was unhappy with the reception he received at the match. The anthems had already been played before he arrived, he was rushed onto the pitch to meet the players, as the referee wanted to start the match early, and he was not seated in the centre seat of his row.[105] The English team and officials also met the Taoiseach, Éamon de Valera, and were granted a tour of Dáil Éireann.[106]

The FAI, later in the year, complained to the IFA for selecting seven players born in the twenty-six counties for the latter's international against Scotland in November.[107] FIFA also queried the IFA for selecting players born in FAI-governed territory for the match against Scotland.[108]

At the International Board meeting in 1947, the English FA's attempt to prohibit each association from selecting players born outside their association was defeated.[109] The English FA still sought a resolution to the impasse, as it desired to 'play matches against the two Irish Associations' and wanted each Irish association to 'restrict the selection of their players to that area over which they have jurisdiction.'[110] Despite the IFA recommending a conference of the associations involved, none took place.[111] One of the reasons the IFA may have been interested in agreeing to a conference, the first time the IFA was willing to do so for over sixteen years, was a new enforcement disallowing any association from selecting players born outside its territory, from 1948. This enforcement was caused by both Irish associations entering the World Cup tournament for the first time.[112] The last time the IFA would select an all-Ireland team was in 1950 against Wales.[113] Although it rarely selected players born outside its own territory, the FAI was mocked in 1949 by the Swedish press for selecting players against Sweden who had previously represented IFA international teams, some accusing the FAI of cheating. The FAI retorted that it was the IFA who had broken FIFA's rules as the players in question were born in the twenty-six counties.[114] The Irish Legation in Stockholm made an official complaint about the overall manner in which the Swedish press showed disrespect to Ireland in reporting on the match in Dublin, by calling Dublin a 'city of beggars and Catholic churches', referring to the 'primitive condition of Dalymount Park' and sarcastically commenting that the Irish President, O'Kelly, shook the hands of the Irish players first, as the Irish players were 'as seldom guests in Dublin as the Swedes' due to the fact that most of the Irish played for British league teams.[115]

Feeling the time was opportune again, the FAI recommended a conference to the IFA in 1950, suggesting 'that the terms of such settlement be on a fifty-fifty basis in all matters pertaining to International Affairs and International Matches, in which Ireland is concerned'. The IFA again rejected the overtures unanimously as it believed 'no new facts or suggestions have been presented' to justify a conference.[116] The IFA's refusal to agree to a conference led to four players, previously capped by the IFA, announcing they would no longer accept international honours from the IFA. Ten players who had not been capped by the IFA also claimed, if such offers were forthcoming, they too would refuse to play, leading the *Limerick Leader* to declare: 'Solve this soccer mix up and you're a genius!'[117] The FAI subsequently stipulated that each player must sign a declaration agreeing to play for an international team only selected by the FAI, in order for a Clearance Certificate to be granted allowing footballers to play for a club under another association.[118] What had been a 'cold war' became a 'complete severance of relations between North and South'.[119] At a meeting between the IFA and the Irish Football League, it was agreed to cancel all inter-league matches between the Irish Football League and the Football League of Ireland; and no club, league or association under the jurisdiction of the IFA was allowed to play against any like club, association or league 'under the jurisdiction of the body calling themselves the Football Association of Ireland.'[120] The junior inter-association matches were also cancelled.[121] The IFA refused to allow Queen's University to participate in the Collingwood Cup,[122] the annual all-Ireland inter-universities competition, and the Irish Schools' Football Association from Northern Ireland cancelled the annual representative match against their equivalent body in the South.[123]

Throughout the 1950s the gulf between the associations widened. It was a decade in which sports and politics would intertwine in soccer and many other sports.

CHAPTER 17

The 1950s – Sport and Politics Intertwine

Soccer was not the only sport affected by partition between North and South during the 1950s. It was a decade that saw many incidents directly related to the political divide in the country impact on sport, some incidents even affecting sports that were unified on an all-Ireland basis.

Under the Civil Authorities (Special Powers) Act of 1933 of the Northern Ireland government, it was illegal to fly the tricolour flag 'purporting to be a flag of an Irish Republic and containing three vertical stripes of green, white and yellow', even though the third colour is orange.[1] A number of high-profile court cases had highlighted the sensitivity relating to this issue. A man was prosecuted in 1950 for displaying the tricolour in Armagh. In his defence, his lawyer highlighted the absurdity of the British government recognising the Republic of Ireland and its flag, and yet the Northern Ireland administration refusing to do so.[2] The Irish Government formally complained to the British for this 'deep offence offered to Irish national sentiment by the continuance of a state of affairs wherein a law is in existence and enforced which purports to render it a criminal offence to display the Irish flag in Ireland.'[3] One of the most high-profile instances of the northern authorities prohibiting the displaying of the tricolour came at an international rugby match between Ireland and Wales held in Ravenhill in Belfast in March 1950. A fan who had travelled from Dublin, on displaying the tricolour prominently before the match commenced, was chased and attacked by RUC men. A photograph showing the man manhandled by the RUC, with one constable planting his knee on the man's neck, pinning him to the ground,

211

was seen around the world.⁴ Motorists travelling over the border
for the match were also ordered to remove the tricolour by the
RUC once they entered the Six Counties.⁵ A similar incident had
occurred two years previously, with the RUC 'snapping' any tri-
colours flown by spectators at an international rugby match in
Ravenhill.⁶ It did not lead to the level of hostility the incident of
1950 did. Many in the press were outraged by the incident, the
Ulster Herald describing it as 'a remarkable illustration of what it
means to live in an armed Police State.'⁷ The *Fermanagh Herald*
believed 'the setting at Ravenhill looked more like as if the game
was being played in an English town, and not in Ireland's second
largest city', such was the prominent display of Union Jack flags.⁸
The *Sunday Independent* believed the IRFU was directly responsible. It urged the union to 'find some remedy which will prevent
the great majority of Irish rugby followers being nauseated' in
future.⁹ Other pro-unionist papers blamed the spectators from the
twenty-six counties for their 'displays of exaggerated nationalism
and political assertiveness wholly out of place at a sporting event
and in exceedingly bad taste.'¹⁰ The *Strabane Weekly News* called
for firm action against displaying the tricolour, describing it as:

> The flag of a bitterly hostile, rebellious foreign country ...
> There can be no objection to the display of any foreign flag in
> Northern Ireland as a mark of respect and courtesy towards
> the countries they represent, but the tricolour can never be
> associated with respect or courtesy. It is the symbol of hatred,
> avarice, dishonour and rebellion, and the emblem of a country
> whose politicians aim at the destruction of the Government of
> Northern Ireland and the subjugation of its people.¹¹

The Northern Ireland government subsequently introduced
legislation to include orange as one of the colours that could be
considered as encompassing the tricolour and it also relaxed its
ruling on the displaying of the tricolour. The flag was no longer
considered illegal: it would only be considered so if it led to 'a
breach of the peace' by provoking 'others to create trouble'.¹²
This act was only repealed in 1987 after the Anglo-Irish Agreement of 1985.¹³

In 1953, the IRFU was accused of insulting 'its country by
having "God Save the Queen" played as the anthem of Ireland, at

an international rugby match between Ireland and France in Ravenhill, the IRFU being described as 'a clique which stands for British rule for part of the northern province of Ireland and which, we feel sure, would like to see the twenty-six counties again occupied by Britain.'[14] It was believed that some of the players from the west of Ireland were 'discussing the form in which they should make a strong protest.'[15] A strike was threatened by the southern players a year later unless the Irish national anthem was played and the tricolour flown, on top of the United Kingdom ones, at rugby internationals held in Ravenhill. A strike was averted when the IRFU agreed to host all future rugby internationals in Dublin.[16]

Other sports governed on an all-Ireland basis, acutely aware of the potential potency of symbols, looked to incorporate the Northern and Southern make-up of their members. At a women's hockey international match between Ireland the Netherlands in 1951, 'O'Donnell Abú' was played instead of the national anthem 'as the situation between their Northern – the Six County members of the team and the others was delicate regarding political loyalties and affiliations and that they feared a split in their Association - at present an all-Ireland Association – if matters were forced'.[17] The dinner that evening featured the tricolour prominently displayed alongside the Dutch flag, as well as the Northern Ireland born non-playing captain offering the Dutch association president a Tara brooch, as she wanted to give 'something really Irish.'[18] The Irish Davis Cup team in tennis played under the flag of the four provinces on a blue background. This was chosen as the flag for their associations as they were keen to preserve Irish unity in tennis.[19] Even though only two of the players representing Ireland at an International Bowls tournament in Brighton in 1953 were from the twenty-six counties, the tricolour was still chosen as the Irish flag.[20] A minor incident was caused in the ranks of the Irish Ladies' Golfing Union in 1958 when the Drogheda-born Philomena Garvey withdrew from the British Isles Curtis Cup team to play the United States because she refused to wear a Union Jack on her blazer. She claimed she 'would be prepared to wear a combination of the Union Jack and Éire Tricolour, or a lion rampant, but I feel I would be disloyal to my country if I wore a Union Jack only.'[21] A compromise was reached the following year when a new badge was designed containing the shields of Ireland, England, Scotland and Wales, and in the centre a small Union Jack, a compromise acceptable to Garvey.[22] Bridge players were also affected by the political divide on the island, with a motion passed at the Contract Bridge Association of Ireland AGM of 1950 not to compete in 'competitions or tournaments in which the Northern Ireland Bridge Union is allowed to complete as a unit.'[23] It was also agreed to explore the possibility of one ruling body for bridge in Ireland, a union that came about in 1954.[24]

The governance of athletics and cycling in Ireland mirrored that of soccer most, with both sports divided on similar lines. The 1950s would see many incidents magnifying the divide. The National Athletics and Cycling Association (NACA) had refused to accept the International Amateur Athletic Federation's (IAAF) ruling of 1934 to 'limit the jurisdiction of its member federations to the political boundaries of the country or nation they represented', and was subsequently suspended from the IAAF in 1935 (see Chapter Eleven).[25] It refused to withdraw its claims to control athletics in Northern Ireland: 'The politics of athletics became identified with the politics of the constitution . . . to accept the IAAF ruling would be to condone partition.'[26]

With the national federations responsible for managing amateur sport on an all-Ireland basis, the Irish Olympic Council decided not to compete in the 1936 Berlin Olympics. Due to the Second World War, the next Olympic Games took place in London in 1948. Clubs unhappy with how NACA was governing athletics in Ireland had established their own athletics body, the Amateur Athletics Union, Éire (AAUE) in 1938. The AAUE became affiliated to the IAAF. Although not sanctioned by the Irish Olympic Council, who supported NACA, ten AAUE athletes competed in London.[27] Talks for unity in Irish athletics were considered in the 1950s, as it was believed that sports that were united on an all-Ireland basis were more competitive internationally than sports that were not:

> The strange thing about Irish sport is that many games are controlled by one body covering both North and South. This is the case with boxing, Rugby and golf, in which they can hold their own with any of the other three home countries. Yet

where there is a split as in athletics and soccer, the Irish have
become the 'poor relations'. Therefore everyone agrees that
Ireland's athletics must be controlled by one organisation.[28]

NACA took issue with the Belfast athlete Thelma Hopkins
winning a gold medal in the high jump while at a race meet in
Berlin representing Britain in 1954. Her sister Moira commented
that, 'although she is representing Britain, the honour and glory is
Ireland's.'[29] Although not allowed to compete for Ireland in athletics, she did represent Ireland in hockey.[30] She won a silver medal
representing Great Britain and Northern Ireland in the 1956
Melbourne Olympics, the same Olympics Ronnie Delany won a
gold medal for Ireland in the 1,500 metres.[31] As Delany was an
AAUE athlete, he did not receive universal acclaim upon his return
to Ireland.[32] Athletics in the Republic of Ireland would only be
healed in 1967 when NACA and AAUE amalgamated to form
Bord Lúthchleas na hÉireann (BLE).[33]

The National Cycling Association (NCA), the cycling arm of
NACA, also did not accept partition, and it too was not recognised by the world governing body of its sport, Union Cycliste
Internationale (UCI). The NCA secretary, Kerry Sloane, sent a circular to all the UCI affiliated associations seeking recognition. He
claimed that the UCI affiliate in Ireland, Cumann Rothaidheachta
na hÉireann (CRE), had only 138 members (including tourists)
compared with the NCA having 1,000 racing cyclists in over one
hundred clubs. The Northern Ireland Cycling Federation (NICF),
also recognised by UCI, allegedly had only about one hundred
members in one or two towns.[34] To highlight the perceived injustice, NCA cyclists were sent to the Rome World Championships
in 1955 and the Melbourne Olympics in 1956 as a mark of protest.
Four NCA cyclists were arrested at the Rome event after a fist
fight ensued between the NCA cyclists and the officially sanctioned Irish team from the CRE. One of the cyclists was detained
for striking an Italian policeman.[35]

Most people in the South were desirous to see soccer governed
on an all-Ireland basis. There was an incident in 1957, though,
that saw both soccer administrators and others from the South
disown any involvement with soccer in Northern Ireland. At an

international match between Italy and Northern Ireland held in Windsor Park in Belfast, it was decided, just before kick-off, to change the fixture from a World Cup qualifier to a friendly match. The match was marred by an ugly attack on the Italian players by local supporters who broke down barriers, battled with the RUC and mobbed the Italian players, who were stoned, kicked and beaten.[36] Italian soccer fans protested in Milan carrying banners that read, 'Ireland, you are no sport.'[37] The unruly attack caused a sensation in the international press with headlines such as the 'Barbarian Irish Football Crowd'[38] and 'Italians Mobbed by Wild Irish'[39] commonplace in many British and international newspapers. The Italian newspaper, *Il Tempo*, commented on the 'Irish public – the "quiet men" whom John Ford made us know and like – invaded the field at the end of the match attacking the Italian athletes.'[40]

There soon followed a rear-guard action from the FAI and the Irish Government, renouncing any involvement in the incidents at Windsor Park. The Minister for External Affairs, Frank Aiken, sent a telegram the day after the match to the Irish embassies in Rome, Paris, Bonn, Brussels, Lisbon, the Hague, Sweden, Switzerland and Madrid stating: 'Explain to Press Belfast part of partitioned Ireland still held by British. All Ireland regrets incident at yesterday's football match.'[41] The FAI protested to the BBC for its use of the name 'Ireland' instead of 'Northern Ireland'.[42] Some commentators were not impressed by the attempts from sections in the South with their 'indecent haste, individuals and organisations vied with each other in their anxiety to disassociate themselves from the "bad boys" of Belfast',[43] some believing 'the "southerners" didn't come so well out of the business with their holier-than-thou and let's-disown-them attitude.'[44] Lord Killanin, president of the Irish Olympic Council and future president of the International Olympic Committee, wrote a letter to *The Times* complaining of its implication that all of Ireland was responsible for the incidents in Belfast when in reality the IFA only governed for the six counties of Northern Ireland. In a wide-ranging letter he commented on how different sports dealt with partition:

216

The overwhelming majority of sports in Ireland are administered internally and affiliated internationally on an all-Ireland basis. The result is that Irishmen from both sides of the border, with divergent but sincere views on what may be politically best for our country play as Irishmen. Among the few exceptions are field and track and Association football. The former all amateur, has cast a shadow over our Olympic endeavours since the split in the mid-1930s. The latter, largely professional, has not only affected the question of entering amateur teams in the Olympic Games but has created problems in the development of sport in this island.[45]

He concluded by pondering on what would happen should Ireland (Republic) and Ireland (North) meet in the finals of the World Cup.[46] The teams would not meet in the 1958 World Cup, with just one of them qualifying, the team from the North.

The Irish Legation in Sweden, host nation of the 1958 World Cup, sought advice from the Department of External Affairs on what attitude should be taken with the Northern Ireland team competing in the World Cup.[47] The following reply was received:

As it is almost certain that the Six County team will be regarded as British, that the Union Jack will be flown, that the British National Anthem will be played and that the principal guest will be the British Ambassador, we feel that you should plead diplomatic illness and not attend the matches in which this team is engaged or any functions in connection with them . . . If approached, you might express pleasure, or regret, at the victory, or loss, of the Northern Ireland team, adding a remark regretting that the team is not representative of all Ireland as in the case of Rugby football.[48]

During the World Cup, there was considerable confusion over the status of the Northern Irish team. The bus to collect the team at Malmö flew the tricolour and was reprimanded by the IFA for doing so, which stated that they were not the FAI. At a shop close to the Northern Ireland training camp, there was a photograph of the Irish team displayed, except it was an FAI and not an IFA team. It was also believed that the team would not have the players to cope with a world tournament.[49] Such beliefs were to be unfounded, as Northern Ireland defied their critics by reaching the quarter-final stages. So frustrated were some with the lack of political capital gained from the team's showing at the World Cup, with most countries referring to them as Ireland and not Northern Ireland, that there were calls for the first time north of the border for the team to be known as Northern Ireland in future.[50]

CHAPTER 18

Hope Rekindled

The animosity that had coloured the whole of the 1950s gave way to a more conciliatory approach adopted by both associations in the 1960s. IFA representatives were in attendance at an international match between the Republic of Ireland and Poland in 1964. It did lead to protests in the North, as the match was held on a Sunday, with some commenting on the hypocrisy of suspending amateur players who played on Sundays whilst officials were allowed to attend matches on the Sabbath day.[1] It was agreed in 1965 to inaugurate an annual fixture between youth teams from the North and the South[2] and in 1967 the Blaxnit All-Ireland cup competition was launched with four teams representing the FAI and four teams the IFA.[3] Despite these advances and the calls from illustrious players, such as George Best, enthusiastically supporting an all-Ireland international team, it was still believed unification was far off due to the 'internal politics of Irish soccer'.[4] A motion was defeated at a council meeting of the FAI in 1969 to approach the IFA with a view to the establishment of an all-Ireland soccer team.[5]

The escalating violence in the North of Ireland from the late 1960s appeared to scupper any chances of healing the split in Irish soccer, with the Blaxnit Cup considered to be in jeopardy as a viable entity in early 1970 due to the Troubles.[6] A boost was received later in the year, though, when a team composed of Republic of Ireland and Northern Ireland players was selected to play against Arsenal in a benefit match for Terry Neill.[7] It was also reported that the FIFA president, Stanley Rous, 'would welcome any move to fuse the Football Association of Ireland and the Irish

A 'SHAMROCK ROVERS ALL-IRELAND XI' TEAM

comprising of players from the Republic of Ireland and Northern Ireland who played against world champions Brazil in Dublin in July 1973. Soon after, a series of conferences was held between the IFA and the FAI to look at the possibility of forming an all-Ireland team.

Courtesy of Sportsfile

Football Association' and that IFA secretary, William Drennan 'agreed that both Irish bodies should be working towards an all-Ireland side.'[8] In the build up to the Terry Neill benefit match, George Best reiterated his call for an all-Ireland international team, claiming he had 'talked to several players from the South and they all want to see a full Irish team. I know the Northern Ireland players think the same way.'[9] With administrators from both associations more open to reconciliation, the fans and the new political realities of Northern Ireland would intervene to maintain the chasm. At the Blaxnit Cup Final of 1971 between Linfield and Cork Hibernians, held in Dalymount Park, crowd trouble coloured the match. The Linfield supporters waved Union Jacks whilst shouting 'Up the UVF' leading to both sections of supporters throwing bottles and stones at each other. The rioting continued after the match.[10] The nationalist-leaning club Derry

City was dealt a significant blow when its ground, the Brandywell, close to the Bogside in Derry, scene of many riots, was considered too dangerous to host games and the club was forced to play its 'home' games in Coleraine, forty miles from the city.[11] Harry Cavan, the IFA president, had previously claimed to the press that it was too unsafe to hold European Cup matches at the Brandywell.[12] The club decided to withdraw from Irish league football in 1972, following in the footsteps of its predecessor, Belfast Celtic.[13]

The FAI commissioned a report on association football which was published in May 1973, on the ills that beset the game in the country. It was chaired by Fianna Fáil TD, David Andrews. On the prospect of reunification, the report stated 'that in the long term a country-wide league competition, including teams from Northern Ireland, be considered'. It also recommended 'that the possibility of fielding an All-Ireland team be examined ... The Football Association of Ireland should set up machinery with the Irish Football Association with a view to the establishment of a country-wide association.'[14] It concluded by stating 'problems involved in fielding an All-Ireland team can be overcome ... the Football Association of Ireland should look ahead and attempt to create an atmosphere of conciliation.'[15]

One event that happened just months later offered encouragement to those who dreamed of an all-Ireland team. Such a team comprising players from Northern Ireland and the Republic of Ireland did play together in July 1973 as a 'Shamrock Rovers All-Ireland XI' against Brazil, a team considered the greatest of all time, having won its third World Cup three years previously.[16] The game, which ended four-three to the Brazilians was enthusiastically supported by 34,000 attendees at Lansdowne Road in Dublin, who heard a rendition of 'A Nation Once Again' by the St Patrick's Brass and Reed Band beforehand.[17] Many observers believed the event would lead to 'an all-Ireland team in action in world competition' in the not too distant future.[18]

The FAI subsequently sent the IFA a letter requesting a meeting 'to discuss matters of mutual interest', a meeting the IFA unanimously agreed to attend.[19] At that conference, held in Belfast on 2 October, 'a very lengthy and amicable discussion' was held, in stark contrast to many of the failed attempts between both associations in years past.[20] Four main topics were discussed at the meeting: the effect and correctness of 'scratch teams'; the possibility of all-Ireland competitions with European ramifications; the possibility of an all-Ireland international team either under the jurisdiction of a joint committee or under the jurisdiction of one association and closer liaison on matters of mutual co-operation such as organising joint competitions like the Blaxnit and Texaco tournaments; and education around coaching courses, referees' courses and school football.[21] At the conclusion of the meeting it was agreed that 'further joint meetings of office bearers be arranged.'[22]

The next meeting between the associations took place in Dublin in January 1974. Both agreed that 'scratch teams' should not be permitted to play matches. On the issue of an all-Ireland league competition, it was felt this venture would not be possible without 'very substantial sponsorship'.[23] On the primary issue of the possibility of an all-Ireland team, Harry Cavan 'pointed out that both Associations at present have the right of entry to the World Cup Competition and the European Football Championship. If there was an All Ireland team, there could only be one entry to both these Competitions.'[24] It was suggested by the FAI that there was

> the possibility of the Irish FA calling on Southern born players for the British International Championship and the FA of Ireland calling on Northern Ireland born players for friendly matches arranged by the FA of Ireland. After further consideration it was agreed that the Irish FA would ascertain the views of the other British Associations . . . and Mr. Cavan would also enquire from FIFA about their reaction to such an arrangement.[25]

No agreement was reached, and talks were still in progress some months later. In deploring the failure of the Scottish Football Association to send its international team to Belfast, the Northern Ireland Minister for Community Relations, Ivan Cooper, commented that discussions were ongoing between the FAI and IFA 'with a view to the possible creation of an all-Ireland soccer team.'[26] By 1974, no international team had played in Northern Ireland, due to the Troubles, for three years; the last team to visit was the Soviet Union in 1971.[27] The Northern Ireland soccer team ultimately played ten 'home' games in Britain from 1972 to 1978 due to civil unrest.[28] The talks of 1973–74 ultimately failed on the question of the IFA looking for the FAI to amalgamate back into the IFA, something the southern body was unwilling to do.[29]

In 1976, the Irish Universities Football Union, comprising twelve universities and colleges from Northern Ireland and the Republic of Ireland, including five from the North, sought grant aid from the IFA and FAI to allow the body to fulfil its remaining fixture against Wales that year.[30] Both associations contributed £100 towards the travelling expenses of the team. The Irish Universities international team was the only all-Ireland soccer team in existence and this was the first occasion it was funded by both associations, another indication that reunion was a distinct possibility.[31]

The IFA agreed to meet after another request was made by the FAI in 1977 'to discuss the possibility of an All Ireland International team.'[32] Cavan, who was also a vice-president of FIFA, said 'he saw no reason why there should not be further discussions on the matter' even if 'there were "practical difficulties"' involved. He also mentioned that 'there might be some difficulty in convincing FIFA of the feasibility of fielding just one national team, representative of two different associations, for competitive games such as the World Cup and European Championship ties.'[33] Commenting on the renewal of talks, David Andrews, who had become Parliamentary Secretary (Minister of State) to the Minister for Foreign Affairs earlier in the year, believed it was 'one of the most encouraging and significant developments on the Irish soccer front in recent years'. He was in favour of a federation of Irish football where a team chosen from both associations would 'play two international friendly matches every year against the top teams in Europe.'[34]

Coinciding with the renewal of talks, was the pairing of Northern Ireland with the Republic of Ireland in Group One of the 1980 European Championship qualifiers in late 1977. England was also drawn in the same group. Considered by *The Irish Times* to be 'a nice touch of irony at a time when moves are afoot to explore the possibility of fielding just one international soccer team', it would lead to the first clash between the teams at senior international level.[35] The first concern that came to most people's minds was the security concerns the clashes in Dublin and Belfast would pose due to the violence that had engulfed Northern Ireland over the previous eight years. One commentator called it 'the worst thing that could possibly happen to soccer football in this country' adding that it could 'set the scene for the most serious football riots of all time since a war broke out over the result of a match in South America (the 'Football War' of 1969 between Honduras and El Salvador).'[36]

It was envisaged the talks would be ongoing over months, perhaps years, to reach an agreement satisfactory to both the IFA and FAI. The most likely solution, it was believed, was an 'all-Ireland Control body which, while guaranteeing the sovereignty of the two associations, will enable them to co-operate for the purpose of promoting international football.'[37] The first session of the 'newest, and clearly, the most determined campaign so far, to attain the long-cherished goal of an all-Ireland team in international football' took place in Dundalk on 2 February 1978.[38] After the four-hour meeting, a joint communique was issued to the press:

> Several options were considered, including the possibility of an All-Ireland Football Federation which would be responsible for international matches. It was agreed that a joint paper be produced setting out these options and the possible difficulties which might arise. The discussions will be continued during the period of the European championship in which the two associations are drawn against each other. The representatives agreed that the meeting had been extremely positive and worthwhile. A further meeting has been arranged for March 8th in Dublin.[39]

The FAI had succeeded in having the emphasis switched from an outright merger of the two associations to the consideration for an all-Ireland football federation, something which would be unprecedented in world football. Cavan gave a qualified endorsement of the outcome of the first day of talks, declaring that 'a lot of points were agreed today but obviously some areas will present problems.'[40] The problems he envisaged included economics, with a joint team playing only half the fixtures both associations played each year resulting in a corresponding drop in income. He also believed it would be hard for the League of Ireland and the Irish League to retain their separate representation in the three European club competitions if only one Irish team was entered in international tournaments. He felt the forthcoming European Championship matches between the Republic of Ireland and Northern Ireland could have a profound influence 'for good or bad' on the talks; the attitude of fans would reflect the feelings at the grass-roots level for a unified team.[41] He concluded on a note of optimism, 'our presence here today is proof that we are convinced there is enough common ground between these two associations to warrant the closest examination of the present situation.'[42] Cavan was also reported as saying he was 'delighted with the way it went and I have high hopes that something good will come out of the talks.'[43]

Frank Davis, the FAI president, was very upbeat after the first session, stating, 'With the goodwill shown around the table today, I believe that, whatever the timing, an all-Ireland team must now come into being . . . The fact that we are drawn together in the European championship is another means of bringing us closer and getting to know each other's options.'[44]

Commenting on the unity talks between the two Irish associations, the *Kerryman* compared the divide in Irish soccer to hockey in Ireland, where a thirty-two county team was due to compete in the men's World Cup Hockey Finals in Argentina that summer. The soccer World Cup Finals were also due to be played in Argentina in 1978. Neither Irish team qualified for the soccer World Cup. The Hockey Association was involved in a controversial episode with the GAA, who disallowed four of its members from participating in a fund-raising function for the Irish hockey team as the latter 'uses "Danny Boy" instead of "Amhrán na bhFiann" as an anthem, and substitutes the flag of the Four Provinces for the Tricolour as a national flag.'[45] The paper claimed an all-Ireland soccer team would be going to Argentina too and if the price of that unity was 'Danny Boy' and a flag of the Four Provinces, it was a price worth paying.[46]

The second session held a month later in Dublin was also considered a positive meeting with the discussions 'taking place in a friendly, cordial atmosphere and that some progress had been made.'[47] Security arrangements were discussed for the upcoming clashes between both Irish associations with the consensus being that the matches posed 'no insurmountable problems'.[48] The meeting concluded with the arrangement for a third meeting in Belfast a month later.[49]

At the IFA AGM of 1979, Harry Cavan, 'the man whom many people in the Republic thought was the principal opponent of the move' for an all-Ireland team, claimed 'that two teams in a small country like this was nonsensical, but he warned that anyone who thought that a united Ireland team would win the World Cup was living in cuckoo land.'[50]

The meetings stuttered along at a torturous pace over the following years. The European Championship clashes between both of the Irish teams passed almost without incident. It was a club match, a European Cup tie between Linfield and Dundalk in 1979 that demonstrated the precarious nature of soccer on the island, and its close links to the political conflict in Northern Ireland, causing one journalist to claim that the 'All-Ireland dream [was] killed by naked tribalism.'[51] The match, held in Oriel Park, Dundalk, had not even started before trouble broke out. Linfield fans destroyed a pub before the match. Their buses were stoned by Dundalk supporters. Throughout the match Linfield fans repeatedly threw stones and sought confrontation. Cliftonville fans had travelled from Northern Ireland just to clash with the Linfield supporters. 'Finally, after an attempt was made midway through the second half to pull down the Tricolour flying over the unreserved stand, Gardaí baton charged the Linfield supporters and cleared them from the ground.'[52] On the way back to their buses, the Linfield fans continued on their rampage, smashing every window within sight. Seventy people were injured in the rioting.[53] UEFA considered the Linfield fans to be the primary culprits, with the Northern club forced to play its 'home' leg, the return fixture, in a neutral venue outside of Ireland or Britain. That match took place in Haarlem in the Netherlands.[54] The FAI, in referring to the 'recent unfortunate occurrences', claimed the incidents at Oriel Park would not de-rail its unification talks with the IFA.[55]

The sixth meeting (since the talks had resumed in 1978) took place between the IFA and the FAI in Belfast in November 1979,

Hope Rekindled

on the eve of the Northern Ireland and Republic of Ireland match to be held in Windsor Park.[56] The campaign to attain an all-Ireland team was considered 'to be almost as difficult as achieving political unity and, in some respects, even more treacherous.'[57] The main stumbling blocks appeared not to be on the sensitive issues of flag and anthem but on money and the financial dilemma the halving of revenue from international fixtures would cause. It was still agreed to meet again in January 1980, grounds for optimism according to Peadar O'Driscoll, FAI secretary, who claimed, 'the longer the talks progress, the better the chances of a solution.'[58]

The following round of talks, held in Dublin in January 1980, would prove to be a turning point, though, bringing the venture that had started in earnest in 1973 'close to total breakdown'.[59] The primary reason for the pessimism was the ongoing conflict in Northern Ireland, manifested during the Linfield-Dundalk riot the previous year. Cavan commented on the

> major problem of community feeling in the North. I went on record a few years ago as saying that something positive in the All Ireland context would be achieved by the IFA's centenary year, which is this year. I didn't realise at the time that the community unrest would still be such a huge problem in 1980.[60]

The problem of reconciling the concept of an all-Ireland team with the rules of FIFA was also mentioned as an obstacle, with FIFA rules prohibiting the formation of one team for competitive purposes where a political border exists between two countries.[61]

Despite attempts by the FAI to renew talks in 1981,[62] the divides were 'still so great, the difficulties so complex and the avenues of finding a solution so long', for any more meaningful attempt to be made at union.[63] Derek Brookes, secretary of Linfield, summed up the main obstacle to unity:

> The problem with people who speak glibly of unity in Irish soccer . . . is that they tend to ignore the facts of life here in the North of Ireland. The concept of one Ireland football team may be exciting but, unfortunately, it does not take account of the fact that we are living in troubled times. People must live six days a week in that environment. It is unreasonable to expect that football can be immune on the seventh.[64]

227

The political factor was eventually acknowledged by the FAI as the primary hindrance to overcome. Its president, John Farrell, stated in 1983, 'there will be no settlement of the split in Irish soccer until such time as the political problems which divide the North and the Republic have been solved.'[65]

The 1980s would see fortunes improve for both associations at international level. The Northern Ireland soccer team won the British Home Championship in 1980 and 1984, the last year it was ever held. The 1981 championship was abandoned due to the civil unrest in Northern Ireland surrounding the hunger strikes in the Maze Prison, with the English and Welsh teams refusing to travel to Belfast.[66] Under Billy Bingham, the international side also qualified for the World Cups of 1982 and 1986, causing one of the biggest upsets in the 1982 competition by defeating the host nation, Spain.[67] The results Northern Ireland was experiencing led Harry Cavan to comment, 'with results like we have had over the last two years, who needs a United Irish soccer side?'[68] Qualification for the World Cup in 1986 would mark the end of Northern Ireland's highly successful run, the team has not qualified for an international tournament since.

By contrast, just two years later the Republic of Ireland made its introduction at international tournaments at the European Championship of 1988 in West Germany. In qualifying for the World Cups in 1990 and 1994, the southern body had overtaken its Northern rival on the field. It would also lessen the appetite of the FAI for unity. Louis Kilcoyne, the FAI president, commenting in 1995 on the prospect of reunion stated, 'if it ain't broken, don't fix it.' He was referring to the thriving state of soccer in both Northern Ireland and the Republic of Ireland.[69]

Sectarian tensions fuelled by the conflict in Northern Ireland also spilled over to soccer during the 1980s and 1990s. At an Irish Cup tie between Linfield and the nationalist-leaning club Donegal Celtic, at Windsor Park in 1990, crowd disturbances led to the intervention of the RUC who fired plastic bullets into the crowd. Forty-five RUC constable's and fifteen civilians were injured.[70] The match had orig-inally been scheduled to be played in Donegal Celtic's home ground in west Belfast. The RUC had felt it couldn't secure public safety there. The IFA decided to reschedule the match to Linfield's home ground, Windsor Park, leading the *Irish News* to condemn the IFA for its 'disgracefully cavalier attitude in riding roughshod over the views of the Donegal Celtic management.'[71]

In 1991 Donegal Celtic was drawn at home against Ards, who had a predominantly Protestant following, in the Irish Cup. Again, the RUC ruled it was too unsafe to stage the match in west Belfast and again the IFA agreed. Donegal Celtic was ordered to play the tie at the Ards ground in Newtownards. Refusing to do so, Donegal Celtic decided to withdraw from the competition. The club's application for membership to the FAI, following the footsteps of Derry City, who joined the FAI governed League of Ireland in 1985, was rejected due to the danger associated with west Belfast.[72]

In 1989, an attempt by Derry City to schedule a benefit match with Linfield was rejected as it was believed both clubs' fans 'would see a Linfield-Derry City friendly as a contradiction in terms.'[73] Buses carrying Derry City fans returning from the FAI Cup Final that year were stoned by Protestant youths carrying Ulster flags.[74]

A survey conducted in 1990 amongst Northern Ireland soccer supporters demonstrated the huge gulf between Catholic and Protestant supporters at the time. One hundred Catholics and one hundred Protestants from the greater Belfast area were surveyed by the University of Ulster student N.P. McGivern, who asked them who they would prefer to see win a British-Irish tournament staged among the two Irish teams, England, Scotland and Wales.[75] Ninety-one per cent of Catholics wanted the Republic of Ireland to come first, with only eight per cent opting for Northern Ireland. Eighty-eight per cent of Protestants wanted Northern Ireland to win the tournament with over sixty per cent desiring for the Republic of Ireland to be placed fourth or last.[76] Eighty-five per cent of Catholics were in favour of an all-Ireland team compared with forty-two per cent of Protestants. Forty-three per cent of Protestants desired an all-UK team.[77]

A frightening example of the deep hatred many in Northern Ireland held towards the Republic of Ireland was starkly demonstrated at the World Cup qualifier in Windsor Park in November 1993 (see Introduction). The prospect for union between both associations had never been further from realisation. Months later, the draw for the qualifying rounds of the 1996 European Champion-ship in England was made with the Republic of Ireland drawn against Northern Ireland yet again. Sean Connolly, FAI secretary remarked, 'This draw doesn't help. We have asked FIFA that in the future the two countries be kept apart'. He was accused by David Bowen, his counterpart in the IFA of 'hysterical scare-mongering'.[78]

Tensions have eased in recent years. Republican and loyalist ceasefires, followed by the signing of the Good Friday Agreement in 1998, have seen an end to the wide-scale violence of the Troubles of Northern Ireland. Both Irish teams have seen their fortunes dwindle on the international stage too and have not met in serious competition since the 1990s. Despite disagree-ments between the IFA and the FAI over the eligibility of Northern Ireland born players such as James McClean and Darron Gibson representing the Republic of Ireland, recent years have seen more cordial relations between both associations.[79] The Setanta Cup, the first cross-border competition since the 1980s, was inaugurated in 2005 and continues to this day.[80] Both associations have also co-operated on issues such as coaching[81] and schooling in the border regions.[82] There have been, though, no clear overtures from either the FAI or the IFA to reconvene talks on unity in soccer. This may change.

The standards of both international teams have dropped sig-nificantly from the 1990s. With the internationalisation of the English Premier League, the league most Irish professionals, North and South, have succeeded in, fewer Irish-born players are finding the opportunity to compete at the highest level in the top division in England. This trend looks set to continue for some time, reducing the likelihood of either Irish team maintaining competitiveness at international level. In turn, this may convince the administrators North and South to reconsider the option of one team representing the whole island.

Conclusion

The permanent split in soccer in Ireland that endures today was neither inevitable nor necessary. When division came about, there were ample opportunities to reach a settlement. There certainly is no strong reason why agreement on one international team representing the island, at the very least, was not achieved.

Politics did play a significant part in driving a wedge between those governing the game North and South. The fractious political atmosphere that engulfed the nation leading up to partition and beyond impacted deeply on soccer in Ireland, most clearly illustrated through the mass riots involving Belfast Celtic and the Linfield and Glentoran clubs. Many of the key administrators in Belfast were unionist in outlook, including the chairman who oversaw the split, James Wilton. A manifestation of their unionism and Protestantism could be seen by their refusal to countenance football on Sundays; football on the Sabbath day was still not an option, even for World Cup matches in the 1950s.[1] Nationalist leaning clubs such as Belfast Celtic, and Leinster soccer administrators had no qualms about playing matches on Sunday.[2] One of the first decisions of the newly formed FAI was to sanction football on Sundays. There was also a belief that the IFA was more prone to side with unionist-leaning clubs than those of the nationalist clubs. The treatment of Belfast Celtic through a number of episodes, particularly in 1920, strengthened this belief. The 'Flag Incident' during the amateur international between Ireland and France in Paris in 1921 also left a sour taste with many in the South, it being seen as another example of the anti-nationalist slant of the IFA. The catalyst that led to Leinster leaving the IFA, Shelbourne being forced back to Belfast for an Irish Cup semi-final replay tie in 1921, also demonstrated deep-rooted unfairness towards clubs in the South compared with those of Ulster. As Mike Cronin points out:

> Soccer had developed originally on an all-Ireland basis, but one that was governed from the North. The IFA saw Ireland as part of the Union, and a home organisation that was no different from that of Scotland or Wales. It organised its own league and cup competitions, indeed had its own international team, but the IFA stressed a national identity, that while Irish, was constructed firmly within a unionist mindset of loyalty to the Crown and State of the mainland.[3]

That there was a Belfast bias within the IFA, there can be no doubt. Players from Ulster clubs (mostly from Belfast) dominated the international team, even after Leinster clubs had become competitive. With the exception of six occasions, all Irish home internationals were played in Belfast, all IFA Council and sub-committee meetings were held in Belfast and the make-up of those committees consisted of personnel mainly from the North-East. Many in the South also felt they were short-changed when the IFA were offering fund assistance and the parent body did little to encourage the growth of the game outside of the North-East.

Many from the North countered that it was from Belfast and its environs that soccer grew, there were more competitive clubs in Belfast, it embraced professionalism long before everywhere else and the success of the Belfast clubs in league and cup competitions was testament to the superiority of football in Belfast. It could also be argued that the attendance record at IFA meetings of representatives from Leinster and Munster was poor in the extreme, justifying the decision not to grant them additional representation on key committees.

There were a number of trying episodes between the IFA and the Leinster Football Association long before the schism of 1921, most notably the saga involving William Sheffield, the former secretary of the Leinster body. If anything, the interference from the IFA in this episode provided a stronger case for secession than the Shelourne–Glenavon incident that did cause the rupture.

Many in the South felt pressurised by the GAA's war on 'foreign games', its cultural nationalism campaign that did not

Conclusion

IFA CHIEF EXECUTIVE, HOWARD WELLS, AND
FAI CHIEF EXECUTIVE, JOHN DELANEY,

share a moment at the launch of the FAI and IFA Third Level Colleges and Universities Football Development Plan in 2008. Although both associations enjoy more cordial relations between each other, no clear overtures have been made to reconvene talks on unity in Irish soccer as of yet.

Courtesy of Inpho Photography

abate after the Free State was formed. Soccer, a game with many nationalists as players and administrators, could not be governed from the North. For the game to survive in the twenty-six counties, particularly in areas where the game had not previously flourished, it was felt separation from the IFA was the only course to take.

Separation from the parent body did see the game spread very quickly in the Free State in the 1920s and to most parts of the fledgling state. It also allowed the FAI to play a vital role in promoting Ireland and the new state to the world. The experience garnered from self-governance during the First World War facilitated in making the Leinster Football Association confident it could go it alone. The experience garnered from governing its own affairs once the FAI was formed, provided the southern body with the confidence and desire to maintain its independence.

The IFA may have wished to be the one governing body for all of Ireland again after the split had happened. This was never a realistic option considering how far the FAI had progressed in the 1920s. The FAI, from then on, believed it to be an equal partner to the IFA. Although only recently established, it governed an area far greater in size than that governed by the IFA. It is simplistic to believe the FAI did not reunify with the IFA because of the new political make-up of the country. There are many incidents showing the FAI would have readily accepted reunion on the basis of equality.

The split was not nurtured by national politics; it was nurtured by power. Both bodies vied for the right to govern soccer in Ireland. The IFA did not see itself just governing for the six counties of Northern Ireland, it saw itself as the national association for all of Ireland. It maintained the name, the Irish Football Association, and selected players from the whole island to assert this claim. The FAI also wanted to govern soccer for all of Ireland. It conceded its right to govern within the six counties only when it saw this as the optimum way to achieve international recognition.

The conferences held between the two bodies from 1923 to 1932 showed this battle for power clearly. The IFA, the fourth-oldest football association in the world, looked to maintain its status, to concede as little as it could. The FAI ultimately would not agree on a settlement unless it was on total equality, right down to a seat on the International Board. In many ways the conferences failed because the IFA was too cautious in relinquishing its power, being forced by the English FA to do so at different junctures. The FAI also contributed significantly to the downfall of the conferences, particularly in 1924 and 1932. The southern body, by adding additional demands just as agreement was close at hand, ensured the collapse of the conferences. The IFA, who genuinely did want a settlement, could rightly be forgiven for thinking the southerners were not serious about amalgamation.

Until the conferences held during the 1970s and 1980s, the years directly after the split offered the best opportunity for resolution. The days before 1921, with soccer governed from Belfast, too biased and unfair in the eyes of many, would never be acceptable again. The chance of an all-Ireland international team with both associations contributing equally could very easily have been achieved and to many, North and South, would have been the most desirable outcome. The fact that the closest soccer has come to union was throughout the Troubles does suggest an agreement can be reached one day. Perhaps the political climate has changed enough and the fortunes of both the Republic of Ireland and Northern Ireland soccer teams might compel the FAI and IFA to reconvene and once again realise an international soccer team for the whole island as there was before.

Notes and References

INTRODUCTION

1   *The Irish Times*, 19 October 1993, p. 4.
2   *The Irish Times*, 17 November 1993, p. 5.
3   *The Irish Times*, 14 November 1993, p. 14.
4   *Irish Independent*, 3 November 1993, p. 12.
5   A. McLoughlin with B. Evans, *A Different Shade of Green: The Alan McLoughlin Story* (Bray, Co. Wicklow: Ballpoint Press, 2014), p. 12.
6   *The Irish Times*, 4 November 1993, p. 1.
7   *Irish Independent*, 17 November 1993, p. 20.
8   *Irish Press*, 15 November 1993, p. 21.
9   *Irish Independent*, 18 November 1993, p. 28.
10 *The Irish Times*, 20 November 1993, p. A1.
11 *Irish Independent*, 18 November 1993, p. 15.
12 *Belfast Telegraph*, 18 November 1993, p. 37.
13 *Belfast Telegraph*, 18 November 1993, p. 1.
14 *Seanad Éireann Debate*, vol. 138, no. 8, 25 November 1993; available from www.oireachtas-debates.gov.ie; accessed 6 January 2015.
15 *Irish News*, 18 November 1993, p. 1.
16 *Irish Press*, 18 November 1993, p. 34.
17 *The Irish Times*, 20 November 1993, p. A1, and 13 December 1993, p. A6.
18 *The Irish Times*, 20 November 1993, p. A1.
19 *Irish News*, 19 November 1993, p. 5.
20 *Irish News*, 20 November 1993, p. 10.
21 P. Byrne, *Green is the Colour: The Story of Irish Football* (London: Carlton Books, 2012), p. 8.
22 McLoughlin with Evans, *A Different Shade of Green: The Alan McLoughlin Story*, p. 18.
23 The passing of the Parliament Act of 1911 allowed the Conservative-controlled House of Lords to veto bills for just two years from thereon, no longer permanently. See R. Fanning, *Fatal Path: British Government and Irish Revolution 1910–1922* (London: Faber and Faber, 2013).
24 J.J. Lee, *Ireland 1912–1985: Politics and Society* (Cambridge: Cambridge University Press, 1989), p. 6.

25 Irish Football Association (hereafter referred to as IFA) Senior Clubs Protest and Appeals Committee, D/4196/K/1–2, 7 March 1921.

CHAPTER ONE – THE NORTH BEGAN

1 *Belfast Newsletter*, 15 November 1785, p. 2 and *Freeman's Journal*, 18 January 1810, p. 3.
2 *Freeman's Journal*, 18 April 1793, p. 4.
3 N. Garnham, *Association Football and Society in Pre-Partition Ireland* (Belfast: Ulster Historcial Foundation, 2004), pp. 3–4.
4 Ibid., p. 4.
5 Ulster History Circle, Dictionary of Ulster Biography, available from http://www.newulsterbiography.co.uk/; accessed on 3 March 2014.
6 Garnham, *Association Football and Society in Pre-Partition Ireland*, p. 4.
7 Ulster History Circle, Dictionary of Ulster Biography, available from http://www.newulsterbiography.co.uk/; accessed on 3 March 2014.
8 R. Robinson, *History of the Queen's Park Football Club 1867–1917* (Glasgow: Hay Nisbet, 1920), p. 27.
9 A. Harvey, *Football: The First Hundred Years: The Untold Story*, (Oxford: Routledge, 2005), p. 171.
10 Robinson, *History of the Queen's Park Football Club 1867–1917*, p. 85.
11 *Belfast Newsletter*, 25 October 1878, p. 8.
12 Ulster History Circle, Dictionary of Ulster Biography, available from http://www.newulsterbiography.co.uk/; accessed on 4 March 2014.
13 S. Reid, 'Identity and cricket in Ireland in the mid-nineteenth century' *Sport in Society: Cultures, Commerce, Media, Politics*, Vol. 15, No. 2 (2012), p. 147.
14 R.V. Comerford, *Ireland: Inventing the Nation* (London: Bloomsbury Academic, 2003), p. 214.
15 J. Sugden and A. Barnier, *Sport, Sectarianism and Society in a Divided Ireland* (Leicester: Leicester University Press, 1993), pp. 47–48.
16 W.P. Hone, *Cricket in Ireland* (Tralee: The Kerryman, 1955), p. 3.
17 *Belfast Newsletter*, 20 September 1879, p. 1.
18 Ulster History Circle, Dictionary of Ulster Biography, available from http://www.newulsterbiography.co.uk/; accessed on 4 March 2014.
19 Ibid.
20 N. Garnham, *The Origins and Development of Football in Ireland: Being a Reprint of R.M. Peter's Irish Football Annual of 1880* (Belfast: Ulster Historical Foundation, 1999), p. 163.
21 Ibid., p. 162.
22 *Belfast Newsletter*, 18 October 1879 p. 4, and 3 January 1880, p. 1
23 *Belfast Newsletter*, 18 October 1880, p. 4.
24 *Belfast Newsletter*, 8 November 1880, p. 8.
25 M. Huggins, *The Victorians and Sport* (London: Bloomsbury Continuum, 2004), p. 225.
26 Byrne, *Green is the Colour: The Story of Irish Football*, p. 13.
27 IFA Minute Book 1880–1886, D/4196/AA/1, 18 November 1880.
28 Ibid.

29 Ibid., 18 November 1880.
30 Garnham, *Association Football and Society in Pre-Partition Ireland*, p. 138.
31 IFA Minute Book 1880–1886, D/4196/AA/1, 18 November 1880.
32 Ibid., 10 January 1881.
33 T. Mason, *Association Football and English Society 1863–1915* (Brighton: Harvester Press, 1980), p. 16.
34 *Belfast Newsletter*, 19 February 1881, p. 3.
35 IFA Minute Book 1880–1886, D/4196/AA/1, 10 January 1881.
36 Ibid., 14 February 1881.
37 Ibid., 7 March 1881.
38 Ibid., 14 February 1881.
39 Ibid., 16 March 1881.
40 *Ireland's Saturday Night*, 3 March 1923, p. 1.
41 Ibid.
42 IFA Minute Book 1880–1886, D/4196/AA/1, 28 April 1881.
43 Ibid., 11 April 1881.
44 *Leeds Mercury*, 26 April 1881.
45 *Belfast Newsletter*, 18 February 1882, p. 3.
46 *Freeman's Journal*, 16 February 1882, p. 6.
47 *Belfast Newsletter*, 18 February 1882, p. 3.
48 *Belfast Newsletter*, 20 February 1882.
49 The Official FA Website, available from www.thefa.com; accessed on 6 March 2014.
50 M. Brodie, *100 Years of Irish Football* (Belfast: Blackstaff Press, 1980), p. 3.
51 *Belfast Newsletter*, 20 February 1882.
52 Garnham, *Association Football and Society in Pre-Partition Ireland*, p. 35.
53 The Football Association Council Meeting and Annual General Meeting 1879–1886, 31 January 1882.
54 Ibid., 25 April 1882.
55 Ibid., 21 September 1882.
56 *Glasgow Herald*, 7 December 1882.
57 The Football Association Council Meeting and Annual General Meeting 1879–1886, 22 February 1883.
58 The International Association Football Board Meeting Minutes, 2 June 1886.
59 *Belfast Newsletter*, 14 January 1884, p. 7.
60 *Belfast Newsletter*, p. 5.
61 Mason, *Association Football and English Society 1863–1915*, p. 16.
62 M. Taylor, *The Association Game: A History of British Football* (Harlow, Middx: Routledge, 2008), p. 40.
63 IFA Minute Book 1880–1886, D/4196/AA/1, 5 December 1881.
64 *Lagan Village Juvenile*, 11 February 1882, and *Belfast Newsletter*, 4 September 1883.
65 *Belfast Newsletter*, 11 February 1884.
66 *Belfast Newsletter*, 25 March 1884.
67 Garnham, *The Origins and Development of Football in Ireland*, p. 14.
68 Garnham, *Association Football and Society in Pre-Partition Ireland*, pp. 8–11.

69 P. Rouse, 'Sport and Ireland in 1881', in A. Barnier (ed.), *Sport and the Irish: Histories, Identities, Issues* (Dublin: UCD Press, 2005), p. 9.
70 Garnham, *Association Football and Society in Pre-Partition Ireland*, p. 5.
71 Ibid., p. 11.
72 Ibid., p. 11.
73 Garnham, *The Origins and Development of Football in Ireland*, p. 8.
74 J. Bardon, 'Belfast at its Zenith', *History Ireland*, Vol. 1, No. 4 (1993), p. 48.
75 Ibid., p. 49.
76 L. O'Callaghan, *Rugby in Munster: A Social and Cultural History* (Cork: Cork University Press, 2011), p. 24.
77 E. Van Esbeck, *The Story of Irish Rugby* (London: Hutchinson, 1986), p. 16. By 1880, the year of the IFA's birth, there were ninety rugby clubs in Ireland, twelve in Belfast. By 1884, this had been reduced to three in Belfast, a reflection of the popularity soccer was gaining during that period.
78 O'Callaghan, *Rugby in Munster: A Social and Cultural History*, p. 25.
79 Van Esbeck, *The Story of Irish Rugby*, p. 24.
80 O'Callaghan, *Rugby in Munster: A Social and Cultural History*, p. 26.
81 Van Esbeck, *The Story of Irish Rugby*, p. 28.
82 Ibid., pp. 32–33.
83 Ibid., p. 33.
84 Ibid., p. 35.
85 O'Callaghan, *Rugby in Munster: A Social and Cultural History*, p. 170.
86 Ibid., p. 39.
87 Ibid., p. 41.
88 D. McAnallen, 'The Story of Gaelic Games in Ulster', Cardinal Tomás Ó Fiaich Memorial Library and Archive (2010), p. 4.

Chapter Two – 'The South has been Invaded'

1 *Freeman's Journal*, 17 September 1880, p. 6.
2 *Freeman's Journal*, 15 October 1883, p. 1.
3 Garnham, *Association Football and Society in Pre-Partition Ireland*, p. 4.
4 *Freeman's Journal*, 29 October 1883, p. 7.
5 Ibid.
6 *Freeman's Journal*, 27 November 1883, p. 2.
7 *Football Sports Weekly*, 23 January 1926, p. 1.
8 *Freeman's Journal*, 31 October 1883, p. 7.
9 Garnham, *Association Football and Society in Pre-Partition Ireland*, p. 11.
10 *Freeman's Journal*, 13 November 1883, p. 6.
11 *Freeman's Journal*, 3 December 1883, p. 8.
12 *Belfast Newsletter*, 11 February 1884, p. 5.
13 *Belfast Newsletter*, 8 November 1884.
14 G. Briggs and J. Dodd, *Leinster Football Association 100 Years Centenary Yearbook 1892–1992* (Dublin: Leinster Football Association, 1993), p. 21.
15 *Belfast Newsletter*, 24 December 1884.
16 Garnham, *Association Football and Society in Pre-Partition Ireland*, p. 19.
17 Ibid., p. 21.

18 *Freeman's Journal*, 1 November 1884, p. 6.
19 Briggs and Dodd, *Leinster Football Association 100 Years Centenary Yearbook 1892–1992*, p. 22.
20 T. Hunt, *Sport and Society in Victorian Ireland: The Case of Westmeath* (Cork: Cork University Press, 2007), p. 171.
21 F. Lynch, *A History of Athlone Town FC: The First 101 Years* (Athlone, 1991), p. 10.
22 Hunt, *Sport and Society in Victorian Ireland*, p. 180.
23 *Clonmel Chronicle*, 26 November 1879.
24 *Clonmel Chronicle*, 3 March 1880.
25 R. McElligott, *Forging a Kingdom: The GAA in Kerry 1884–1934* (Cork: The Collins Press, 2013), p. 101.
26 Garnham, *Association Football and Society in Pre-Partition Ireland*, p. 19.
27 Ibid., p. 25.
28 Briggs and Dodd, *Leinster Football Association 100 Years Centenary Yearbook 1892–1992*, p. 22.
29 Lynch, *A History of Athlone Town FC: The First 101 Years*, p. 5.
30 Garnham, *Association Football and Society in Pre-Partition Ireland*, p. 21.
31 Ibid., p. 67.
32 Ibid., p. 29.
33 Briggs and Dodd, *Leinster Football Association 100 Years Centenary Yearbook 1892–1192*, p. 22.
34 Byrne, *Green is the Colour: The Story of Irish Football*, p. 17.
35 Briggs and Dodd, *Leinster Football Association 100 Years Centenary Yearbook 1892–1992*, p. 22.
36 Ibid., p. 22.
37 Ibid., p. 26.
38 Ibid., p. 26.
39 Ibid., p. 30.
40 *Shelbourne Football Club 1895–1945: Golden Jubilee Souvenir* (Dublin: The Parkside Press, 1945), p. 11.
41 Briggs and Dodd, *Leinster Football Association 100 Years Centenary Yearbook 1892–1992*, p. 27.
42 Leinster Football Association Papers, Leinster Football Association Minute Book 1899–1902, 8 January 1900.
43 Briggs and Dodd, *Leinster Football Association 100 Years Centenary Yearbook 1892–1992*, p. 28.
44 Byrne, *Green is the Colour: The Story of Irish Football*, p. 23.
45 Leinster Football Association Papers, Leinster Football Association Minute Book 1899–1902, 21 March 1900.
46 *Freeman's Journal*, 14 May 1900, p. 16.
47 Garnham, *Association Football and Society in Pre-Partition Ireland*, p. 69.
48 Ibid., p. 6.
49 Ibid., p. 162.
50 Leinster Football Association Papers, Leinster Football Association Minute Book 1899–1902, 6 May 1901.

51 Ibid., 6 February 1902.

52 Leinster Football Association Papers, Leinster Football Association Minute Book 1902–1904, 12 February 1902.

53 Ibid., 12 March 1902.

54 Ibid., 12 March 1902.

55 Ibid., 3 April 1902.

56 Ibid., 9 April 1902.

CHAPTER THREE – AN UNEASY ALLIANCE

1 Garnham, *Association Football and Society in Pre-Partition Ireland*, p. 43.

2 Byrne, *Green is the Colour: The Story of Irish Football*, p. 36.

3 IFA Annual General Meetings 1910–1987, D/4196/U/1, 14 May 1910.

4 Garnham, *Association Football and Society in Pre-Partition Ireland*, p. 166.

5 IFA Annual General Meetings 1910–1987, D/4196/U/1, 14 May 1910.

6 Ibid., 13 May 1911.

7 D. O'Sullivan, *Sport in Cork: A History* (Dublin: The History Press, 2010), p. 99.

8 *The Irish Times*, 2 April 1910, p. 23.

9 Garnham, *Association Football and Society in Pre-Partition Ireland*, p. 20.

10 Ibid.

11 J.J. Walsh, *Recollections of a Rebel* (Tralee: The Kerryman, 1944), p. 17.

12 *Sunday Independent*, 23 September 1906, p. 9.

13 IFA Minute Book 1909–1928, D/4196/A/3, 20 May 1913.

14 Ibid., 2 September 1913.

15 Ibid., 18 November 1913.

16 Garnham, *Association Football and Society in Pre-Partition Ireland*, p. 31.

17 Briggs and Dodd, *Leinster Football Association 100 Years Centenary Yearbook 1892–1992*, p. 32.

18 Leinster Football Association Papers, Leinster Football Association Minute Book 1899–1902, 13 November 1901.

19 Garnham, *Association Football and Society in Pre-Partition Ireland*, p. 71.

20 Ibid., p. 86.

21 Ibid., p. 73.

22 Leinster Football Association Papers, Leinster Football Association Minute Book 1902–1904, 8 May 1902.

23 Ibid., 17 September 1902.

24 Ibid., 22 October 1902.

25 B. Flynn, *Political Football: The Life and Death of Belfast Celtic* (Dublin: Nonsuch Ireland, 2009), p. 48.

26 *Shelbourne Football Club 1895–1945: Golden Jubilee Souvenir*, p. 17.

27 Briggs and Dodd, *Leinster Football Association 100 Years Centenary Yearbook 1892–1992*, p. 30.

28 Leinster Football Association Papers, Leinster Football Association Minute Book 1906–1915, 13 January 1909.

29 Leinster Football Association Papers, Leinster Football Association Minute Book 1899–1902, 12 June 1901.

30 Ibid., 21 May 1902.
31 Ibid., 8 May 1902 and 11 May 1904.
32 Ibid., 18 February 1903.
33 Leinster Football Association Papers, Leinster Football Association Minute Book 1906–1915, 3 April 1907.
34 Ibid., 15 May 1907.
35 *The Irish Times*, 6 December 1906, p. 4.
36 Leinster Football Association Papers, Leinster Football Association Minute Book 1906–1915, 15 May 1907.
37 Ibid.
38 Ibid., 29 May 1907.
39 Ibid., 29 January 1908.
40 Ibid., 9 March 1908.
41 Ibid., 14 September 1908.
42 Ibid., 1 October 1908.
43 Ibid., 13 April 1908.
44 Ibid., 1 April 1908.
45 Ibid., 1 October 1908.
46 Ibid., 21 October 1908.
47 Ibid., 13 April 1909.
48 Ibid., 13 April 1909.
49 Ibid., 15 May 1909.
50 Ibid., 8 September 1909.
51 Ibid., 15 May 1909.

CHAPTER FOUR – THE FIRST RUPTURE

1 Garnham, *Association Football and Society in Pre-Partition Ireland*, p. 142.
2 *The Irish Times*, 16 May 1904, p. 7.
3 *Freeman's Journal*, 15 May 1905, p. 9.
4 Ibid.
5 *Irish Independent*, 14 May 1906, p. 5.
6 IFA Annual General Meetings 1910–1987, D/4196/U/1, 14 May 1910.
7 *Sunday Independent*, 15 May 1910, p. 7.
8 *The Irish Times*, 21 May 1910, p. 14.
9 *The Irish Times*, 16 May 1910, p. 3.
10 Garnham, *Association Football and Society in Pre-Partition Ireland*, p. 147.
11 *The Irish Times*, 20 May 1911, p. 21.
12 *Freeman's Journal*, 15 February 1912, p. 12.
13 Ibid.
14 *Irish Independent*, 15 February 1912, p. 8.
15 *Sport*, 17 February 1912, p. 2.
16 *Irish Independent*, 20 February 1912, p. 6.
17 *Sport*, 24 February 1912, p. 2.
18 *Sport*, 24 February 1912, p. 2.
19 *Irish Independent*, 16 February 1912, p. 7.
20 *Irish Independent*, 20 February 1912, p. 6.

21 *Sport*, 24 February 1912, p. 2.
22 *The Times*, 24 February 1912, p. 15.
23 Leinster Football Association Papers, Leinster Football Association Minute Book 1906–1915, 27 February 1912.
24 Ibid., 13 March 1912.
25 IFA Minute Book 1909–1928, D/4196/A/3, 7 May 1912.
26 *Sport*, 2 March 1912, p. 2.
27 *Sport*, 24 February 1912, p. 2.
28 *Sport*, 16 March 1912, p. 2.
29 *Sport*, 2 March 1912, p. 2.
30 Leinster Football Association Papers, Leinster Football Association Minute Book 1906–1915, 27 February 1912.
31 *Sport*, 16 March 1912, p. 2.
32 *Sport*, 2 March 1912, p. 2.
33 *Sport*, 9 March, 6 April, 13 April, 27 April and 4 May 1912.
34 *Sport*, 18 May 1912, p. 2.
35 *Sport*, 30 March 1912, p. 2.
36 The International Football Association Board Annual Meeting Minutes, 8 June 1912.
37 The Football Association, International Selection Committee Meeting Minutes, 19 July 1912.
38 *Sport*, 20 April 1912, p. 2.
39 *Sport*, 27 April 1912, p. 2.
40 Byrne, *Green is the Colour: The Story of Irish Football*, p. 47.
41 Irish Football League Minute Book 1909–1913, D4511/1/30, 23 May 1913.
42 *Sport*, 23 March 1912, p. 2.
43 *Sport*, 11 May 1912, p. 2.
44 *Sport*, 23 March 1912, p. 2.
45 *Sport*, 11 May 1912, p. 2.
46 IFA Annual General Meetings 1910–1987, D/4196/U/1, 11 May 1912.
47 Ibid.
48 Ibid.
49 *The Irish Times*, 13 May 1912, p. 4.
50 *Sport*, 18 May 1912, p. 2.
51 IFA Minute Book 1909–1928, D/4196/A/3, 25 June 1912.
52 *The Times*, 15 August 1912, p. 9.
53 IFA Minute Book 1909–1928, D/4196/A/3, 9 July 1912.
54 Ibid., 3 September 1912.
55 Leinster Football Association Papers, Leinster Football Association Minute Book 1906–1915, 11 September 1912.
56 Byrne, *Green is the Colour: The Story of Irish Football*, p. 47.
57 *Skibbereen Eagle*, 4 October 1913, p. 12.
58 Gaelic Athletic Association (hereafter GAA) Central Council Meeting Minutes/GAA/CC/01/02, 14 September 1913.
59 *Gaelic Athlete*, 24 January 1914, p. 3.

CHAPTER FIVE – 1912

1 Fanning, *Fatal Path: British Government and Irish Revolution 1910–1922*, p. 12.
2 Ibid., p. xiii.
3 M. Foy, 'Ulster Unionist Propaganda against Home Rule 1912–1914', *History Ireland*, Vol. 4, No. 1 (1996), p. 50.
4 A. Bryson, Dictionary of Irish Biography, available from http://dib.cambridge.org/; accessed on 14 July 2014.
5 Foy, 'Ulster Unionist Propaganda against Home Rule 1912–1914', p. 50.
6 A. Bryson, Dictionary of Irish Biography, available from http://dib.cambridge.org/; accessed on 14 July 2014.
7 IFA Annual General Meetings 1910–1987, D/4196/U/1.
8 G. Simpson, 'William Pirrie, the Titanic and Home Rule', *History Ireland*, Vol. 20, No. 2 (2012), p. 34.
9 Ibid.
10 Ibid.
11 *House of Lords Debate*, 20 February 1912, Vol. 11, cc132-6132, available from http://hansard.millbanksystems.com; accessed on 14 July 2014.
12 Flynn, *Political Football: The Life and Death of Belfast Celtic*, p. 53.
13 A.F. Parkinson, *Friends in High Places: Ulster's Resistance to Irish Home Rule, 1912–14* (Belfast: Ulster Historical Foundation, 2012), p. 22.
14 *Freeman's Journal*, 5 February 1912, p. 7.
15 *The Irish Times*, 3 February 1912, p. 8.
16 *Freeman's Journal*, 5 February 1912, p. 7.
17 *House of Lords Debate*, 12 February 1914, Vol. 15, cc148-217, available from http://hansard.millbanksystems.com; accessed on 15 July 2014.
18 Garnham, *Association Football and Society in Pre-Partition Ireland*, p. 139.
19 *Freeman's Journal*, 5 February 1912, p. 7.
20 Flynn, *Political Football: The Life and Death of Belfast Celtic*, p. 54.
21 *Freeman's Journal*, 5 February 1912, p. 7.
22 *Skibbereen Eagle*, 24 February 1912, p. 10.
23 *House of Lords Debate*, 20 February 1912, Vol. 11, cc132–6132, available from http://hansard.millbanksystems.com; accessed on 15 July 2014.
24 *Skibbereen Eagle*, 24 February 1912, p. 10.
25 *The Irish Times*, 17 February 1912, p. 1.
26 Ibid.
27 Parkinson, *Friends in High Places: Ulster's Resistance to Irish Home Rule, 1912–14*, p. 23.
28 *The Irish Times*, 17 February 1912, p. 1.
29 Ibid.
30 Ibid.
31 Ibid.
32 Ibid.
33 *Southern Star*, 10 February 1912, p. 1.
34 *Donegal News*, 10 February 1912, p. 5.
35 *Freeman's Journal*, 9 February 1912, p. 7.

36 *Southern Star*, 10 February 1912, p. 1.
37 *House of Commons Debate*, 19 February 1912, Vol. 34, cc310–418, available from http://hansard.millbanksystems.com; accessed on 15 July 2014.
38 Bardon, 'Belfast at its Zenith', p. 50.
39 Simpson, 'William Pirrie, the Titanic and Home Rule', p. 31.
40 Flynn, *Political Football: The Life and Death of Belfast Celtic*, p. 52.
41 IFA Minute Book 1909–1928, D/4196/A/3, 7 May 1912.
42 IFA Annual General Meetings 1910–1987, D/4196/U/1, 11 May 1912.
43 Byrne, *Green is the Colour: The Story of Irish Football*, p. 47.
44 The Football Association Council Meeting and Annual General Meeting 1912, 25 April 1912.
45 J. Kay and W. Vamplew, 'Beyond Altruism: British football and charity, 1877–1914', *Soccer and Society*, Vol. 11, No. 3 (2010), p. 193.
46 *House of Commons Debate*, 11 April 1912, Vol. 36, c1399, available from http://hansard.millbanksystems.com; accessed on 16 July 2014.
47 Public Record Office of Northern Ireland (PRONI), Edward Carson's Souvenir Parchment Covenant, D1496/3.
48 Flynn, *Political Football: The Life and Death of Belfast Celtic*, p. 38.
49 Garnham, *Association Football and Society in Pre-Partition Ireland*, p. 47.
50 Flynn, *Political Football: The Life and Death of Belfast Celtic*, p. 22.
51 Garnham, *Association Football and Society in Pre-Partition Ireland*, p. 64.
52 Ibid., p. 99.
53 Ibid., p. 64.
54 Flynn, *Political Football: The Life and Death of Belfast Celtic*, p. 39.
55 Ibid., pp. 40–41.
56 Ibid., p. 42.
57 Garnham, *Association Football and Society in Pre-Partition Ireland*, p. 122.
58 Ibid.
59 *The Irish Times*, 19 December 1903, p. 7.
60 *The Times*, 28 December 1903, p. 5.
61 Garnham, *Association Football and Society in Pre-Partition Ireland*, pp. 123–124.
62 Ibid.
63 Flynn, *Political Football: The Life and Death of Belfast Celtic*, p. 57.
64 *Donegal News*, 21 September 1912, p. 6.
65 *The Irish Times*, 21 September 1912, p. 1.
66 Flynn, *Political Football: The Life and Death of Belfast Celtic*, p. 59.
67 *Sunday Independent*, 15 September 1912, p. 1.
68 *Donegal News*, 21 September 1912, p. 6.
69 *The Irish Times*, 21 September 1912, p. 6.
70 Flynn, *Political Football: The Life and Death of Belfast Celtic*, p. 59.
71 *Freeman's Journal*, 16 September 1912, p. 7.
72 Bureau of Military History, 1913–21, document no. WS 919, available from http://www.bureauofmilitaryhistory.ie; accessed on 16 July 2014.
73 *The Irish Times*, 21 September 1912, p.1.
74 *Sport*, 21 September 1912, p. 3.

75 Flynn, *Political Football: The Life and Death of Belfast Celtic*, p. 61.
76 *Skibbereen Eagle*, 21 September 1912, p. 2.
77 *The Irish Times*, 21 September 1912, p. 6.
78 Ibid.
79 Flynn, *Political Football: The Life and Death of Belfast Celtic*, pp. 65–66.
80 P. Coyle, *Paradise Lost and Found: The Story of Belfast Celtic* (Edinburgh: Mainstream Publishing, 1999), p. 28, and *Irish News*, 16 September 1912.
81 *The Gaelic Athlete*, 21 September 1912, p. 1.
82 *Sport*, 21 September 1912, p. 3.
83 Ibid.
84 *Sport*, 28 September 1912, p. 3.
85 Flynn, *Political Football: The Life and Death of Belfast Celtic*, p. 68.
86 *The Irish Times*, 5 October 1912, p. 6.
87 *Sport*, 5 October 1912, p. 3.
88 *Sport*, 23 November 1912, p. 3.
89 Garnham, *Association Football and Society in Pre-Partition Ireland*, p. 128.

CHAPTER SIX – IRELAND – SOCCER CHAMPIONS OF THE WORLD

1 R. Samuel, *The British Home Football Championships 1884–1984* (Cleethorpes, Lincs.: Soccer Books, 2003).
2 Garnham, *Association Football and Society in Pre-Partition Ireland*, p. 162.
3 Samuel, *The British Home Football Championships 1884–1984*, p. 31.
4 Taylor, *The Association Game: A History of British Football*, pp. 104–105.
5 The International Football Association Board Annual Meeting Minutes, 12 June 1909.
6 IFA Minute Book 1909–1928, D/4196/A/3, 14 May 1910.
7 Samuel, *The British Home Football Championships 1884–1984*, p. 37.
8 Irish Football Association (hereafter IFA) International Minutes 1909–1966, D/4196/D/1, 3 March 1913.
9 IFA Annual General Meetings 1910–1987, D4196/U/1, 10 May 1913.
10 *Sport*, 10 January 1914, p. 2.
11 *The Irish Times*, 24 January 1914, p. 19.
12 J. Quinn, Dictionary of Irish Biography, available from http://dib.cambridge.org/; accessed on 6 May 2014.
13 *Freeman's Journal*, 14 February 1914, p. 11.
14 Ibid.
15 C. Kerrigan, 'Ireland's greatest football team?', *History Ireland*, Vol. 13, No. 3 (2005), p. 28.
16 Ibid.
17 Ibid.
18 M. Coleman, Dictionary of Irish Biography, available from http://dib.cambridge.org/; accessed on 6 May 2014.
19 Kerrigan, 'Ireland's Greatest Football Team?' pp. 28–29.
20 J. Shanahan, Dictionary of Irish Biography, available from http://dib.cambridge.org/; accessed on 6 May 2014.
21 *Sport*, 21 February 1914, p. 2.

22 *Irish Independent*, 16 February 1914, p. 4.
23 *Freeman's Journal*, 16 February 1914, p. 11.
24 *The Irish Times*, 21 February 1914, p. 19.
25 IFA Minute Book 1909–1928, D4196/A/3, 3 March 1914.
26 *Freeman's Journal*, 14 March 1914, p. 10.
27 *Irish Independent*, 14 March 1914, p. 8.
28 *Sport*, 14 March 1914, p. 2.
29 *Sport*, 21 March 1914, p. 2.
30 *Sport*, 24 January 1914, p. 2.
31 IFA International Minutes 1909–1966, D/4196/D/1, 2 March 1914.
32 *Manchester Guardian*, 9 March 1914, p. 10.
33 *Freeman's Journal*, 11 March 1914, p. 1.
34 Kerrigan, 'Ireland's greatest football team?', p. 29.
35 *Irish Independent*, 16 March 1914, p. 8.
36 *Sport*, 21 March 1914, p. 2.
37 Ibid.
38 Ibid.
39 *Sport*, 28 March 1914, p. 2.
40 *Irish Independent*, 16 March 1914, p. 4.
41 IFA Minute Book 1909–1928, D4196/A/3, 28 April 1914.
42 IFA Annual General Meetings 1910–1987, D4196/U/1, 9 May 1914.
43 *Sport*, 9 May 1914, p. 2.
44 For composition of Irish teams, see *Sport, Irish Independent, Freeman's Journal, The Irish Times*, IFA International Minutes 1909–1966, D/4196/D/1, and Northern Ireland Footballing Greats, available from http://nifootball.blogspot.ie/.

CHAPTER SEVEN – THE WORLD GOES TO WAR

 1 J.E.A. Connell Jr, 'British Army First World War Recruitment in Ireland' *History Ireland*, Vol. 22, No. 4 (2014), p. 66.
 2 C. Pennell, 'Going to war', *Our War: Ireland and the Great War* (ed. J. Horne) (Dublin: Royal Irish Academy, 2008), p. 37.
 3 Fanning, *Fatal Path: British Government and Irish Revolution 1910–1922*, p. 126.
 4 Pennell, 'Going to war', *Our War: Ireland and the Great War*, p. 37.
 5 Ibid., p. 39.
 6 J. Horne, 'Our War, our History', *Our War: Ireland and the Great War*, p. 8.
 7 D. Fitzpatrick, 'Home front and everyday life', *Our War: Ireland and the Great War*, p. 133.
 8 E. Madigan, '"A Seamless Robe of Irish Experience": the First World War, the Irish Revolution and centenary commemoration', *History Ireland*, Vol. 22, No. 4 (2014), p. 14.
 9 Madigan, '"A Seamless Robe of Irish Experience": the First World War, the Irish Revolution and centenary commemoration', p. 14, and K. Myers, 'Crunching the Numbers and Busting Myths', *History Ireland*, Vol. 22, No. 4 (2014), p. 40.
10 P. Orr, '200,000 volunteer soldiers', *Our War: Ireland and the Great War*, p. 66.
11 *Sport*, 30 October 1915, p. 1.

12 Ibid.

13 Orr, '200,000 volunteer soldiers', *Our War: Ireland and the Great War*, p. 65.

14 Fitzpatrick, 'Home front and everyday life', *Our War: Ireland and the Great War*, p. 133.

15 M. Laffan, 'Two Irish States' *The Crane Bag*, Vol. 8, No. 1, Ireland: Dependence and Independence (1984), p. 29.

16 Pennell, 'Going to war', *Our War: Ireland and the Great War*, p. 39.

17 Orr, '200,000 volunteer soldiers', *Our War: Ireland and the Great War*, p. 66.

18 Briggs and Dodd, *Leinster Football Association 100 Years Centenary Yearbook 1892–1992*, p. 40.

19 Madigan, '"A Seamless Robe of Irish Experience": the First World War, the Irish Revolution and centenary commemoration', p. 14.

20 Pennell, 'Going to war', *Our War: Ireland and the Great War*, p. 40.

21 Ibid., p. 41.

22 Ibid., p. 43.

23 Fitzpatrick, 'Home front and everyday life', *Our War: Ireland and the Great War*, p. 137.

24 Ibid., p. 139.

25 Ibid., p. 138.

26 Van Esbeck, *The Story of Irish Rugby*, p. 82.

27 *Sport*, 19 September 1914, p. 2.

28 Ibid.

29 *Sport*, 17 October 1914, p. 2.

30 O'Callaghan, *Rugby in Munster: A Social and Cultural History*, p. 46.

31 W. Murphy, 'The GAA During the Irish Revolution, 1913–1923', M. Cronin, W. Murphy, P. Rouse (eds), *The Gaelic Athletic Association 1884–2009* (Dublin: Irish Academic Press, 2009), p. 67.

32 Courtesy of Dónal McAnallen, Ulster GAA.

33 GAA Annual Congress Meeting Minutes, 4 April 1915.

34 *Gaelic Athlete*, 27 March 1915, p. 2.

35 *Gaelic Athlete*, 29 August 1914, p. 1.

36 D. Goldblatt, *The Ball is Round: A Global History of Football* (London: Penguin, 2006), p. 79.

37 The Football Association Minute Book 1914–1915, 31 August 1914.

38 Ibid., 31 August 1914.

39 IFA Minute Book 1909–1928, D4196/A/3, 8 September 1914.

40 Ibid., 31 August 1914.

41 The Football Association Minute Book 1914–1915, 4 and 10 September 1914.

42 Goldblatt, *The Ball is Round: A Global History of Football*, p. 80.

43 U. Hesse-Lichtenberger, *Tor!: The Story of German Football* (London: WSC Books, 2003), p. 40.

44 Goldblatt, *The Ball is Round: A Global History of Football*, pp. 80–81.

45 *House of Commons Debate*, 23 November 1914, Vol. 68, cc762–3, available from http://hansard.millbanksystems.com; accessed on 20 July 2014.

46 *House of Commons Debate*, 19 November 1914, Vol. 68, cc576–653, available from http://hansard.millbanksystems.com; accessed on 20 July 2014.

47 *House of Commons Debate*, 26 November 1914, Vol. 68, cc1305, available from http://hansard.millbanksystems.com; accessed on 20 July 2014.

48 The Football Association Minute Book 1914–1915, 12 October 1914.

49 *House of Commons Debate*, 1 March 1915, Vol. 70, cc589–623, available from http://hansard.millbanksystems.com; accessed on 20 July 2014.

50 *Sport*, 19 September 1914, p. 5.

51 The Football Association Minute Book 1914–1915, 5 December 1914.

52 *The Irish Times*, 12 December 1914, p. 10.

53 The Football Association Minute Book 1914–1915, 14 December 1914.

54 IFA Minute Book 1909–1928, D4196/A/3, 12 January 1915.

55 Ibid., 17 November 1914.

56 Ibid., 17 November 1914.

57 IFA Annual General Meetings 1910–1987, D/4196/U/1, 8 May 1915.

58 *Sport*, 26 September 1914, p. 2.

59 *Sport*, 19 December 1914, p. 2.

60 Byrne, *Green is the Colour: The Story of Irish Football*, p. 53.

61 Briggs and Dodd, *Leinster Football Association 100 Years Centenary Yearbook 1892–1992*, p. 40.

62 *Sport*, 17 April 1915, p. 2.

63 *Sport*, 23 January 1915, p. 2.

64 *Sport*, 13 February 1915, p. 2.

65 *Sport*, 24 April 1915, p. 2.

66 Northern Ireland Footballing Greats, available from http://nifootball.blogs pot.ie; accessed on 31 August 2014.

67 D. Needham, *Ireland's First Real World Cup: The Story of the 1924 Ireland Olympic Football Team* (Dublin: The Manuscript Publisher, 2012), p. 149.

68 *Sport*, 29 May 1915, p. 3.

69 *Sport*, 31 July 1915, p. 3.

70 *Sport*, 28 August 1915, p. 2.

71 IFA Annual General Meetings 1910–1987, D/4196/U/1, 13 May 1916.

72 Ibid., 12 May 1917.

73 Leinster Football Association Minute Book 1906–1915, 9 September 1914.

74 *Sport*, 17 April 1915, p. 2.

75 *Sport*, 22 May 1915, p. 2.

76 IFA Minute Book 1909–1928, D4196/A/3.

77 *Sport*, 1 May 1915, p. 2.

78 *Sport*, 26 September 1914, p. 2.

79 *Sport*, 20 March 1915, p. 2.

80 *Sport*, 3 October 1914, p. 2.

81 *Sport*, 17 October 1914, p. 2.

82 *Sport*, 26 December 1914, p. 2.

83 IFA Minute Book 1909–1928, D4196/A/3, 12 January 1915.

84 *Sport*, 23 January 1914, p. 2.

85 *Sport*, 6 March 1915, p. 2.

86 *Sport*, 17 April 1915, p. 2.

87 IFA Minute Book 1909–1928, D4196/A/3, 20 April 1915.

88 *Sport*, 26 December 1914, p. 2.

89 IFA Minute Book 1909–1928, D4196/A/3, 7 December 1914.

90 IFA Annual General Meetings 1910–1987, D/4196/U/1, 8 May 1915.

91 Ibid.

92 Ibid.

93 *Sport*, 13 February 1915, p. 2.

94 Ibid.

95 Goldblatt, *The Ball is Round: A Global History of Football*, p. 81.

96 *Sport*, 24 April 1915, p. 2.

97 *Sport*, 29 May 1915, p. 3.

98 *Sport*, 19 June 1915, p. 3.

99 *Sport*, 26 June 1915, p. 3.

100 *Sport*, 24 July 1915, p. 3.

101 *Irish Independent*, 31 August 1916, p. 5.

102 *Irish Independent*, 23 October 1915, p. 3.

103 IFA Minute Book 1909–1928, D4196/A/3, 10 August 1915.

104 *Freeman's Journal*, 11 August 1915, p. 9.

105 *Sport*, 21 August 1915, p. 3.

106 Ibid.

107 Irish Football League Papers, Belfast and District Football League 1915–1916, D4511/8/1, 15 September 1915.

108 *Sport*, 18 September 1915, p. 3.

109 IFA Annual General Meetings 1910–1987, D/4196/U/1, 13 May 1916.

110 IFA Minute Book 1909–1928, D4196/A/3, 30 May 1916.

111 Briggs and Dodd, *Leinster Football Association 100 Years Centenary Yearbook 1892–1992*, p. 40.

112 IFA Annual General Meetings 1910–1987, D/4196/U/1, 12 May 1917.

113 Ibid., 11 May 1918.

CHAPTER EIGHT – 'THE USELESS TAIL OF AN INEPT AND MORIBUND ORGANISATION'

1 Orr, '200,000 volunteer soldiers', *Our War: Ireland and the Great War*, p. 75.

2 *Dáil Éireann Debates*, Vol. F, 21 January 1919, available from www.oireachtas-debates.gov.ie; accessed 29 July 2014.

3 IFA Minute Book 1909–1928, D4196/A/3, 12 January 1915.

4 *Sport*, 23 January 1915, p. 2.

5 *Sport*, 24 April 1915, p. 2.

6 Ibid.

7 *Sport*, 8 May 1915, p. 2.

8 IFA Annual General Meetings 1910–1987, D/4196/U/1, 8 May 1915.

9 *Sport*, 29 May 1915, p. 3.

10 *Freeman's Journal*, 20 November 1918, p. 6.

11 IFA Minute Book 1909–1928, D4196/A/3, 19 November 1918.

12 Brodie, *100 Years of Irish Football*, p. 14.

13 IFA Annual General Meetings 1910–1987, D/4196/U/1, 10 May 1919.

14 *Sunday Independent*, 11 May 1919, p. 7.
15 IFA Annual General Meetings 1910–1987, D/4196/U/1, 10 May 1919.
16 *Sunday Independent*, 11 May 1919, p. 7.
17 *The Irish Times*, 12 May 1919, p. 6.
18 IFA Annual General Meetings 1910–1987, D/4196/U/1, 10 May 1919.
19 Ibid.
20 IFA Minute Book 1909–1928, D4196/A/3, 20 May 1919.
21 Ibid., 25 February 1918.
22 Ibid., 24 June 1919.
23 Garnham, *Association Football and Society in Pre-Partition Ireland*, p. 175.
24 IFA Minute Book 1909–1928, D4196/A/3, 24 June 1919.
25 Marcus de Búrca, *The GAA: A History* (Dublin: Gill and Macmillan, 1980), p. 108.
26 *Freeman's Journal*, 20 September 1917, p. 6.
27 GAA Central Council Meeting Minutes, GAA/CC/01/02, 20 July 1918.
28 *Meath Chronicle*, 27 July 1918, p. 1.
29 IFA Minute Book 1909–1928, D4196/A/3, 24 June 1919.
30 Ibid., 11 November 1919.
31 Garnham, *Association Football and Society in Pre-Partition Ireland*, p. 175, and Byrne, *Green is the Colour: The Story of Irish Football*, p. 56.
32 IFA Minute Book 1909–1928, D4196/A/3, 11 November 1919.
33 Byrne, *Green is the Colour: The Story of Irish Football*, p. 57.
34 Garnham, *Association Football and Society in Pre-Partition Ireland*, p. 176.
35 Ibid., p. 175.
36 Byrne, *Green is the Colour: The Story of Irish Football*, p. 60.
37 Flynn, *Political Football: The Life and Death of Belfast Celtic*, p. 80.
38 *The Irish Times*, 10 March 1919, p. 3.
39 Flynn, *The Life and Death of Belfast Celtic*, p. 80.
40 Ibid., p. 83.
41 *The Irish Times*, 5 January 1920, p. 8.
42 IFA Minute Book 1909–1928, D4196/A/3, 13 January 1920.
43 *The Kerryman*, 20 March 1920, p. 1.
44 Flynn, *The Life and Death of Belfast Celtic*, p. 90.
45 *The Irish Times*, 18 March 1920, p. 5.
46 Ibid.
47 Flynn, *The Life and Death of Belfast Celtic*, p. 88.
48 IFA Protests and Appeals 1912–1922, D4196/K/1-2, 19 March 1920.
49 Ibid.
50 Ibid.
51 *The Irish Times*, 27 March 1920, p. 4.
52 *Freeman's Journal*, 29 March 1920, p. 4.
53 IFA Minute Book 1909–1928, D4196/A/3, 30 March 1920.
54 Ibid.
55 IFA Annual General Meetings 1910–1987, D/4196/U/1, 8 May 1920.
56 IFA Minute Book 1909–1928, D4196/A/3, 20 May 1920.

57 *The Irish Times*, 15 June 1920, p. 3.
58 IFA Senior Clubs' Protests and Appeals 1912–1922, D4196/K/1-2, 13 September 1920.
59 Ibid., 8 October 1920.
60 *Sport*, 14 May 1921, p. 3.
61 *The Irish Times*, 29 May 1920, p. 8.
62 Flynn, *Political Football: The Life and Death of Belfast Celtic*, p. 14.
63 R. Lynch, 'The People's Protectors?: The Irish Republican Army and the "Belfast Pogrom", 1920–1922', *Journal of British Studies*, Vol. 47, No. 2 (2008), p. 375.
64 Ibid.
65 Seán MacEntee TD, *Dáil Éireann Debates*, Vol. F, No. 16, 2 July 1931, available from www.oireachtas-debates.gov.ie; accessed 16 January 2015.
66 *Christian Science Monitor*, 14 October 1920, p. 6.
67 IFA Senior Clubs Protests and Appeals 1912–1922, D4196/K/1-2, 13 January 1921.
68 *Sport*, 8 January 1921, p. 9.
69 *Northern Whig and Belfast Post*, 19 February 1921, p. 3.
70 *Sport*, 12 March 1921, p. 14.

CHAPTER NINE – 'CUT THE PAINTER'

1 IFA Minute Book 1909–1928, D4196/A/3, 13 January 1920.
2 Ibid., 26 August 1920.
3 Garnham, *Association Football and Society in Pre-Partition Ireland*, p. 150.
4 *Gaelic Athlete*, 22 March 1913, p. 1.
5 IFA Minute Book 1909–1928, D4196/A/3, 1 April 1913.
6 IFA Annual General Meetings 1910–1987, D/4196/U/1, 11 May 1912 and 11 May 1918.
7 IFA Annual General Meetings 1910–1987, D/4196/U/1, for lists of all committee and sub-committee membership make-ups from 1910 to 1921.
8 IFA Annual General Meetings 1910–1987, D/4196/U/1, 10 May 1912.
9 Ibid., 14 May 1921.
10 IFA Protests and Appeals 1912–1922, D4196/K/1–2, 13 January 1921.
11 *Irish News*, 28 February 1921, p. 2.
12 IFA Minute Book 1909–1928, D4196/A/3, 22 March 1921.
13 *Irish Field*, 8 January 1921, p. 4.
14 Byrne, *Green is the Colour: The Story of Irish Football*, p. 62.
15 Ibid., p. 64.
16 Ibid., p. 62.
17 Garnham, *Association Football and Society in Pre-Partition Ireland*, p. 193.
18 *Irish Field*, 8 January 1921, p. 4.
19 See the *Belfast Telegraph* and the *Irish News* from January to March 1921 where a disproportionate number of violent incidents in Dublin compared with Belfast were reported.
20 *Belfast Telegraph*, 15 February 1921, p. 3, and 28 February 1921, p. 6.

21 *The Irish Times*, 14 January 1921, p. 5.

22 *The Irish Times*, 31 January 1921, p. 4.

23 *The Irish Times*, 3 February 1921, p. 5.

24 *The Irish News*, 24 February 1921, p. 2.

25 *The Irish Times*, 7 February 1921, p. 5.

26 *The Irish Times*, 14 February 1921, p. 4.

27 *The Irish Times*, 31 March 1921, p. 5.

28 *The Irish Times*, 15 March 1921, p. 5.

29 *Irish News*, 5 March 1921, p. 5.

30 D.W. Cunnane, 'The Troubles in Belfast: An Anatomy of Sectarian and Political Violence, 1920–1922' (Yale University PhD thesis, 2005), pp. 94–95.

31 Ibid., p. 133.

32 *Sport*, 22 January 1921, p. 2.

33 *Shelbourne Football Club 1895–1945: Golden Jubilee Souvenir*, p. 23.

34 IFA Senior Clubs Protests and Appeals 1912–1922, D4196/K/1–2, 7 March 1921.

35 *Sport*, 12 March 1921, p. 14.

36 Ibid.

37 *Evening Herald*, 8 March 1921, p. 4.

38 *Irish Field*, 12 March 1921, p. 6.

39 *Irish News*, 14 March 1921, p. 2.

40 *Football Sports Weekly*, 2 July 1927, p. 3.

41 *Northern Whig and Belfast Post*, 19 March 1921, p. 3.

42 IFA Senior Club Protests and Appeals 1912–1922, D4196/K/1–2, 17 March 1921.

43 Ibid., 17 March 1921.

44 Leinster Football Association Papers, Leinster Football Association Minute Book 1915–1922, 14 March 1921

45 Ibid., 14 March 1921.

46 *Sport*, 19 March 1921, p. 3.

47 *Sport*, 1 May 1915, p. 2.

48 *Irish Field*, 19 March 1921, p. 12.

49 IFA Annual General Meetings 1910–1987, D/4196/U/1, 14 May 1921.

50 IFA Emergency Minutes 1909–1943, D4196/N/1, 17 March 1921.

51 *Evening Herald*, 15 March 1921, p. 4; *Irish News*, 14 March 1921, p. 2, and *Irish Field*, 19 March 1921, p. 12.

52 *Northern Whig and Belfast Post*, 23 March 1921, p. 3.

53 IFA Minute Book 1909–1928, D4196/A/3, 22 March 1921.

54 *The Irish Times*, 9 February 1921, p. 3.

55 Garnham, *Association Football and Society in Pre-Partition Ireland*, p. 185.

56 Needham, *Ireland's First Real World Cup: The Story of the 1924 Ireland Olympic Football Team*, p. 32.

57 *Evening Herald*, 15 February 1921, p. 3.

58 *The Irish Times*, 24 March 1921, p. 7.

59 *Irish News*, 23 March 1921, p. 2.
60 *The Irish Times*, 24 March 1921, p. 7.
61 Garnham, *Association Football and Society in Pre-Partition Ireland*, p. 185.
62 *Irish Field*, 16 April 1921, p. 5.
63 *The Irish Times*, 9 February 1946, p. 5.
64 *The Irish Times*, 1 June 1935, p. 12.
65 *The Irish Times*, 21 May 1935, p. 8.
66 *Irish Independent*, 9 June 1936.
67 *The Irish Times*, 25 May 1938, p. 7.
68 *Irish News*, 23 March 1921, p. 2.
69 Ibid.
70 IFA Minute Book 1909–1928, D4196/A/3, 22 March 1921.
71 Ibid.
72 *Sport*, 2 April 1921, p. 3.
73 Ibid.
74 Ibid.
75 Leinster Football Association Papers, Leinster Football Association Minute Book 1915–1922, 7 April 1921.
76 *Sport*, 16 April 1921, p. 4.
77 Ibid.
78 *Sport*, 23 April 1921, p. 10.
79 Leinster Football Association Papers, Leinster Football Association Minute Book 1915–1922, 4 May 1921.
80 Ibid.
81 Census of Ireland 1911, available at www.census.nationalarchives.ie; accessed on 1 August 2014.
82 Leinster Football Association Papers, Leinster Football Association Minute Book 1915–1922, 11 May 1921.
83 Briggs and Dodd, *Leinster Football Association 100 Years Centenary Yearbook 1892–1992*, p. 43.
84 *Sport*, 21 May 1921, p. 3.
85 IFA Emergency Minutes 1909–1943, D4196/N/1, 6 April 1921.
86 IFA Annual General Meetings 1910–1987, D/4196/U/1, 14 May 1921.
87 *Sport*, 21 May 1921, p. 3.
88 IFA Annual General Meetings 1910–1987, D/4196/U/1, 14 May 1921.
89 Ibid.
90 Ibid.
91 Ibid.
92 Ibid.
93 Ibid.
94 Byrne, *Green is the Colour: The Story of Irish Football*, p. 74.
95 *Sport*, 14 May 1921, p. 10.
96 *Sport*, 28 May 1921, p. 3.
97 Ibid.
98 *Irish Independent*, 2 June 1921, p. 7.
99 *Freeman's Journal*, 2 June 1921, p. 7.

100 Irish Football League Minute Book, 1913–1923, D4511/1/31, 27 May 1921.
101 *Irish News*, 28 May 1921, p. 2.
102 *Irish Independent*, 2 June 1921, p. 7.
103 Ibid.
104 *Freeman's Journal*, 2 June 1921, p. 7.
105 Ibid.
106 *Irish Independent*, 2 June 1921, p. 7.
107 *Ireland's Saturday Night*, 4 June 1921, p. 4.
108 IFA Minute Book 1909–1928, D4196/A/3, 7 June 1921.
109 IFA Emergency Minutes 1909–1943, D4196/N/1, 26 June 1921.
110 Ibid.

CHAPTER TEN – THE FOOTBALL ASSOCIATION OF IRELAND IS BORN

1 Garnham, *Association Football and Society in Pre-Partition Ireland*, p. 178.
2 T.P. Walsh, *Twenty Years of Irish Soccer* (Dublin: Sports Publicity Services, 1941), p. 24.
3 Ibid.
4 *Irish Independent*, 3 September 1921, p. 7.
5 IFA Emergency Minutes 1909–1943, D4196/N/1, 26 June 1921.
6 Ibid., 22 July 1921.
7 Ibid., 19 August 1921.
8 IFA Minute Book 1909–1928, D4196/A/3, 30 August 1921.
9 M. Brodie, *Linfield: 100 Years* (Belfast: Linfield Football and Athletic Club, 1985), p. 4.
10 *Ireland's Saturday Night*, 23 July 1921, p. 4.
11 Ibid., p. 1.
12 *Ireland's Saturday Night*, 26 November 1921, p. 1.
13 IFA Minute Book 1909–1928, D4196/A/3, 30 August 1921.
14 Ibid., 3 October 1921.
15 *The Irish Times*, 21 September 1921, p. 4.
16 *Ireland's Saturday Night*, 8 October 1921, p. 4
17 *The Irish Times*, 21 September 1921, p. 4.
18 *Ireland's Saturday Night*, 20 August 1921, p. 4.
19 The Football Association of Ireland (hereafter FAI) Papers, International Minute Book, P137/1, 17 March 1922.
20 Garnham, *Association Football and Society in Pre-Partition Ireland*, p. 178.
21 *Ireland's Saturday Night*, 3 December 1921, p. 6.
22 *Ireland's Saturday Night*, 20 August 1921, p. 4.
23 Garnham, *Association Football and Society in Pre-Partition Ireland*, p. 178.
24 *Sunday Independent*, 7 February 1954, p. 10.
25 IFA Minute Book 1909–1928, D4196/A/3, 8 November 1921.
26 Ibid., 14 November 1922.
27 Walsh, *Twenty Years of Irish Soccer*, p. 24.
28 Ibid.
29 *The Irish Times*, 10 April 1922, p. 7.
30 S. Ryan, *The Official Book of the FAI Cup* (Dublin: Liberties Press, 2011), p. 14.

31 Walsh, *Twenty Years of Irish Soccer*, p. 24.
32 *Ireland's Saturday Night*, 25 March 1922, p. 4.
33 Ryan, *The Official Book of the FAI Cup*, p. 12.
34 The FAI Papers, International Minute Book, P137/1, 17 March 1922.
35 Byrne, *Green is the Colour: The Story of Irish Football*, p. 74.
36 Briggs and Dodd, *Leinster Football Association 100 Years Centenary Yearbook 1892–1992*, pp. 43–44.
37 IFA Minute Book 1909–1928, D4196/A/3, 7 February 1922.
38 Ibid.
39 Ibid., 7 March 1922.
40 The Football Association Council Meeting and Annual General Meeting 1921–1922, 27 March 1922.
41 IFA Annual General Meetings 1910–1987, D/4196/U/1, 13 May 1922.
42 Ibid.
43 *Ireland's Saturday Night*, 20 May 1922, p. 5.
44 Ibid.
45 *Sunday Independent*, 14 May 1922, p. 5.
46 *Ireland's Saturday Night*, 20 May 1922, p. 5.
47 *Sunday Independent*, 14 May 1922, p. 5.
48 IFA Minute Book 1909–1928, D4196/A/3, 11 April 1922.
49 *Freeman's Journal*, 15 May 1922, p. 8.
50 IFA Minute Book 1909–1928, D4196/A/3, 6 June 1922.
51 IFA Annual General Meetings 1910–1987, D/4196/U/1, 13 May 1922.
52 *Ireland's Saturday Night*, 27 May 1922, p. 2.
53 *Ireland's Saturday Night*, 15 July 1922, p. 2.
54 IFA Minute Book 1909–1928, D4196/A/3, 12 December 1922.
55 Brodie, *Linfield: 100 Years*, p. 4.
56 IFA Minute Book 1909–1928, D4196/A/3, 12 December 1922.
57 Byrne, *Green is the Colour: The Story of Irish Football*, p. 78.
58 Garnham, *Association Football and Society in Pre-Partition Ireland*, p. 194.
59 Needham, *Ireland's First Real World Cup: The Story of the 1924 Ireland Olympic Football Team*, p. 23.
60 Ibid., p. 24.
61 IFA Minute Book 1909–1928, D4196/A/3, 22 January 1923.
62 The FAI Papers, International Minute Book, P137/1, 7 February 1922.
63 The International Football Association Board Annual Meeting Minutes, 10 June 1922.
64 *Ireland's Saturday Night*, 17 June 1922, p. 3.
65 GAA Central Council Meeting Minutes, GAA/CC/01/02, 15 October 1921.

CHAPTER ELEVEN – SPORT IN A DIVIDED ISLAND

1 *Ireland's Saturday Night*, 18 November 1922, p. 1.
2 P. Reynolds, '"A First-Class Split": political conflict in Irish athletes, 1924–1940', *History Ireland*, Vol. 20, No. 4 (2012), p. 30.
3 *Ireland's Saturday Night*, 27 May 1922, p. 4.
4 *Ireland's Saturday Night*, 17 June 1922, p. 3.

5 P. Griffin, *The Politics of Irish Athletics 1850–1990* (Ballinamore, County Leitrim: Marathon Publications, 1990), p. 68.

6 Reynolds, '"A First-Class Split": political conflict in Irish athletes, 1924–1940', p. 30.

7 Griffin, *The Politics of Irish Athletics 1850–1990*, p. 72.

8 *Football Sports Weekly*, 5 September 1925, p. 4.

9 Reynolds, '"A First-Class Split": political conflict in Irish athletes, 1924–1940', p. 31.

10 Ibid.

11 *Football Sports Weekly*, 5 September 1925, p. 4.

12 *Football Sports Weekly*, 3 October 1925, p. 19.

13 Griffin, *The Politics of Irish Athletics 1850–1990*, p. 77.

14 Reynolds, '"A First-Class Split": political conflict in Irish athletes, 1924–1940', p. 31.

15 *Football Sports Weekly*, 29 August 1925, p.2.

16 Reynolds, '"A First-Class Split": political conflict in Irish athletes, 1924–1940', pp. 31–32.

17 Ibid., p. 32.

18 T. Hunt, '"In our case, it seems obvious the British Organising Committee piped the tune": the campaign for recognition of "Ireland" in the Olympic Movement, 1935–1956', *Sport in Society: Cultures, Commerce, Media, Politics*, published online 2 January 2015, p. 2.

19 Reid, 'Identity and cricket in Ireland in the mid-nineteenth century', pp. 147–149.

20 *The Irish Times*, 8 May 1890, p. 7.

21 *The Irish Times*, 5 April 1890.

22 J.C. Hiles, *A History of Senior Cricket in Ulster* (Comber, County Down: Hiltop Publications, 2003), p. 93.

23 *The Irish Times*, 17 August 1901, p. 18.

24 Hiles, *A History of Senior Cricket in Ulster*, p. 93.

25 *The Irish Times*, 9 March 1909, p. 8.

26 *The Irish Times*, 5 June 1909, p. 5.

27 *The Irish Times*, 14 June 1909, p. 4.

28 Hiles, *A History of Senior Cricket in Ulster*, p. 94.

29 Ibid., p. 95.

30 *The Irish Times*, 17 September 1923, p. 4.

31 *Ireland's Saturday Night*, 10 November 1923, p. 3.

32 Hone, *Cricket in Ireland*, p. 154.

33 Hiles, *A History of Senior Cricket in Ulster*, p. 94.

34 T. Wynne (Comp.) and C. Glennon (ed.), *Ninety Years of the Irish Hockey Union* (Naas: Leinster Leader, 1985), p. 66 and p. 70.

35 Sugden and Barnier, *Sport, Sectarianism and Society in a Divided Ireland*, p. 63.

36 Ibid.

37 W.A. Menton, *The Golfing Union of Ireland 1891–1991* (Dublin: Gill and Macmillan, 1991), p. 54.

38 D. Ferriter, *Judging Dev: A Reassessment of the Life and Legacy of Éamon de Valera*, (Dublin: Royal Irish Academy, 2007), p. 222.

39 Van Esbeck, *The Story of Irish Rugby*, p. 83.

40 O'Callaghan, *Rugby in Munster: A Social and Cultural History*, pp. 166–167.

41 Census of Ireland 1911, available at www.census.nationalarchives.ie; accessed on 21 August 2014.

42 *Ireland's Saturday Night*, 22 September 1923, p. 5.

43 Van Esbeck, *The Story of Irish Rugby*, p. 88.

44 *Ireland's Saturday Night*, 29 September 1923, p. 6.

45 N. Garnham, 'Accounting for the Early Success of the Gaelic Athletic Association', *Irish Historical Studies*, Vol. 34, No. 133, (2004), p. 71.

46 O'Callaghan, *Rugby in Munster: A Social and Cultural History*, p. 173.

47 Van Esbeck, *The Story of Irish Rugby*, p. 96.

48 O'Callaghan, *Rugby in Munster: A Social and Cultural History*, p. 80.

49 Ibid., p. 177.

50 Van Esbeck, *The Story of Irish Rugby*, p. 97.

51 O'Callaghan, *Rugby in Munster: A Social and Cultural History*, p. 173.

52 *Irish Press*, 2 July 1934, p. 7.

53 *Football Sports Weekly*, 14 November 1925, p. 5.

54 *Football Sports Weekly*, 7 November 1925, pp. 1–2.

55 *Gaelic Athlete*, 7 November 1925, p. 2.

56 *Irish Independent*, 5 January 1932, p. 1.

57 O'Callaghan, *Rugby in Munster: A Social and Cultural History*, p. 172.

58 Richard Walsh TD, 'Public Business: Finance Bill, 1931', *Dáil Éireann Debates*, Vol. 39, 2 July 1931, available from www.oireachtas-debates.gov.ie; accessed 21 August 2014.

59 National Archives of Ireland (hereafter NAI), Department of Foreign Affairs and Trade, DFA/2/1/38, *National Flag at International Rugby Football Matches, Lansdowne Road*, 5 February 1932.

60 Van Esbeck, *The Story of Irish Rugby*, p. 98.

61 Sugden and Barnier, *Sport, Sectarianism and Society in a Divided Ireland*, p. 44.

62 de Búrca, *The GAA: A History*, p. 132.

63 Ibid., p. 133.

64 P. Rouse, 'Sport and the Politics of Culture: A History of the GAA Ban 1884–1971' (UCD master's thesis, 1991) and C. Moore, *The GAA V Douglas Hyde: The Removal of Ireland's First President as GAA Patron* (Cork: The Collins Press, 2012).

65 *Gaelic Athlete*, 11 April 1925, p. 2.

66 *Gaelic Athlete*, 21 March 1925, p. 2.

67 M. Tynan, 'Association Football and Irish Society During the Inter-War Period, 1918–1939' (NUI, Maynooth, PhD thesis, 2013), p. 191.

68 Ibid., p. 193.

69 Ibid., p. 185.

70 F. McGarry, *Eoin O'Duffy: A Self-Made Hero* (Oxford: Oxford University Press, 2005), p. 45.

71 Tynan, 'Association Football and Irish Society During the Inter-War Period, 1918–1939', p. 195.

CHAPTER TWELVE – THE FOOTBALL ASSOCIATION OF THE IRISH FREE STATE IS BORN

1 IFA Minute Book 1909–1928, D4196/A/3, 22 January 1923.
2 Garnham, *Association Football and Society in Pre-Partition Ireland*, p. 179.
3 *Irish Independent*, 2 February 1923, p. 9.
4 Ibid.
5 Ibid.
6 Ibid.
7 P. Yeates, *A City in Turmoil: Dublin 1919–1921* (Dublin: Gill and Macmillan, 2012), p. 141.
8 *Evening Herald*, 10 March 1921, p. 1.
9 *Evening Herald*, 13 April 1921, p. 3.
10 *The Scotsman*, 21 August 1920, p. 10.
11 *The Observer*, 26 September 1920, p. 14.
12 *Manchester Guardian*, 12 March 1921, p. 11.
13 NAI, Department of an Taoiseach, S1095, *Belfast Boycott*, 24 January 1924.
14 NAI, North Eastern Boundary Bureau, NEBB/1/1/3, *Belfast Pogrom Statistics*, 24 May 1922.
15 The Football Association International Selection Committee Meeting Minutes 1922–1923, 9 April 1923.
16 *Irish Independent*, 2 February 1923, p. 9.
17 *The Irish Times*, 13 February 1923, p. 8.
18 *Ireland's Saturday Night*, 17 February 1923, p. 2.
19 Ibid.
20 Ibid., p. 1.
21 IFA Minute Book 1909–1928, D4196/A/3, 12 February 1923.
22 IFA Annual General Meetings 1910–1987, D/4196/U/1, 12 May 1923.
23 *Freeman's Journal*, 14 May 1923, p. 8.
24 Ibid.
25 Ibid.
26 IFA Annual General Meetings 1910–1987, D/4196/U/1, 12 May 1923.
27 *Ireland's Saturday Night*, 26 May 1923, p. 3.
28 *Ireland's Saturday Night*, 2 June 1923, p. 3.
29 IFA Emergency Minutes 1909–1943, D4196/N/1, 6 June 1923.
30 Ibid., 21 June 1923.
31 Ibid., 21 June 1923.
32 *Ireland's Saturday Night*, 16 June 1923, p. 3.
33 *Ireland's Saturday Night*, 23 June 1923, p. 3.
34 *Ireland's Saturday Night*, 16 June 1923, p. 3.
35 IFA Emergency Minutes 1909–1943, D4196/N/1, 5 July 1923.
36 *Ireland's Saturday Night*, 21 July 1923, p. 4.
37 *Ireland's Saturday Night*, 28 July 1923, p. 3.
38 IFA Emergency Minutes 1909–1943, D4196/N/1, 13 August 1923.

39 Byrne, *Green is the Colour: The Story of Irish Football*, p. 79.
40 A. Tomlinson, *FIFA (Fédération Internationale de Football Association): The Men, The Myths and The Money* (Oxford: Routledge, 2014), p. 14.
41 A. Tomlinson, 'FIFA and the men who made it', *Soccer and Society* (2007), p. 56.
42 Ibid.
43 Tomlinson, *FIFA (Fédération Internationale de Football Association): The Men, The Myths and The Money*, p. 14.
44 Tomlinson, 'FIFA and the men who made it', p. 57.
45 IFA Minute Book 1909–1928, D4196/A/3, 3 December 1912.
46 International Football Association Board, Minutes of Special Meeting, 22 February 1913.
47 Tomlinson, 'FIFA and the men who made it', p. 57.
48 Tomlinson, *FIFA (Fédération Internationale de Football Association): The Men, The Myths and The Money*, p. 54.
49 IFA Minute Book 1909–1928, D4196/A/3, 16 August 1919.
50 The Football Association, Council Meeting Minutes 1923–1924, 27 August 1923.
51 The FAI Papers, International Minute Book, P137/1, 10 May 1923.
52 Ibid., 17 March 1922.
53 Ibid., P137/1, 22 December 1922.
54 The FAI Papers, International Minute Book, P137/2, 30 December 1922.
55 The FAI Papers, International Minute Book, P137/3.
56 *Freeman's Journal*, 11 April 1923, p. 6.
57 The FAI Papers, International Minute Book, P137/3.
58 Ibid.
59 The FAI Papers, International Minute Book, P137/1, 10 May 1923.
60 Ibid.
61 K. McCarthy, *Gold, Silver and Green: The Irish Olympic Journey 1896–1924* (Cork: Cork University Press, 2011), p. 312.
62 The FAI Papers, International Minute Book, P137/1, 3 May 1923.
63 Ibid., 3 May 1923.
64 P.J. Dempsey and S. Boylan, Dictionary of Irish Biography, available from http://dib.cambridge.org/; accessed on 9 August 2014.
65 The Football Association, Council Meeting Minutes 1923–1924, 16 May 1923.
66 The FAI Papers, International Minute Book, P137/2.
67 The FAI Papers, International Minute Book, P137/3, 5 June 1923.
68 Ibid.
69 Ibid.
70 *The Irish Times*, 26 May 1923, p. 5.
71 *Ireland's Saturday Night*, 9 June 1923, p. 3.
72 Ryan, *The Official Book of the FAI Cup*, p. 16.
73 *Ireland's Saturday Night*, 24 March 1923, p. 3.
74 The Football Association, Council Meeting Minutes 1923–1924, 7 June 1923.
75 The International Football Association Board Annual Meeting Minutes, 9 June 1923.

76 *Sunday Independent*, 10 June 1923, p. 7.
77 The FAI Papers, International Minute Book, P137/2, 13 July 1923.
78 Ibid., 20 July 1923.
79 Ibid., 28 September 1923.
80 The Football Association, Council Meeting Minutes 1923–1924, 10 August 1923.
81 Ibid.
82 Byrne, *Green is the Colour: The Story of Irish Football*, p. 88.
83 The Football Association, Council Meeting Minutes 1923–1924, 9 July 1923.
84 *Ireland's Saturday Night*, 14 July 1923, p. 3.
85 Ibid.
86 IFA Minute Book 1909–1928, D4196/A/3, 21 August 1923.
87 The Football Association, Council Meeting Minutes 1923–1924, 27 August 1923.
88 The FAI Papers, International Minute Book, P137/2, 18 October 1923.
89 Ibid.
90 Ibid.
91 *Ireland's Saturday Night*, 27 October 1923, p. 6.
92 *Freeman's Journal*, 22 October 1923, p. 9.
93 *The Irish Times*, 1 November 1923, p. 3.
94 *Ireland's Saturday Night*, 22 December 1923, p. 4.
95 Byrne, *Green is the Colour: The Story of Irish Football*, p. 92.
96 *The Irish Times*, 28 November 1923, p. 8.

CHAPTER THIRTEEN – FALSE DAWN

1 The FAI Papers, International Minute Book, P137/1, 20 December 1923.
2 Ibid., 10 January 1924.
3 Walsh, *Twenty Years of Irish Soccer*, p. 25.
4 *Football Sports Weekly*, 24 October 1925, p. 1.
5 Walsh, *Twenty Years of Irish Soccer*, p. 25.
6 The Football Association, International Selection Committee Meeting Minutes 1923–1924, 17 December 1923.
7 IFA Minute Book 1909–1928, D4196/A/3, 27 November 1923.
8 Ibid., 10 December 1923.
9 *The Irish Times*, 9 January 1924, p. 3.
10 Ibid.
11 IFA Minute Book 1909–1928, D4196/A/3, 8 January 1924.
12 Ibid., 12 February 1924.
13 Ibid., D4196/A/3, 11 March 1924.
14 *The Irish Times*, 15 March 1924, p. 13.
15 *The Irish Times*, 10 March 1924, p. 9.
16 *Sport*, 15 March 1924, p. 4.
17 *The Irish Times*, 10 March 1924, p. 9.
18 *Sport*, 15 March 1924, p. 3.
19 IFA Minute Book 1909–1928, D4196/A/3, 11 March 1924.
20 The FAI Papers, International Minute Book, P137/1, 10 March 1924.

21 The FAI Papers, International Minute Book, P137/3.
22 IFA Minute Book 1909–1928, D4196/A/3, 1 April 1924.
23 IFA Annual General Meetings 1910–1987, D/4196/U/1, 10 May 1924.

Chapter Fourteen – First Olympians

1 McCarthy, *Gold, Silver and Green: The Irish Olympic Journey 1896–1924*, p. 314.
2 P. O'Sullivan, 'Ireland and the Olympic Games', *History Ireland*, Vol. 6, No. 1 (1998), p. 42.
3 Wynne (Comp.) and Glennon (ed.), *Ninety Years of the Irish Hockey Union*, p. 72.
4 Byrne, *Green is the Colour: The Story of Irish Football*, p. 95.
5 IFA Emergency Minutes 1909–1943, D4196/N/1, 15 April 1924.
6 The Football Association, Council Meeting Minutes 1923–1924, 22 October 1923.
7 *The Times*, 29 October 1927, p. 7.
8 The FAI Papers, International Minute Book, P137/1, 16 April 1924.
9 Ibid.
10 Byrne, *Green is the Colour: The Story of Irish Football*, p. 95.
11 The FAI Papers, International Minute Book, P137/1.
12 T. Carey, 'Ireland's Footballers at the Paris Olympics, 1924', *History Ireland*, Vol. 20, No. 4 (2012), p. 23.
13 The FAI Papers, International Minute Book, P137/1, 7 May 1924.
14 Carey, 'Ireland's Footballers at the Paris Olympics, 1924', p. 23.
15 D. Toms, '"Notwithstanding the Discomfort Involved": Fordson's Cup Win in 1926 and how "the Old Contemptible" were Represented in Ireland's Public Sphere During the 1920s', *Sport in History* (2013), p. 6.
16 Walsh, *Twenty Years of Irish Soccer*, pp. 25–26.
17 Carey, 'Ireland's Footballers at the Paris Olympics, 1924', p. 23.
18 The FAI Papers, International Minute Book, P137/1, 19 April 1924.
19 NAI, Department of Foreign Affairs and Trade, DFA/GR 37, *Jeux Olympiques, "Olympian Games"*, 21 May 1924.
20 Ibid., 27 May 1924.
21 Needham, *Ireland's First Real World Cup: The Story of the 1924 Ireland Olympic Football Team*, p. 149.
22 Carey, 'Ireland's Footballers at the Paris Olympics, 1924', p. 23.
23 *New York Times*, 16 June 1924.
24 NAI, Department of an Taoiseach, S3767, *National Anthem: Adoption of the Soldier's Song*, 1 February 1924.
25 Ibid., 24 April 1924.
26 Ibid., 1 February 1924.
27 Ibid., 12 July 1926.
28 R. Sherry, 'The Story of the National Anthem', *History Ireland*, Vol. 4, No. 1 (1996), p. 40.
29 Press clipping of *Irish Statesman* article in NAI, Department of an Taoiseach, S6536, *Trinity College Sports 1928–1932*, 15 June 1929.

30 NAI, Department of an Taoiseach, S3767, *National Anthem: Adoption of the Soldier's Song*, 19 October 1928.

31 NAI, Department of an Taoiseach, S6536, *Trinity College Sports 1928–1932*, 17 September 1928.

32 Sherry, 'The Story of the National Anthem', p. 42.

33 Carey, 'Ireland's Footballers at the Paris Olympics, 1924', p. 24.

34 Needham, *Ireland's First Real World Cup: The Story of the 1924 Ireland Olympic Football Team*, p. 167.

35 M. Cronin, 'Projecting the Nation through Sport and Culture: Ireland, Aonach Tailteann and the Irish Free State, 1924–1932', *Journal of Contemporary History*, Vol. 38, No. 3 (2003), p. 396.

36 Carey, 'Ireland's Footballers at the Paris Olympics, 1924', p. 23–24.

37 Ibid., p. 24.

38 Les Jeux de la 'VIII Olympiade, Paris 1924', p. 171.

39 Carey, 'Ireland's Footballers at the Paris Olympics, 1924', p. 25.

40 *The Irish Times*, 11 June 1924, p. 4.

41 The FAI Papers, International Minute Book, P137/2, 14 July 1924.

42 Needham, *Ireland's First Real World Cup: The Story of the 1924 Ireland Olympic Football Team*, p. 202.

43 *Sunday Independent*, 15 September 1924, p. 11.

CHAPTER FIFTEEN – MONOPOLISING THE NAME 'IRELAND'

1 The FAI Papers, International Minute Book, P137/1, 22 August 1924.

2 IFA Emergency Minutes – 1909–1943, D4196/N/1, 25 November 1924.

3 IFA Minute Book 1909–1928, D/4196/A/3, 30 December 1924.

4 Ibid.

5 The FAI Papers, International Minute Book, P137/1, 11 March 1925.

6 Ibid.

7 IFA Minute Book 1909–1928, D/4196/A/3, 31 March 1925.

8 *The Times*, 16 March 1925, p. 6.

9 IFA Annual General Meetings 1910–1987, D/4196/U/1, 9 May 1925.

10 *Football Sports Weekly*, 5 September 1925, p. 6.

11 IFA Emergency Minutes 1909–1943, D4196/N/1, 25 November 1924.

12 *Football Sports Weekly*, 1 October 1925, p. 1.

13 *Football Sports Weekly*, 19 September 1925, p. 12.

14 *Football Sports Weekly*, 3 October 1925, p. 1.

15 The FAI Papers, International Minute Book, P137/1, 11 May 1925.

16 The Football Association Minute Book 1925–1926, 11 July 1925.

17 IFA Minute Book 1909–1928, D/4196/A/3, 10 August 1925.

18 The Football Association Minute Book 1925–1926, 5 September 1925.

19 *Football Sport Weekly*, 12 September 1925, p. 2.

20 Ibid., p. 4.

21 *Football Sports Weekly*, 19 September 1925, p. 3.

22 *House of Commons Debate*, 8 March 1922, Vol. 151, cc1362-433, available from http://hansard.millbanksystems.com; accessed on 22 August 2014.

23 *Football Sports Weekly*, 3 October 1925, p. 7.

24 *Football Sports Weekly*, 29 August 1925, p. 7.
25 *Football Sports Weekly*, 12 December 1925, p. 1.
26 Toms, '"Notwithstanding the Discomfort Involved": Fordson's Cup Win in 1926 and how "the Old Contemptible" were Represented in Ireland's Public Sphere During the 1920s', p. 6.
27 *Football Sports Weekly*, 29 August 1925, p. 9.
28 Walsh, *Twenty Years of Irish Soccer*, p. 25.
29 Briggs and Dodd, *Leinster Football Association 100 Years Centenary Yearbook 1892–1992*, p. 45.
30 Ryan, *The Official Book of the FAI Cup*, p. 22.
31 Ibid., pp. 14–30.
32 Walsh, *Twenty Years of Irish Soccer*, p. 26.
33 Toms, '"Notwithstanding the Discomfort Involved": Fordson's Cup Win in 1926 and how "the Old Contemptible" were Represented in Ireland's Public Sphere During the 1920s', p. 7.
34 *Football Sports Weekly*, 5 June 1926, p. 1.
35 IFA Annual General Meetings 1910–1987, D4196/U/1, 13 May 1922, 12 May 1923 and 10 May 1924.
36 Ryan, *The Official Book of the FAI Cup*, p. 24.
37 Walsh, *Twenty Years of Irish Soccer*, p. 26.
38 *Football Sports Weekly*, 7 November 1925, p. 1.
39 *Football Sports Weekly*, 24 October 1925, p. 1.
40 *Football Sports Weekly*, 19 December 1925, p. 1.
41 *Football Sports Weekly*, 20 March 1926, p. 5.
42 Walsh, *Twenty Years of Irish Soccer*, p. 29.
43 *The Irish Times*, 15 March 1926, p. 11.
44 *Football Sports Weekly*, 14 August 1926, p. 11.
45 *The Irish Times*, 15 March 1926, p. 11.
46 *Football Sports Weekly*, 1 May 1926, p. 4.
47 *Football Sports Weekly*, 5 December 1925, p. 2.
48 The FAI Papers, International Minute Book, P137/1, 29 April 1925.
49 Ibid., 18 July 1925.
50 Ibid., 13 August 1925.
51 *Football Sports Weekly*, 10 October 1925, p. 2.
52 *Football Sports Weekly*, 17 October 1925, p. 1.
53 *Football Sports Weekly*, 5 December 1925, p. 2.
54 Byrne, *Green is the Colour: The Story of Irish Football*, p. 100.
55 The FAI Papers, International Minute Book, P137/1, 2 October 1925.
56 Byrne, *Green is the Colour: The Story of Irish Football*, p. 104.
57 S. Ryan, *The Boys in Green: The FAI International Story* (Edinburgh: Mainstream Publishing, 1997), p. 14.
58 Byrne, *Green is the Colour: The Story of Irish Football*, p. 106.
59 Ryan, *The Boys in Green: The FAI International Story*, p. 13.
60 Byrne, *Green is the Colour: The Story of Irish Football*, p. 105.
61 Ryan, *The Boys in Green: The FAI International Story*, p. 16.
62 Ibid., p. 17.

63 *Football Sports Weekly*, 27 March 1926, p. 2.

64 Byrne, *Green is the Colour: The Story of Irish Football*, p. 107.

65 Briggs and Dodd, *Leinster Football Association 100 Years Centenary Yearbook 1892–1992*, p. 45.

66 *The Irish Times*, 18 November 1926, p. 10.

67 Ibid.

68 Ibid.

69 IFA Emergency Minutes 1909–1943, D4196/N/1, 14 December 1926.

70 Ibid.

71 *Irish Independent*, 25 November 1926, p. 9.

72 Ibid.

73 *Football Sports Weekly*, 27 November 1926, p. 3.

74 IFA Emergency Minutes 1909–1943, D4196/N/1, 22 February 1927.

75 Ibid.

76 *Football Sports Weekly*, 12 March 1927, p. 1.

77 *Football Sports Weekly*, 5 March 1927, p. 7.

78 *Football Sports Weekly*, 19 March 1927, p. 16.

79 Ibid.

80 *Football Sports Weekly*, 26 March 1927, p. 1.

81 Ibid.

82 The Football Association Minute Book 1927–1928.

83 Byrne, *Green is the Colour: The Story of Irish Football*, p. 110.

84 The FAI Papers, International Minute Book, P137/3.

85 *Football Sports Weekly*, 11 June 1927, p. 7.

86 The FAI Papers, International Minute Book, P137/3.

87 *The Irish Times*, 1 August 1929, p. 8.

88 Walsh, *Twenty Years of Irish Soccer*, p. 133.

89 Byrne, *Green is the Colour: The Story of Irish Football*, p. 116.

CHAPTER SIXTEEN – TOWARDS ANTIPATHY

1 Briggs and Dodd, *Leinster Football Association 100 Years Centenary Yearbook 1892–1992*, p. 47.

2 Byrne, *Green is the Colour: The Story of Irish Football*, p. 134.

3 Briggs and Dodd, *Leinster Football Association 100 Years Centenary Yearbook 1892–1992*, p. 48.

4 IFA Annual General Meetings 1910–1987, D4196/U/1, 8 May 1926.

5 Ibid., 12 May 1928.

6 Ibid., 10 May 1930, 9 May 1931 and 14 May 1932.

7 Walsh, *Twenty Years of Irish Soccer*, p. 32.

8 Ibid.

9 *Football Sports Weekly*, 25 September 1926, p. 11.

10 *Football Sports Weekly*, 18 December 1926, p. 10.

11 *Football Sports Weekly*, 25 September 1926, p. 11.

12 *Football Sports Weekly*, 5 February 1927, p. 2.

13 Ryan, *The Boys in Green: The FAI International Story*, p. 217.

14 Walsh, *Twenty Years of Irish Soccer*, p. 133.

15 *The Times*, 29 October 1927, p. 7.

16 The Football Association Minute Book 1927–1928, 17 February 1928.

17 Ibid.

18 Byrne, *Green is the Colour: The Story of Irish Football*, p. 117.

19 The FAI Papers, International Minute Book, P137/3.

20 Ibid.

21 Ibid.

22 *The Irish Times*, 30 April 1930, p. 11.

23 Byrne, *Green is the Colour: The Story of Irish Football*, p. 104.

24 D. Cullen, *Freestaters: The Republic of Ireland Soccer Team 1921–1939* (Southend-on-Sea, Essex: Desert Island Books, 2007), pp. 187–192.

25 P.M. Geoghegan, Dictionary of Irish Biography, available from http://dib.cambridge.org/; accessed on 28 August 2014.

26 *The Irish Times*, 15 September 1931, p. 11.

27 P.M. Geoghegan, Dictionary of Irish Biography, available from http://dib.cambridge.org/; accessed on 28 August 2014.

28 Byrne, *Green is the Colour: The Story of Irish Football*, p. 120.

29 *The Irish Times*, 31 December 1930, p. 10.

30 Ibid.

31 Ibid.

32 The International Football Association Board Annual Meeting Minutes, 13 June 1931.

33 *Irish Independent*, 12 November 1936, p. 17.

34 *The Irish Times*, 23 February 1931, p. 11.

35 Ibid.

36 The International Football Association Board Annual Meeting Minutes, 13 June 1931.

37 *The Irish Times*, 27 January 1932, p. 11.

38 *The Irish Times*, 3 March 1932, p. 11.

39 Byrne, *Green is the Colour: The Story of Irish Football*, p. 127.

40 IFA Minute Book 1929–1944, D1496/A/4, 2 March 1932.

41 *The Irish Times*, 3 March 1932, p. 11.

42 *The Irish Times*, 14 March 1932, p. 11.

43 Ibid.

44 Ibid.

45 IFA Minute Book 1929–1944, D4196/A/4, 5 April 1932.

46 IFA Annual General Meetings 1910–1987, D4196/U/1, 14 May 1932.

47 Ibid.

48 Byrne, *Green is the Colour: The Story of Irish Football*, p. 135.

49 Walsh, *Twenty Years of Irish Soccer*, p. 35.

50 Tynan, 'Association Football and Irish Society During the Inter-War Period, 1918–1939', p. 159

51 *Irish Press*, 25 May 1934, p. 10.

52 *The Irish Times*, 30 May 1934, p. 11.

53 *The Irish Times*, 7 June 1934, p. 10.

54 IFA Emergency Minutes 1909–1943, D4196/N/1, 26 June 1934.

55 Walsh, *Twenty Years of Irish Soccer*, p. 38.
56 Tynan, 'Association Football and Irish Society during the Inter-War Period, 1918–1939', p. 157.
57 *Irish Press*, 19 September 1935, p. 8.
58 IFA Emergency Minutes 1909–1943, D4196/N/1, 9 October 1935.
59 Ibid., 15 November 1935.
60 Ibid., 15 November 1935.
61 Ibid., 16 November 1935.
62 *Irish Independent*, 29 November 1935, p. 13, *The Irish Times*, 7 December 1935, p. 26.
63 *Irish Independent*, 12 November 1936, p. 17.
64 *Munster Express*, 4 February 1938, p. 3.
65 *The Irish Times*, 22 June 1938, p. 11.
66 IFA Emergency Minutes 1909–1943, D4196/N/1, 4 May 1937.
67 Tynan, 'Association Football and Irish Society during the Inter-War Period, 1918–1939', p. 75.
68 IFA Emergency Minutes – 1909–1943, D4196/N/1, 7 May 1938.
69 Ibid., 2 August 1938.
70 Ibid., 16 August 1938.
71 Ibid., 24 August 1938.
72 Walsh, *Twenty Years of Irish Soccer*, p. 38.
73 IFA Emergency Minutes 1909–1943, D4196/N/1, 25 February 1938.
74 Ibid.
75 M. Daly, 'The Irish Free State/Éire/Republic of Ireland/Ireland: "A Country by Any Other Name"?' *Journal of British Studies*, Vol. 46, No. 1 (2007), p. 72.
76 IFA Emergency Minutes 1909–1943, D4196/N/1, 25 February 1938.
77 Daly, 'The Irish Free State/Éire/Republic of Ireland/Ireland: "A Country by Any Other Name"?', p. 72.
78 NAI, Department of Foreign Affairs and Trade, DFA/301/2, *Name of the State: Use, Translation and Pronunciation of 'Eire'. Use of 'Ireland' in the English Language*, 21 July 1938 and 29 January 1939.
79 Ibid., 21 July 1938.
80 Ibid., 25 March 1942.
81 *Manchester Guardian*, 16 April 1946, p. 4.
82 Daly, 'The Irish Free State/Éire/Republic of Ireland/Ireland: "A Country by Any Other Name"?' p. 73.
83 Public Record Office of Northern Ireland (PRONI), Northern Ireland: A Divided Community, 1921–1972, Cabinet Papers of the Stormont Administration, CAB 4/389, 7 December 1937.
84 NAI, Department of Foreign Affairs and Trade, DFA/305/14/162, *Partition in Sport*, 27 January 1951.
85 Hunt, '"In our case, it seems obvious the British Organising Committee piped the tune": the campaign for recognition of "Ireland" in the Olympic Movement, 1935–1956', p. 5.

86 NAI, Department of Foreign Affairs and Trade, DFA/301/2, *Name of the State: Use, Translation and Pronunciation of 'Éire'. Use of 'Ireland' in the English Language*, 1 July 1949.

87 *The Irish Times*, 21 April 1941, p. 3.

88 *Irish Press*, 9 August 1940, p. 8.

89 *Irish Examiner*, 1 May 1941, p. 6.

90 *Sunday Independent*, 27 April 1941, p. 6.

91 *Irish Press*, 25 March 1942, p. 5.

92 *Irish Press*, 27 February 1943, p. 4.

93 *The Irish Times*, 2 February 1943, p. 2.

94 *Irish Press*, 25 March 1942, p. 5.

95 *Irish Independent*, 25 April 1944, p. 4.

96 IFA Emergency Minutes – 1943–1995, D4196/N/2, 9 May 1946.

97 *The Irish Times*, 18 April 1946, p. 4.

98 Tomlinson, *FIFA (Fédération Internationale de Football Association): The men, The myths and The money*, p. 56.

99 IFA Emergency Minutes 1943–1995, D4196/N/2, 17 September 1946.

100 Ibid., 17 September 1946.

101 Ibid.

102 *The Irish Times*, 24 September 1946, p. 2.

103 M. Coleman, Dictionary of Irish Biography, available from http://dib.cambridge.org/; accessed on 25 January 2015.

104 NAI, Office of President, PRES1/P2888, *International soccer matches: attendance of President*, 21 September 1946.

105 Ibid., 1 October 1946.

106 Ibid.

107 *The Irish Times*, 21 November 1946, p. 2.

108 IFA Emergency Minutes 1943–1995, D4196/N/2, 10 December 1946.

109 Ibid., 11 November 1947.

110 Ibid., 29 July 1948.

111 Ibid., 12 August 1948.

112 *The Scotsman*, 11 October 1950.

113 Sugden and Barnier, *Sport, Sectarianism and Society in a Divided Ireland*, p. 74.

114 *Irish Examiner*, 30 May 1949, p. 6.

115 NAI, Department of an Taoiseach, S14650A, *President of Ireland: Attendance at International Football Matches*, 14 September 1949.

116 IFA Emergency Minutes 1943–1995, D4196/N/2, 24 January 1950.

117 *Limerick Leader*, 1 April 1950, p. 12.

118 *Irish Independent*, 30 December 1950, p. 9.

119 Ibid.

120 IFA Emergency Minutes 1943–1995, D4196/N/2, 4 October 1950.

121 *The Scotsman*, 10 October 1950.

122 Press clipping of Northern Whig article in NAI, Department of Foreign Affairs and Trade, DFA/305/14/162, Partition in Sport, 6 December 1950, and IFA Emergency Minutes 1943–1995, D4196/N/2, 10 January 1952.

123 Press clipping of *Belfast Newsletter* article in NAI, Department of Foreign Affairs and Trade, DFA/305/14/162, *Partition in Sport*, 19 December 1950.

CHAPTER SEVENTEEN – THE 1950S – SPORT AND POLITICS INTERTWINE

1 PRONI, CAB 4/844, 25 April 1951.
2 NAI, Department of an Taoiseach, S14749A, *Prosecution of Flying of National Flag in Six Counties*, 17 February 1950.
3 Ibid.
4 NAI, Department of Foreign Affairs and Trade, DFA/305/14/125, *Six-County Ban on Flying of Tri-Colour*, 24 March 1950.
5 *Sunday Independent*, 12 March 1950, p. 1.
6 *Mayo News*, 27 March 1948, p. 3.
7 *Ulster Herald*, 18 March 1950, p. 7.
8 *Fermanagh Herald*, 18 March 1950, p. 5.
9 *Sunday Independent*, 19 March 1950, p. 10.
10 Press clipping of *Belfast Newsletter* article in NAI, Department of Foreign Affairs and Trade, DFA/305/14/125, *Six-County Ban on Flying of Tri-Colour*, 13 March 1950.
11 Press clipping of *Strabane Weekly News* article in NAI, Department of Foreign Affairs and Trade, DFA/305/14/125, *Six-County Ban on Flying of Tri-Colour*, 25 March 1950.
12 PRONI, CAB 4/846, 10 May 1951.
13 Sugden and Barnier, *Sport, Sectarianism and Society in a Divided Ireland*, p. 59.
14 *Connacht Sentinel*, 27 January 1953, p. 2.
15 Ibid.
16 Sugden and Barnier, *Sport, Sectarianism and Society in a Divided Ireland*, p. 59.
17 NAI, Department of Foreign Affairs and Trade, DFA/305/14/183, *All Ireland Teams in International Sport*, 16 May 1951.
18 Ibid.
19 Ibid.
20 Ibid., 11 July 1953.
21 Press clipping of *Belfast Telegraph* article in NAI, Department of Foreign Affairs and Trade, DFA/305/14/162/2, *Partition in Sport: Soccer Matches*, 28 June 1958.
22 *Irish Press*, 24 September 1959, p. 1.
23 NAI, Department of Foreign Affairs and Trade, DFA/305/14/162, *Partition in Sport*, 23 May 1950.
24 Ibid., 28 March 1954.
25 Hunt, '"In our case, it seems obvious the British Organising Committee piped the tune": The campaign for recognition of "Ireland" in the Olympic Movement, 1935–1956', p. 2.
26 Comerford, *Ireland: Inventing the Nation*, p. 233.
27 Hunt, '"In our case, it seems obvious the British Organising Committee piped the tune": The campaign for recognition of "Ireland" in the Olympic Movement, 1935–1956', p. 6.

28 Press clipping of *Sunday Graphic* article in NAI, Department of Foreign Affairs and Trade, DFA/305/14/162, *Partition in Sport*, 10 January 1954.
29 Press clipping of *Irish Press* article in NAI, Department of Foreign Affairs and Trade, DFA/305/14/162, *Partition in Sport*, 31 August 1954.
30 *Irish Independent*, 8 March 1954, p. 10.
31 Press clipping of *The Irish Times* article in NAI, Department of Foreign Affairs and Trade, DFA/305/14/162, *Partition in Sport*, 3 December 1956.
32 Comerford, *Ireland: Inventing the Nation*, p. 234.
33 Ibid.
34 NAI, Department of Foreign Affairs and Trade, DFA/305/14/162, *Partition in Sport*, 31 August 1958.
35 Press clipping of *Irish Press* article in NAI, Department of Foreign Affairs and Trade, DFA/305/14/162, *Partition in Sport*, 28 August 1955.
36 *Los Angeles Times*, 5 December 1957, p. C4.
37 *Irish Press*, 5 December 1957, p. 1.
38 *The Times*, 6 December 1957, p. 8.
39 *Irish Pictorial*, 14 December 1957, p. 2.
40 NAI, Department of Foreign Affairs and Trade, DFA/305/14/162/2, *Partition in Sport: Soccer Matches*, 6 December 1957.
41 Ibid., 5 December 1957.
42 Ibid., 7 December 1957.
43 Press clipping of *Sunday Review* article in NAI, Department of Foreign Affairs and Trade, DFA/305/14/162/2, *Partition in Sport: Soccer Matches*, 8 December 1957.
44 *Irish Pictorial*, 14 December 1957, p. 2.
45 *The Times*, 10 December 1957, p. 11.
46 Ibid.
47 NAI, Department of Foreign Affairs and Trade, DFA/305/14/162/2, *Partition in Sport: Soccer Matches*, 7 April 1958.
48 Ibid., 16 April 1958.
49 Press clipping of *Sunday Review* article in NAI, Department of Foreign Affairs and Trade, DFA/305/14/162/2, *Partition in Sport: Soccer Matches*, 22 June 1958.
50 Press clipping of *Derry Journal* article in NAI, Department of Foreign Affairs and Trade, DFA/305/14/162/2, *Partition in Sport: Soccer Matches*, 4 July 1958.

CHAPTER EIGHTEEN – HOPE REKINDLED

1 *Irish Independent*, 28 October 1964, p. 14.
2 *Irish Independent*, 27 October 1965, p. 14.
3 *Irish Independent*, 26 November 1967, p. 14.
4 *The Irish Times*, 28 November 1967, p. 3.
5 *Sunday Independent*, 16 November 1969, p. 15.
6 *The Irish Times*, 3 January 1970, p. 3.
7 *Irish Press*, 13 August 1970, p. 18.
8 Ibid.

9 *Irish Press*, 19 August 1970, p. 19.

10 *The Irish Times*, 22 May 1971, p. 8.

11 Sugden and Barnier, *Sport, Sectarianism and Society in a Divided Ireland*, p. 85.

12 IFA Minute Book 1970–1977, D4196/A/11, 30 March 1971.

13 *The Irish Times*, 14 October 1972, p. 4.

14 *The Irish Times*, 10 May 1973, p. 3.

15 Ibid.

16 S. Tobin, 'All-Ireland Samba: Shamrock Rovers All-Ireland XI 3–4 Brazil Lansdowne Road, Tuesday 3 July 1973', *History Ireland*, Vol. 16, No. 4, Ireland and Latin America (2008), p. 46.

17 *The Irish Times*, 5 July 1973, p. 3.

18 *The Irish Times*, 4 July 1973, p. 3.

19 IFA Minute Book 1970–1977, D4196/A/11, 28 August 1973.

20 Ibid., 2 October 1973.

21 Ibid., 2 October 1973.

22 *Irish Press*, 3 October 1973, p. 18.

23 IFA Minute Book 1970–1977, D4196/A/11, 29 January 1974.

24 Ibid.

25 Ibid.

26 *The Irish Times*, 8 March 1974, p. 10.

27 *The Irish Times*, 30 October 1974, p. 3.

28 Sugden and Barnier, *Sport, Sectarianism and Society in a Divided Ireland*, p. 70.

29 *The Irish Times*, 3 February 1978, p. 3.

30 IFA Minute Book 1970–1977, D4196/A/11, 30 March 1976.

31 *Irish Independent*, 11 March 1976, p. 11.

32 IFA Minute Book 1970–1977, D4196/A/11, 30 August 1977.

33 *The Irish Times*, 31 August 1977, p. 3.

34 *The Irish Times*, 12 October 1977, p. 3.

35 *The Irish Times*, 1 December 1977, p. 4.

36 *The Irish Times*, 6 December 1977, p. 3.

37 *The Irish Times*, 2 February 1978, p. 3.

38 *The Irish Times*, 3 February 1978, p. 3.

39 Ibid.

40 Ibid.

41 Ibid.

42 Ibid.

43 *Irish Independent*, 3 February 1978, p. 13.

44 *The Irish Times*, 3 February 1978, p. 3.

45 *The Kerryman*, 10 February 1978, p. 8.

46 Ibid.

47 *The Irish Times*, 9 March 1978, p. 3.

48 Ibid.

49 *Irish Press*, 9 March 1978, p. 16.

50 *Donegal News*, 7 July 1979, p. 5.

51 *The Irish Times*, 30 August 1979, p. 4.

52 *The Argus*, 31 August 1979, p. 1.
53 Ibid.
54 *The Argus*, 7 September 1979, p. 28.
55 *The Irish Times*, 8 September 1979, p. 4.
56 *Irish Press*, 20 November 1979, p. 7.
57 *The Irish Times*, 23 November 1979, p. 3.
58 Ibid.
59 *The Irish Times*, 10 January 1980, p. 3.
60 *Irish Press*, 10 January 1980, p. 16.
61 *The Irish Times*, 10 January 1980, p. 3.
62 *The Irish Times*, 27 June 1981, p. 22.
63 *Irish Press*, 10 September 1981, p. 13.
64 *The Irish Times*, 31 December 1981, p. 12.
65 *The Irish Times*, 4 May 1983, p. 1.
66 Samuel, *The British Home Football Championships 1884–1984*, pp. 95, 96 and 99.
67 Byrne, *Green is the Colour: The Story of Irish Football*, p. 229.
68 P. Agnew, 'Irish Football's Two Contrasting States', *Fortnight*, No. 200, (1984), p. 23.
69 *Irish Independent*, 29 March 1995, p. 13.
70 *The Irish Times*, 19 February 1990, p. 11.
71 Sugden and Barnier, *Sport, Sectarianism and Society in a Divided Ireland*, p. 88.
72 Ibid., p. 89.
73 E. McCann, 'Two Tribes on the Terraces?', *Fortnight*, No. 274 (1989), p. 25.
74 Ibid., p. 25.
75 *Irish Press*, 29 March 1995, p. 35.
76 Sugden and Barnier, *Sport, Sectarianism and Society in a Divided Ireland*, p. 79.
77 Ibid., p. 80.
78 *Irish Voice*, 1 February 1994, p. 2.
79 *Ulster Herald*, 8 November 2007, p. 12.
80 *Irish Independent*, 5 January 2005, p. 1.
81 *Ulster Herald*, 13 December 2007, p. 76.
82 *Donegal News*, 20 February 2009, p. 62.

CONCLUSION

1 *Sunday Independent*, 26 May 1927, p. 9.
2 *The Irish Times*, 16 May 1904, p. 7.
3 M. Cronin, *Sport and Nationalism in Ireland: Gaelic Games, Soccer and Irish Identity since 1884* (Dublin: Four Courts Press, 1999), pp. 123–124.

Sources and Bibliography

Primary Sources

PUBLIC RECORD OFFICE OF NORTHERN IRELAND
2 Titanic Boulevard, Titanic Quarter,
Belfast, BT3 9HQ

Edward Carson's Souvenir Parchment Covenant, D1496/3
Northern Ireland: A Divided Community, 1921–1972, Cabinet Papers of
the Stormont Administration

IRISH FOOTBALL ASSOCIATION ARCHIVE

Minute Book 1880–1886, D4196/AA/1
Minute Book 1909–1928, D4196/A/3
Minute Book 1970–1977, D4196/A/11
Senior Clubs Protest and Appeal Committee, D4196/K/1-2
Annual General Meetings 1910–1987, D4196/U/1
International Minutes 1909–1966, D4196/D/1
Emergency Minutes 1909–1943, D4196/N/1
IFA Emergency Minutes 1943–1995, D4196/N/2

IRISH FOOTBALL LEAGUE ARCHIVE

Belfast and District Football League 1915–1916, D4511/8/1
Minute Book 1909–1913, D4511/1/30
Minute Book 1913–1923, D4511/1/31

THE FOOTBALL ASSOCIATION
Wembley Stadium, London, SW1P 9EQ
United Kingdom

Council Meeting and Annual General Meeting 1879–1886
International Selection Committee Meeting Minutes
Council Meeting and Annual General Meeting 1912
Minute Book 1914–1915
Council Meeting and Annual General Meeting 1921–1922
Council Meeting Minutes 1923–1924

Sources and Bibliography

THE GAELIC ATHLETIC ASSOCIATION ARCHIVE
Croke Park, Dublin 3

GAA Central Council Meeting Minute Book (1911–1925), GAA/CC/01/02
GAA Annual Congress Meeting Minute Book

NATIONAL ARCHIVES OF IRELAND, Bishop Street, Dublin 8
Department of an Taoiseach
S1095, *Belfast Boycott*
S3767, *National Anthem: Adoption of the Soldier's Song*
S6536, *Trinity College Sports 1928–1932*
S14650A, *President of Ireland: Attendance at International Football Matches*
S14749A, *Prosecution of Flying of National Flag in Six Counties*
Department of Foreign Affairs and Trade
DFA/GR 37, *Jeux Olympiques, 'Olympian Games'*
DFA/2/1/38, *National Flag at International Rugby Football Matches, Lansdowne Road*
DFA/301/2, *Name of the State: Use, Translation and Pronunciation of 'Éire'. Use of 'Ireland' in the English Language*
DFA/305/14/162, *Partition in Sport*
DFA/305/14/162/2, *Partition in Sport: Soccer Matches*
DFA/305/14/125, *Six-County Ban on Flying of Tri-Colour*
DFA/305/14/183, *All Ireland Teams in International Sport*
Office of President
PRES1/P2888, *International soccer matches: attendance of President*
North Eastern Boundary Bureau
NEBB/1/1/3, *Belfast Pogrom Statistics*

UCD ARCHIVES,
School of History and Archives,
University College, Dublin 4

Leinster Football Association Papers, Leinster Football Association Minute Book 1899–1902, p.239/21
Leinster Football Association Papers, Leinster Football Association Minute Book 1902–1904, p.239/22
Leinster Football Association Papers, Leinster Football Association Minute Book 1906–1915, p.239/24
Leinster Football Association Papers, Leinster Football Association Minute Book 1915–1922, p.239/25
The International Minute Book of the Football Association of Ireland Papers, P137/1-3

NEWSPAPERS AND MAGAZINES

Belfast Newsletter

Sources and Bibliography

Belfast Telegraph
Christian Science Monitor
Clonmel Chronicle
Connacht Sentinel
Derry Journal
Donegal News
Evening Herald
Fermanagh Herald
Football Sports Weekly
Freeman's Journal
Gaelic Athlete
Glasgow Herald
Ireland's Saturday Night
Irish Examiner
Irish Field
Irish Independent
Irish News
Irish Pictorial
Irish Press
Irish Statesman
Irish Voice
Lagan Village Juvenile
Leeds Mercury
Limerick Leader
Los Angeles Times
Manchester Guardian
Mayo News
Meath Chronicle
Munster Express
New York Times
Northern Whig and Belfast Post
Skibbereen Eagle
Southern Star
Sport
Strabane Weekly News
Sunday Graphic
Sunday Independent
Sunday Review
The Argus
The Irish Times
The Kerryman
The Observer

The Scotsman
The Times
Ulster Herald

Secondary Sources

BOOKS

Barnier, A. (ed.), *Sport and the Irish: Histories, Identities, Issues* (Dublin: UCD Press, 2005)

Briggs, G. and Dodd, J., *Leinster Football Association 100 Years Centenary Yearbook 1892–1992* (Dublin: Leinster Football Association, 1993)

Brodie, M., *100 Years of Irish Football* (Belfast: Blackstaff Press, 1980)

Brodie, M., *Linfield: 100 Years* (Belfast: Linfield Football and Athletic Club, 1985)

Byrne, P., *Green is the Colour: The Story of Irish Football* (London: Carlton Books, 2012)

Comerford, R.V., *Ireland: Inventing the Nation* (London: Bloomsbury Academic, 2003)

Coyle, P., *Paradise Lost and Found: The Story of Belfast Celtic* (Edinburgh: Mainstream Publishing, 1999)

Cronin, M., *Sport and Nationalism in Ireland: Gaelic Games, Soccer and Irish Identity since 1884* (Dublin: Four Courts Press, 1999)

Cronin, M., Murphy, W., Rouse, P. (eds), *The Gaelic Athletic Association 1884–2009* (Dublin: Irish Academic Press, 2009)

Cullen, D., *Freestaters: The Republic of Ireland Soccer Team 1921–1939* (Southend-on-Sea, Essex: Desert Island Books, 2007)

de Búrca, M., *The GAA: A History* (Dublin: Gill and Macmillan, 1980)

Fanning, R., *Fatal Path: British Government and Irish Revolution 1910–1922* (London: Faber and Faber, 2013)

Ferriter, D., *Judging Dev: A Reassessment of the Life and Legacy of Éamon de Valera* (Dublin: Royal Irish Academy, 2007)

Flynn, B., *Political Football: The Life and Death of Belfast Celtic* (Dublin: Nonsuch Ireland, 2009)

Garnham, N., *Association Football and Society in Pre-Partition Ireland* (Belfast: Ulster Historical Foundation, 2004)

Garnham, N., *The Origins and Development of Football in Ireland: Being a Reprint of R.M. Peter's Irish Football Annual of 1880* (Belfast: Ulster Historical Foundation, 1999)

Goldblatt, D., *The Ball is Round: A Global History of Football* (London: Penguin, 2006)

Griffin, P., *The Politics of Irish Athletics 1850–1990* (Ballinamore, County Leitrim: Marathon Publications, 1990)

Harvey, A., *Football: The First One Hundred Years: The Untold Story* (Oxford: Routledge, 2005)

Hesse-Lichtenberger, U., *Tor!: The Story of German Football* (London: WSC Books, 2003)

Hiles, J.C., *A History of Senior Cricket in Ulster* (Comber, County Down: Hiltop Publications, 2003)

Hone, W.P., *Cricket in Ireland* (Tralee: The Kerryman, 1955)

Horne, J. (ed.), *Our War: Ireland and the Great War* (Dublin: Royal Irish Academy, 2008)

Huggins, M., *The Victorians and Sport* (London: Bloomsbury Continuum, 2004)

Hunt, T., *Sport and Society in Victorian Ireland: The Case of Westmeath* (Cork: Cork University Press, 2007)

Lee, J.J., *Ireland 1912–1985: Politics and Society* (Cambridge: Cambridge University Press, 1989)

Lynch, F., *A History of Athlone Town FC: The First 101 Years* (Athlone, 1991)

Mason, T., *Association Football and English Society 1863–1915* (Brighton: Harvester Press, 1980)

McCarthy, K., *Gold, Silver and Green: The Irish Olympic Journey 1896–1924* (Cork: Cork University Press, 2011)

McElligott, R., *Forging a Kingdom: The GAA in Kerry 1884–1934* (Cork: The Collins Press, 2013)

McGarry, F., *Eoin O'Duffy: A Self-Made Hero* (Oxford: Oxford University Press, 2005)

McLoughlin, A. with Evans, B., *A Different Shade of Green: The Alan McLoughlin Story* (Bray, County Wicklow: Ballpoint Press, 2014)

Menton, W.A., *The Golfing Union of Ireland 1891–1991* (Dublin: Gill and Macmillan, 1991)

Moore, C., *The GAA v Douglas Hyde: The Removal of Ireland's First President as GAA Patron* (Cork: The Collins Press, 2012)

Needham, D., *Ireland's First Real World Cup: The Story of the 1924 Ireland Olympic Football Team* (Dublin: The Manuscript Publisher, 2012)

O'Callaghan, L., *Rugby in Munster: A Social and Cultural History* (Cork: Cork University Press, 2011)

O'Sullivan, D., *Sport in Cork: A History* (Dublin: The History Press, 2010)

Parkinson, A.F., *Friends in High Places: Ulster's Resistance to Irish Home Rule, 1912–14* (Belfast: Ulster Historical Foundation, 2012)

Robinson, R., *History of the Queen's Park Football Club 1867–1917* (Glasgow: Hay Nisbet, 1920)

Ryan, S., *The Boys in Green: The FAI International Story* (Edinburgh: Mainstream Publishing, 1997)

Ryan, S., *The Official Book of the FAI Cup* (Dublin: Liberties Press, 2011)

Sources and Bibliography

Samuel, R., *The British Home Football Championships 1884–1984* (Cleethorpes, Lincs.: Soccer Books Limited, 2003)

Sugden, J. and Barnier, A., *Sport, Sectarianism and Society in a Divided Ireland* (Leicester: Leicester University Press, 1993)

Taylor, M., *The Association Game: A History of British Football* (Harlow, Middx.: Routledge, 2008)

Tomlinson, A., *FIFA (Fédération Internationale de Football Association): The Men, The Myths and The Money* (Oxford: Routledge, 2014)

Van Esbeck, E., *The Story of Irish Rugby* (London: Hutchinson, 1986)

Walsh, J.J., *Recollections of a Rebel* (Tralee: The Kerryman, 1944)

Walsh, T.P., *Twenty Years of Irish Soccer* (Dublin: Sports Publicity Services, 1941)

Wynne, T. (Comp.) and Glennon, C. (ed.), *Ninety Years of the Irish Hockey Union* (Kildare: Leinster Leader, 1985)

Yeates, P., *A City in Turmoil: Dublin 1919–1921* (Dublin: Gill and Macmillan, 2012)

JOURNALS AND PERIODICALS

Agnew, P., 'Irish Football's Two Contrasting States', *Fortnight*, No. 200 (1984)

Bardon, J., 'Belfast at its Zenith', *History Ireland*, Vol. 1, No. 4 (1993)

Carey, T., 'Ireland's Footballers at the Paris Olympics, 1924', *History Ireland*, Vol. 20, No. 4 (2012)

Connell Jr, J.E.A., 'British Army First World War Recruitment in Ireland', *History Ireland*, Vol. 22, No. 4 (2014)

Cronin, M., 'Projecting the Nation through Sport and Culture: Ireland, Aonach Tailteann and the Irish Free State, 1924–1932', *Journal of Contemporary History*, Vol. 38, No. 3 (2003)

Daly, M., 'The Irish Free State/Éire/Republic of Ireland/Ireland: "A Country by Any Other Name"?', *Journal of British Studies*, Vol. 46, No. 1 (2007)

Foy, M., 'Ulster Unionist Propaganda against Home Rule 1912–1914' *History Ireland*, Vol. 4, No. 1 (1996)

Garnham, N., 'Accounting for the Early Success of the Gaelic Athletic Association', *Irish Historical Studies*, Vol. 34, No. 133 (2004)

Hunt, T., '"In our case, it seems obvious the British Organising Committee piped the tune": The campaign for recognition of "Ireland" in the Olympic Movement, 1935–1956', *Sport in Society: Cultures, Commerce, Media, Politics* (2015)

Kay, J. and Vamplew, W., 'Beyond Altruism: British football and charity, 1877–1914', *Soccer and Society*, Vol. 11, No. 3 (2010)

Kerrigan, C., 'Ireland's Greatest Football Team?' *History Ireland*, Vol. 13, No. 3 (2005)

Sources and Bibliography

Laffan, M., 'Two Irish States' *The Crane Bag*, Vol. 8, No. 1, Ireland: Dependence and Independence (1984)

Lynch, R., 'The People's Protectors? The Irish Republican Army and the "Belfast Pogrom", 1920–1922', *Journal of British Studies*, Vol. 47, No. 2 (2008)

Madigan, E., '"A Seamless Robe of Irish Experience": the First World War, the Irish Revolution and centenary commemoration', *History Ireland*, Vol. 22, No. 4 (2014)

McAnallen, D., 'The Story of Gaelic Games in Ulster', Cardinal Tomás Ó Fiaich Memorial Library and Archive (2010)

McCann, E., 'Two Tribes on the Terraces?', *Fortnight*, No. 274, (1989)

Myers, K., 'Crunching the Numbers and Busting Myths', *History Ireland*, Vol. 22, No. 4 (2014)

O'Sullivan, P., 'Ireland and the Olympic Games', *History Ireland*, Vol. 6, No. 1 (1998)

Reid, S., 'Identity and cricket in Ireland in the mid-nineteenth century', *Sport in Society: Cultures, Commerce, Media, Politics*, Vol. 15, No. 2 (2012)

Reynolds, P., '"A First-Class Split": political conflict in Irish athletes, 1924–1940', *History Ireland*, Vol. 20, No. 4 (2012)

Sherry, R., 'The Story of the National Anthem', *History Ireland*, Vol. 4, No. 1 (1996)

Simpson, G., 'William Pirrie, The Titanic and Home Rule' *History Ireland*, Vol. 20, No. 2 (2012)

Tobin, S., 'All-Ireland Samba: Shamrock Rovers All-Ireland XI 3–4 Brazil, Lansdowne Road, Tuesday 3 July 1973', *History Ireland*, Vol. 16, No. 4, Ireland and Latin America (2008)

Tomlinson, A., 'FIFA and the men who made it', *Soccer and Society* (2007)

Toms, D., '"Notwithstanding the Discomfort Involved": Fordson's Cup Win in 1926 and How "the Old Contemptible" Were Represented in Ireland's Public Sphere During the 1920s', *Sport in History* (2013)

ELECTRONIC SOURCES

British Parliamentary Debates, http://hansard.millbanksystems.com

Bureau of Military History, http://www.bureauofmilitaryhistory.ie/

Census of Ireland 1911, www.census.nationalarchives.ie

Dáil Éireann Debates, www.oireachtas-debates.gov.ie

Dictionary of Irish Biography, http://dib.cambridge.org/

Dictionary of Ulster Biography, http://www.newulsterbiography.co.uk/

Northern Ireland Footballing Greats, http://nifootball.blogspot.ie/

Les Jeux de la VIIIe Olympiade, Paris 1924, http://www.olympic.org/paris-1924-summer-olympics

The International Football Association Board Meeting Minutes 1886–1931, http://ssbra.org/html/laws/ifab.html

Sources and Bibliography

The Official FA Website, www.thefa.com

OTHER

Shelbourne Football Club 1895–1945: Golden Jubilee Souvenir (Dublin, 1945)

Cunnane, D. W., 'The Troubles in Belfast: An Anatomy of Sectarian and Political Violence, 1920–1922' (Yale University PhD thesis, 2005)

Rouse, P., 'Sport and the Politics of Culture: A History of the GAA Ban 1884–1971' (UCD master's thesis, 1991)

Tynan, M., 'Association Football and Irish Society During the Inter-War Period, 1918–1939' (NUI, Maynooth, PhD thesis, 2013)

Appendix A: IFA Sub-Committee Membership Make-Up, 1909/1910–1920/1921*

	Leinster	Munster	North-East	North-West	Mid-Ulster	Fermanagh & Western	Junior Committee	Honorary Treasurer	Total
1909–1910									
Protests & Appeals	0	0	3	1	2	1	0	0	7
Finance	0	1	4	2	1	0	1	0	9
Emergency	0	0	3	2	0	1	0	0	6
International	1	0	3	1	1	1	0	0	7
1910–1911									
Protests & Appeals	1	0	3	1	2	1	0	0	8
Finance	1	1	3	2	1	0	1	0	9
Emergency	0	0	3	2	0	1	0	0	6
International	1	0	3	1	1	1	0	0	7
1911–1912									
Protests & Appeals	1	0	3	1	2	0	0	0	7
Finance	1	0	4	1	1	0	1	0	8
Emergency	0	1	4	2	0	0	0	0	7
International	1	0	3	1	1	1	0	0	7
Referees	1	1	4	2	1	1	1	0	11
Rules Revision	1	1	5	2	1	0	1	0	11
1912–1913									
Protests & Appeals & Reinstatements	1	0	3	1	1	0	1	0	7

Appendix A (cont.)

	Leinster	Munster	North-East	North-West	Mid-Ulster	Fermanagh & Western	Junior Committee	Honorary Treasurer	Total
Finance	0	0	4	0	2	0	1	1	8
Emergency	0	0	3	1	1	0	0	1	6
International	1	0	3	1	1	1	0	0	7
Senior League Clubs Protests & Appeals	0	0	5	0	0	0	0	0	5
Rules Revision	0	0	2	1	0	0	0	0	0
Advisory	1	0	2	1	1	0	0	1	6
1913 – 1914									
Protests & Appeals & Reinstatements	0	1	3	2	1	0	0	0	7
Finance	0	1	5	0	2	0	0	1	9
Emergency	0	0	3	1	1	0	0	1	6
International	1	0	5	1	0	0	0	0	7
Senior League Clubs Protests & Appeals	0	0	6	0	0	0	0	0	6
Rules Revision	0	0	1	2	1	0	0	1	5
1914 – 1915									
Protests & Appeals & Reinstatements	0	1	3	2	2	0	0	0	8
Finance	0	0	4	1	1	0	0	1	7
Emergency	0	0	3	0	0	0	0	1	4
Senior League Clubs Protests & Appeals	0	0	5	0	0	0	0	0	5
Rules Revision	0	0	1	3	0	0	0	0	4

Appendix A (cont.)

	Leinster	Munster	North-East	North-West	Mid-Ulster	Fermanagh & Western	Junior Committee	Honorary Treasurer	Total
1915 – 1916									
Protests & Appeals & Reinstatements	1	0	2	1	1	0	0	0	5
Finance	0	0	3	1	1	0	0	1	6
Emergency	0	0	4	1	0	0	0	1	6
Senior League Clubs Protests & Appeals	0	0	5	0	0	0	0	0	5
Rules Revision	0	0	1	2	1	0	0	1	5
1916 – 1917									
Protests & Appeals & Reinstatements	1	0	3	1	2	0	0	0	7
Finance	1	0	5	1	1	0	0	1	9
Emergency	1	0	6	1	0	0	0	1	9
Senior League Clubs Protests & Appeals	1	0	5	0	1	0	0	0	7
Rules Revision	0	0	3	1	1	0	0	1	6
1917 – 1918									
Protests & Appeals & Reinstatements	1	0	4	1	2	0	0	0	8
Finance	1	0	3	0	1	0	1	1	7
Emergency	1	0	7	1	0	0	0	1	10
Senior League Clubs Protests & Appeals	1	0	6	0	1	0	0	0	8
Rules Revision	0	0	4	1	1	0	0	1	7
Referees	1	0	4	1	0	0	0	1	7

Appendix A (cont.)

	Leinster	Munster	North-East	North-West	Mid-Ulster	Fermanagh & Western	Junior Committee	Honorary Treasurer	Total
1918 – 1919									
Protests & Appeals & Reinstatements	0	0	4	1	1	0	0	0	6
Finance	1	0	4	1	1	0	1	1	9
Emergency	2	0	8	2	0	0	0	1	13
Senior League Clubs Protests & Appeals	2	0	7	0	0	0	0	0	9
Rules Revision	0	0	4	2	0	0	0	1	7
Referees	1	0	3	2	0	1	0	1	8
International	1	0	2	1	0	0	0	0	4
1919 – 1920									
Protests & Appeals & Reinstatements	1	0	4	2	0	0	0	0	7
Finance	1	0	4	2	0	0	1	0	8
Emergency	2	0	5	3	0	0	0	0	10
Senior League Clubs Protests & Appeals	3	0	5	0	1	0	0	0	9
Rules Revision	0	0	5	3	0	0	0	0	8
Referees	1	0	5	2	1	1	0	0	10
International	1	0	4	1	1	0	0	0	7
Spread of the Game	2	0	6	2	1	0	0	0	11

Appendix A (cont.)

1920 – 1921	Leinster	Munster	North-East	North-West	Mid-Ulster	Fermanagh & Western	Junior Committee	Honorary Treasurer	Total
Protests & Appeals & Reinstatements	1	0	4	2	0	0	0	0	7
Finance	1	0	4	2	0	0	1	0	8
Emergency	2	0	7	3	0	0	0	0	12
Senior League Clubs Protests & Appeals	2	0	5	0	1	0	0	0	8
Rules Revision	1	0	6	3	1	0	0	0	11
Referees	1	0	5	2	1	1	0	0	10
International	1	0	4	1	1	0	0	0	7

* IFA Annual General Meetings, 1910–1987, D/4196/U/1

Appendix B: Leinster and Munster Delegate Attendance Record at IFA Council and Sub-Committee Meetings, 1910–1921*

1909 – 1910	
IFA Council Meetings – 10 Meetings Held	
Leinster	*Meetings Attended*
W. Cleary	6
T. Farrell	6
P.H. Stewart	2
Wm. Fitzsimons	7
H. Wigoder	6
W.H. Taylor	2
L.C. Sheridan	2
G.B. McErlean	2
J.F. Bridgeman	1
Munster	
T. McCann	10
Rev. R.N. Ruttle	5
W.B. Smith	1
Finance Committee – 8 Meetings Held	
Munster	
T. McCann	6
International Committee – 4 Meetings Held	
Leinster	
Wm. Fitzsimons	4
1910 – 1911	
IFA Council Meetings – 6 Meetings Held	
Leinster	
P.H. Stewart	5
Wm. Fitzsimons	5
W. Cleary	3
L.C. Sheridan	3
W.H. Taylor	2
G.B. McErlean	2
T. Farrell	1
H. Wigoder	1
J.F. Bridgeman	0
C.C. Robertson	0
Munster	
T. McCann	6
Lieut. & Qr. Master E.A. Parker	2
W.B. Smith	1
Rev. R.N. Ruttle	1
Protest and Appeals – 20 Meetings Held	
Leinster	

L.C. Sheridan	0
Finance – 4 Meetings Held	
Leinster	
P.H. Stewart	0
Munster	
T. McCann	4
International – 4 Meetings Held	
Leinster	
Wm. Fitzsimons	4

1911 – 1912

IFA Council Meetings – 7 Meetings Held	
Leinster	
P.H. Stewart	3
Wm. Fitzsimons	4
T. Collins	4
L.C. Sheridan	2
T.B. Keogh	2
G.B. McErlean	1
W. Cleary	2
J.F. Bridgeman	2
C.C. Robertson	0
Munster	
T. McCann	1
Rev. R.N. Ruttle	4
Lieut. & Qr. Master E.A. Parker	3
Protests and Appeals – 14 Meetings Held	
Leinster	
L.C. Sheridan	3
Finance – 3 Meetings Held	
Leinster	
P.H. Stewart	0
Emergency – 16 Meetings Held	
Munster	
Rev. Ruttle	12
International – 4 Meetings Held	
Leinster	
Wm. Fitzsimons	4
Referees – 1 Meeting Held	
Leinster	
P.H. Stewart	0
Munster	
Rev. Ruttle	0
Rules Revision – 7 Meetings Held	
Leinster	
Wm. Fitzsimons	3
Munster	
Rev. Ruttle	2

1912 – 1913

IFA Council Meetings – 8 Meetings Held

Leinster	
P.H. Stewart	1
Wm. Fitzsimons	7
R.W. Neville	4
L.C. Sheridan	4
T.B. Keogh	1
G.B. McErlean	1
A. Donnelly	3
J.F. Bridgeman	2
D. Mulcahy	2
Munster	
Rev. R.N. Ruttle	3
H. Wigoder	3

Protests and Appeals and Reinstatements – 12 Meetings Held

Leinster	
L.C. Sheridan	0

International – 4 Meetings Held

Leinster	
L.C. Sheridan	2

Advisory – 4 Meetings Held

Leinster	
Wm. Fitzsimons	1

1913 – 1914

IFA Council Meetings – 6 Meetings Held

Leinster	
R.W. Neville	6
R.E.T. Richey	3
Sergt. McLean	3
L.C. Sheridan	2
J.B.M. Wilson	2
Wm. Fitzsimons	2
T. Collins	2
T.J. Murray	2
P.H. Stewart	1
D. Mulcahy	1
Munster	
H. Wigoder	5
Rev. R.N. Ruttle	3
J. McAnerney	5

Protests and Appeals and Reinstatements – 11 Meetings Held

Munster	
J. McAnerney	6

Finance – 7 Meetings Held

Munster	
H. Wigoder	3
Emergency – 16 Meetings Held	
Munster	
International – 5 Meetings Held	
Leinster	
Wm. Fitzsimons	2

1914 – 1915

IFA Council Meetings – 5 Meetings Held	
Leinster	
H. Wigoder	5
R.E.T. Richey	3
L.C. Sheridan	3
J.T. Murray	2
P.H. Stewart	2
T. Collins	2
Wm. Fitzsimons	1
J.M.B. Wilson	1
G. McLean	1
R.W. Neville	1
Munster	
J. McAnerney	2
Rev. R.N. Ruttle	1
Protests and Appeals and Reinstatements – 12 Meetings Held	
Munster	
J. McAnerney	1

1915 – 1916

IFA Council Meetings – 3 Meetings Held	
Leinster	
R.E.T. Richey	2
T.J. Murray	2
H. Wigoder	1
P.H. Stewart	0
L.C. Sheridan	0
T. Collins	0
R.R. Stewart	0
Protests and Appeals and Reinstatements – 6 Meetings Held	
Leinster	
T.J. Murray	2

1916 – 1917

IFA Council Meetings – 3 Meetings Held	
Leinster	
R.R. Stewart	2
T. Collins	2

H. Wigoder	2
R.E.T. Richey	2
T.J. Murray	2
P.H. Stewart	0
L.C. Sheridan	0
Protests and Appeals and Reinstatements – 13 Meetings Held	
Leinster	
T.J. Murray	3
Finance – 2 Meetings Held	
Leinster	
R.E.T. Richey	0
Emergency – 13 Meetings Held	
Leinster	
T. Collins	2
Senior League Clubs Protest and Appeals – 9 Meetings Held	
Leinster	
R.R. Stewart	4

1917 – 1918

IFA Council Meetings – 6 Meetings Held	
Leinster	
H. Wigoder	3
R.E.T. Richey	4
P.H. Stewart	3
R.R. Stewart	3
T.J. Murray	1
R.A. Duff	1
T. Collins	1
L.C. Sheridan	0
Protests and Appeals and Reinstatements – 13 Meetings Held	
Leinster	
T.J. Murray	2
Finance – 2 Meetings Held	
Leinster	
R.E.T. Richey	0
Emergency – 11 Meetings Held	
Leinster	
R.R. Stewart	2
Senior League Clubs Protest and Appeals – 5 Meetings Held	
Leinster	
R.R. Stewart	4
Referees – 2 Meeting Held	
Leinster	
H. Wigoder	0

1918 – 1919

IFA Council Meetings – 4 Meetings Held	
Leinster	

H. Wigoder	1
R.E.T. Richey	2
P.H. Stewart	0
R.R. Stewart	3
J. Walsh	0
J.F. Harrison	1
L.C. Sheridan	0
Finance – 5 Meetings Held	
Leinster	
R.E.T. Richey	1
Emergency – 11 Meetings Held	
Leinster	
R.R. Stewart	3
J. Walsh	2
Senior League Clubs Protest and Appeals – 10 Meetings Held	
Leinster	
R.R. Stewart	3
J. Walsh	1
International – 4 Meeting Held	
Leinster	
L.C. Sheridan	1

1919 – 1920

IFA Council Meetings – 7 Meetings Held

Leinster	
H. Wigoder	6
R.E.T. Richey	5
P.H. Stewart	3
R.R. Stewart	2
J. Walsh	3
J.S. Smurthwaite	3
J.F. Harrison	3
L.C. Sheridan	3
G.P. Fleming	0
J. McDonald	0
Protests and Appeals and Reinstatements – 17 Meetings Held	
Leinster	
H. Wigoder	9
Finance – 8 Meetings Held	
Leinster	
R.E.T. Richey	2
Emergency – 7 Meetings Held	
Leinster	
G.P. Fleming	0
J. Walsh	1
Senior League Clubs Protest and Appeals – 15 Meetings Held	
Leinster	
R.R. Stewart	3
J. Walsh	5

G.P. Fleming	0

Referees – 1 Meeting Held

Leinster	
H. Wigoder	0

International – 10 Meetings Held

Leinster	
P.H. Stewart	4

Spread of the Game – 4 Meetings Held

Leinster	
R.R. Stewart	1
H. Wigoder	1

1920 – 1921

IFA Council Meetings – 3 Meetings Held

Leinster	
H. Wigoder	3
R.E.T. Richey	2
P.H. Stewart	1
G.P. Fleming	0
J. Walsh	1
J.S. Smurthwaite	1
J.F. Harrison	1
L.C. Sheridan	2

Protests and Appeals and Reinstatements – 13 Meetings Held

Leinster	
H. Wigoder	3

Finance – 4 Meetings Held

Leinster	
R.E.T. Richey	0

Emergency – 8 Meetings Held

Leinster	
G.P. Fleming	0
J. Walsh	0

Senior League Clubs Protest and Appeals – 10 Meetings Held

Leinster	
J. Walsh	4
G.P. Fleming	0

Rules Revision – 1 Meeting Held

Leinster	
G.P. Fleming	0

Referees – 1 Meeting Held

Leinster	
H. Wigoder	0

International – 10 Meetings Held

Leinster	
P.H. Stewart	7

* IFA Annual General Meetings, 1910–1987, D/4196/U/1

Appendices

Appendix C: Number of International Caps based on Location of Player's Club, 1882–1921*

Year	Leinster	Ulster	Overseas	Total
1882	0	22	0	22
1883	0	22	0	22
1884	0	32	1	33
1885	6	27	0	33
1886	3	30	0	33
1887	0	33	0	33
1888	0	33	0	33
1889	2	31	0	33
1890	0	33	0	33
1891	1	32	0	33
1892	0	33	0	33
1893	0	33	0	33
1894	0	33	0	33
1895	2	31	0	33
1896	3	30	0	33
1897	0	33	0	33
1898	0	33	0	33
1899	3	25	5	33
1900	3	25	5	33
1901	5	25	3	33
1902	2	21	10	33
1903	1	19	13	33
1904	2	18	13	33
1905	2	13	18	33
1906	5	21	7	33
1907	5	20	8	33
1908	5	16	12	33
1909	3	10	20	33
1910	2	11	20	33
1911	5	7	21	33
1912	4	8	21	33
1913	6	6	21	33
1914	4	9	20	33
1919	0	6	5	11
1920	1	10	22	33
1921	0	7	26	33
Overall Total	75	798	271	1,144

* For composition of Irish teams, see *Belfast Newsletter, Sport, Irish Independent, Freeman's Journal, The Times,* IFA International Minutes, 1909–1966, D/4196/D/1, Brodie, *100 Years of Irish Football* and *Northern Ireland's Footballing Greats,* available from http://nifootball.blogspot.ie

Index

Note: illustrations are indicated by page numbers in bold.

297

Index

Index

305

Index

Index

Index